Winston Churchill at
The Telegraph

Winston Churchill at
The Telegraph

Edited by Dr Warren Dockter

Foreword by Boris Johnson

Aurum
Press

First published in Great Britain
2015 by Aurum Press Ltd
74–77 White Lion Street
Islington
London N1 9PF
www.aurumpress.co.uk

A catalogue record for this book is available from the British Library.

ISBN 978 1 78131 452 4
ebook ISBN 978 1 78131 469 2

1 3 5 7 9 10 8 6 4 2
2015 2017 2019 2018 2016

Typeset in Fournier by SX Composing DTP, Rayleigh, Essex
Printed and bound by CPI Group (UK) Ltd, Croydon, CR0 4YY

CONTENTS

Foreword

When the *Daily Telegraph* celebrated its 100th birthday in 1955, the newspaper received a message of congratulation from Winston Churchill pointing out that he was the oldest and longest serving member of the paper's staff. He was quite right.

It was a relationship that had begun in 1897, when he went off with Sir Bindon Blood to serve and observe the forces of the British Empire. He sent back several gut-wrenching accounts of the fighting, vividly describing the frenzy of the Pashtun tribesmen in what is now the badlands of Pakistan, and the awful carnage wreaked by the British machine-guns. His byline was 'a young officer', and he was paid £5 per piece.

He was initially disappointed not to be properly credited with the articles – but enough people knew the truth (thanks partly to his mother; she probably slept with the extravagantly moustachioed Bindon Blood to get her boy the job), and his reputation started to grow. So did his relationship with the great Conservative paper.

It was the *Daily Telegraph* that had the immeasurable moral distinction, in the 1930s, of sticking with Churchill – and publishing his views on Germany – even when they were unfashionable, and when other London newspapers were either refusing his copy (the *Evening Standard* springs to mind) or actively promoting appeasement of Hitler (the *Daily Mail*). It was the *Telegraph* that published his denunciations of Nazism right up until the outbreak of war, and it was Viscount Camrose of the *Daily Telegraph* who was indispensable to the solution of Churchill's financial problems, setting up the trust that enabled him to continue to live at his beloved Chartwell.

Winston Churchill owed a huge amount to the *Telegraph* – and the world owes an incalculable debt to that journalistic relationship. Why did Winston Churchill see so clearly the peril of Nazi Germany? Why was he almost alone, for so long, in his warnings?

It was at least partly because he had actually been out to Germany, in the early 1930s. He had seen the spooky marches of the blond-headed young men and women, the black and red swastika bunting in the streets. Indeed, he tried (though thankfully failed) to secure an interview with Hitler. It was the same instinct that took him to Cuba, to Malakand, to the Sudan, to the Boer War and to the trenches – the same urge that made him try to join the fleet at D-Day.

It wasn't just a quest for military glory; it was a lust to see for himself, to clarify his thoughts by his own observation, and to articulate what was going on with his own extraordinary gifts of expression. He was, in other words, a superb reporter; and it was Churchill the reporter who enabled Churchill the statesman to get it right about Hitler.

The *Daily Telegraph* can claim a significant and honourable role in helping to launch that career, and in supporting him at an absolutely critical juncture. It was a symbiosis that should come as no surprise, when you consider that Churchill and the

Telegraph shared much in their political character – romantic, imperialist, fervently pro-British, but basically soft-hearted and with a sympathy for the underdog.

Boris Johnson

Introduction

This year marks the fiftieth anniversary of the passing of one of the most iconic and major figures of the twentieth century, Sir Winston Churchill. His legacy looms large in the British national psyche and commands reverence from all quarters of the globe. He is best remembered as the man who saved Britain, if not the whole world, from the Nazi war machine during the Second World War. His awe-inspiring oratory gave the British lion its roar and his speeches have been immortalised in the annals of history.

Winston Churchill was born when the British Empire was arguably at its zenith, in 1874, and left power for the last time in 1955, when the inevitable break-up of the British Empire was under way. He was prime minister in the Second World War and helped steer Britain through the early phases of the Cold War. But more than that, he was a soldier, a journalist, a novelist, an historian and a politician. During his career, Churchill, like Britain, had to come to grips with the forces of modernity. This often led to him holding complex and, at times, paradoxical views. For instance, he was an affirmed believer in Empire but loathed the punitive 'butcher and bolt' campaigns which were employed on the frontiers of the British

Empire. He believed in free markets (so much so that he left the Tories in 1904 when they began to experiment with imperial protectionism), but he also championed social reforms (along with Lloyd George) that helped lay the foundation for the welfare state. He was at once principled and a political opportunist; a progressive Victorian but a reactionary modern statesman. In short, Winston Churchill's legacy is wedded to Britain's.

His political legacy is remarkable. He invented the concept of the 'summit', where leaders of the highest rank would meet and solve problems, he forged an alliance with the United States and he championed international organisations like the League of Nations and later the UN. His parliamentary career spanned sixty-four years. Not including his own premierships, Churchill served under thirteen prime ministers, represented five different constituencies and was a member of two major parties throughout his long life in British politics. Though Churchill's political legacy undoubtedly resonates more with the right than the left, political ideologies compete to share in his achievements. The right celebrate Churchill's devotion to Britain, free trade and tradition, while the left venerate his championing of social reform during the early 1900s and his inclusive approach to the formation of his wartime government.

Beyond Churchill's considerable life in politics, it is often forgotten that he was also a journalist of note, much like his father Lord Randolph Churchill. Churchill developed a knack for writing very early on. In 1895, he went to observe the Cuban War of Independence and was commissioned by the *Daily Graphic* to report on what he had seen. It was a profound trip for Churchill. While he was there he came under fire for the first time and he learned to love the excitement of battle.

He also developed a taste for Cuban cigars which would stay with him all his life and become a part of his iconic appearance. However, Churchill longed to make his name in the British military and soon he was given a post in British India. This was where his relationship with the *Telegraph* began. Churchill had volunteered to go on a mission to the Malakand valley in the Swat region of what is now Pakistan. He was anxious to see action and to report it. So he forged a relationship with the *Telegraph* to act as a war correspondent on the Northwest Frontier of India. His articles were widely acclaimed and formed the basis of his first book, *The Story of the Malakand Field Force: An Episode of Frontier War* (1898).

This began a lasting relationship with the *Telegraph* which was bolstered later by Churchill's personal relationship with Lord William Camrose, the proprietor of the *Daily Telegraph* from 1927. Initially, Lord Camrose was not particularly fond of Churchill, perhaps owing to Churchill's failed military campaign at the Dardanelles and Gallipoli in the First World War. In the *Sunday Times* in 1917, he dismissed Churchill as a 'gambler' and 'adventurer' and warned that Churchill's readmission into the government would 'constitute a grave danger to the Administration and to the Empire as whole'.

However, this state of affairs changed rather rapidly. After the fall of Lloyd George's coalition government in the general election of 1922, Churchill was without political office or even a parliamentary seat. He had become estranged from the Liberal Party, and Conservatives were still very suspicious of him. Churchill's political career seemed to hang in the balance. But Lord Camrose offered Churchill a speaking event at Aldwych Publicity Club in May 1923 which provided him with a political platform and helped relaunch his career. Churchill never forgot this act of kindness and wrote to Lord Camrose after the Second World War, 'My Dear Bill, who has never wavered nor varied in your fruitful friendship during all those long and baffling and finally tumultuous years when you took the Chair for me at that luncheon'.

This assured a firm friendship between the two for years to come. Churchill and his friend F.E. Smith invited Lord Camrose to join the 'Other Club', a dining society which they founded in 1911, and they often played bridge together. This helped ensure that Churchill's relationship with the *Telegraph* was also solid. Not only did Churchill write as a freelance journalist for the paper, he also regularly wrote in to express his opinion on stories or the paper itself. In February 1930, the *Telegraph* changed its print style and layout, to some consternation. Churchill happily wrote in to say that 'In its new form the *Daily Telegraph* is a most convenient paper to handle and I hope it may long continue to flourish in its faithful support of the Conservative cause.' Churchill continued this tradition throughout his life. In November 1950, he wrote to the editor of the *Telegraph* to correct the horse-racing column, 'From the Course', which had printed that Churchill's favourite horse, Colonist II, was a gelding, when in fact Colonist II was a colt.

It was during the 1930s that Churchill's journalistic relationship with the *Telegraph* really flourished. He wrote a series of articles on his impressions of the United States, then a series based on his five-volume history of the First World War, *The World Crisis* (published 1923–31), including a separate collection of articles on the naval aspects of the war, which he published as the often-overlooked series, 'U-boat War'. However, during this period Churchill's most significant contribution to the *Telegraph* was a collection of articles on British foreign policy and international affairs , which captures Europe's slow decline into war during the late 1930s.

These articles began when Churchill wrote to Lord Camrose in April 1938 to inquire if the *Telegraph* would be interested in publishing his articles on foreign policy. Churchill had been writing for the *Evening Standard*, but his outspoken objections to appeasement had caused them to terminate his contract because, as Churchill told Lord Camrose, his views were 'not in accordance with the policy of the paper'. Naturally, Camrose jumped at the opportunity and the series of articles was begun. These later went on to form the backbone of Churchill's book *Step by Step* (1939). By then the *Telegraph* had lost faith in the Chamberlain Government and clearly supported Churchill, Anthony Eden and other opponents of appeasement in the hopes they might form a government.

During the Second World War, Churchill remembered this by taking special care of the *Telegraph*. In 1943, during the astringent days of censorship, Churchill even personally saved the paper from persecution. In May that year, the *Telegraph* published news of three RAF pilots who escaped from Germany; this violated the D-notice forbidding publication of potentially sensitive material. The Army and Air Council wrote to Brendan Bracken, the Minster of Information, demanding charges be brought against the paper. The Ministry of Information took a hard line but Churchill wrote to them explaining that the *Telegraph* was a 'friendly paper' and that Lord Camrose was 'a patriotic man'; Churchill continued, 'would it not be well to see him first and explain that we have no choice unless he can give absolute assurance for the future'.

Shortly after the war, Lord Camrose repaid the favour by helping Churchill after he had hit some financial difficulty. Churchill had been in serious debt prior to the war, and wanted to put his beloved country home, Chartwell, up for sale to raise money to pay them off. This was before he had published his Second World War memoirs, so Churchill had little income at the time. In August 1945, Lord Camrose asked if Churchill would sell the house privately to friends, who would then let him live out the rest of his days there. Churchill agreed and Lord Camrose was able to raise the funds among a small group of friends, saving Chartwell from the market and preserving it for future generations, by arranging that the house would eventually go to the National Trust.

In the meantime, Churchill continued to write for the *Telegraph*. He published articles on the notion of a United Europe and his six-volume Second World War memoirs were serialised. In addition, he published a collection of articles in 1958 on the state of international affairs, which became a postscript to his war memoirs. Though he left public life after the close of his second premiership in 1955, the public were still very interested in him and several articles were written about him, from his frequent painting trips to the welfare of his pets, during the twilight of his life.

This period became a time of reflection for Churchill. While 1955 was the year he left No.10 for the last time, it was also a year when the *Telegraph* was celebrating its one hundredth anniversary. Churchill took this opportunity to reflect on his life as a journalist by writing to congratulate the paper. His words illuminate his relationship with the *Telegraph* and go some way to revealing the extent to which its legacy was intertwined with his own. It therefore seems very fitting that Churchill's own words should serve as an introduction to this thematic collection of articles:

As the oldest living member of the *Daily Telegraph* and *Morning Post* staff I am glad to send my warmest greetings and congratulations to the paper on reaching its century. It is fifty-eight years since I was a *Daily Telegraph* Correspondent in the days of the first Lord Burnham during the Malakand Campaign. In those enlightened times a combination of military and journalistic functions were possible. Over fifty-five years ago, through my friendship with Oliver Borthwick, I became a *Morning Post* Correspondent in South Africa; and only recently my old and revered friend, the late Lord Camrose, serialised for six years in the paper my Memoirs of the Second World War.

I therefore take an almost filial interest in the fortune of what is by any standards a great national newspaper; which plays for its side and plays fair. It is now venerable in years but young in method and spirit. Experience and enterprise are the combination capable of ensuring the continued advance which it is my heartfelt wish it may be destined to enjoy.

Chapter 1

Churchill as a Soldier

It was as a soldier that Winston Churchill's relationship with the *Telegraph* began. Though he had already seen action in Cuba, it was on Northwest Frontier of British India (now in Pakistan) where Churchill first wrote for the paper. He had been in India since October 1896 as a junior cavalry officer with the 4th Queen's Own Hussars. By 1897, Churchill was to lobby his way to the front in the Malakand Valley, where he fought against a Pashtun tribal uprising led by Mullah Sadullah. The Mullah had been nicknamed the 'Mad Fakir', and was described by Churchill as a 'wild enthusiast, convinced of his Divine mission and miraculous powers, [who] preached a crusade, or Jihad, against the infidel'. Churchill went on to fight in Sudan and then South Africa, where the *Telegraph* reported on his acts of bravery and his rising star.

ON THE INDIAN FRONTIER
By a Young Officer [Churchill]
6 October 1897

As the correspondent approaches the theatre of war he will naturally endeavour to observe every sign along the line of communications which indicates an unusual state of affairs. The first incident that suggested the great mobilisation on the frontier happened as I was leaving Bangalore. The 6th Madras Infantry were going to the front. It was a striking and, in some ways, a moving spectacle. The Madras Army is a very much-married army. The Madras Sepoy is a domesticated person. Women of every age and class hung, weeping, to the departing soldiers, their husbands or sons, who were going to some distant and mysterious danger, perhaps never to return. But the sadness was relieved by a striking and – if I may use an epithet adapted to the sentiment of the year – an Imperial thought. For hundreds of years the waves of conquest have swept across India from the North. Now the tale was to be different. The despised and often-conquered Southern Indians, under his white officers, would be carried by the railway to teach the sons of those who had made his fathers slaves that at last there were fighting men in the South.

At the station I was confronted by a fact which brings home with striking force the size of the Indian Empire. On asking the booking clerk – a sleek Babu – how far it was to Nowshera, he replied, with composure, that it was 2,027 miles. I rejoiced to think of the disgust with which a Little Englander would contemplate this fact. And then followed five weary days of train, the monotony of the journey only partially relieved by the changing scenes which the window presents. Northwards, through the arid tracts that lie between Guntahal and Wadi Junction, through the green and fertile slopes of the Central Provinces, to more dry and unpropitious country at the foot of the great mountains, with the never-ceasing rattle of the railway irritating the nerves and its odious food cloying the palate, I am swiftly carried. At Umballa a wing of the Dorsetshire Regiment is waiting, deterred from moving to Peshawar by several cholera cases; a few rest-camps near the line, a few officers hurrying to join their regiments, half-a-dozen nursing sisters travelling North, on an errand of mercy, are the only signs so far of the war. But as Rawal Pindi is neared the scene displays more significant features. Long trains of transport show the incessant passage of supplies to the front. One, in particular, of camels presented a striking picture. Six or seven of these animals are crowded into an open truck. Their knees are bound to prevent them moving on the journey, and their long necks, which rise in a cluster in the middle, have a strange and ridiculous aspect. Sometimes, I am told, curiosity, or ambition, or restlessness, or some other cause induces a camel to break his bonds and stand up, and as there are several tunnels on the line, the spectacle of a headless 'oont' is sometimes to be seen when the train arrives at Rawal Pindi.

This great northern cantonment usually contains a large garrison, but now most of its occupants are at Peshawar or Kohat, and those who remain are anxiously and eagerly expecting their orders. Situated at the junction of two strategic railways, Rawal Pindi must necessarily attract the attention of all who take an intelligent interest in the defences of the British Empire – of whatever nationality they may be. It is defended by a strong permanent fort, and the railways enable troops to be thrown either on the Kohat or Peshawar lines, as circumstances may decide. But when I recall the dusty roads, the burnt-up grass, the intense heat and the deserted barracks, I am unable to recommend it as a resting-place for either the sybarite, the invalid, or the artist.

Six hours' rail from 'Pindi' brings one to Nowshera, the base of the operations of the Malakand Field Force. Here the train is left, with a feeling of relief, which is, however, soon dispelled by the jolting of the tonga. A large and well-filled field hospital here presents the unpleasing and sombre side of a campaign. Fever, dysentery and bullets have accumulated more than three hundred poor fellows in the different wards, and the daily deaths mark the process of what tacticians and strategists have called 'the waste of war'.

It is fifty miles from Nowshera to the Malakand Pass, and the journey occupies seven hours in a tonga and involves much beating of galled and dilapidated ponies. Everywhere are the tricks of an army. A gang of prisoners chained hand to hand, escorted by a few Sikhs, marched sullenly by in the blazing heat. Suspicious characters, I am informed, being deported across the frontier into British territory until things are more settled. Some dead transport animals lay by the roadside, their throats hurriedly cut. The different stages – Mardom, a Jelala, Dargai – are marked by rest-camps and small mud forts, while droves of slaughter cattle and camels and scores of mules attest the necessary but unpicturesque business of the Commissariat.

After Dargai the Malakand Pass is reached, and henceforth the road winds upwards, until a two hours' climb brings the tonga to rest beneath the hill on which the fort stands. The ground is as broken and confused as can be imagined. On every side steep and often precipitous hills, covered with boulders and stunted trees, rise in confused irregularity. A hollow in the middle – the crater – is the camp of the West Kent Regiment. The slopes are dotted with white tents, perched on platforms cut in the side of the hill. On one of these platforms my own is now pitched, and its situation commands a view of the ground on which, a month ago, the fighting took place. In front is the signal station – a strong tower held by a picket – from which all day long the heliograph is flickering and blinking its messages to Nowshera, India, and on to the tape machines at the London clubs. To the left is Guides Hill, stormed in '95 by the corps who have given it its name, and who are now at Khar, four miles down the valley. To the right is the point from which Sir Bindon Blood, a month ago, delivered that turning and flanking movement – one of those obvious moves that everybody thinks of afterwards – which cleared the valley at one stroke from the tribesmen, and opened the way to the relief of Chakdara. Soldiers of many kinds are moving among the trees and tents. The tall Sikh, the red in his turban relieving the businesslike brown of the kharki; the British infantryman, with his white pouches and belts, none the whiter for six weeks' service; an occasional Lancer of the General's red escort, and crowds of followers in every conceivable costume, beginning at nothing but a rag and often ending abruptly, combine to produce a picture full of interest and animation.

Since the return of the column from the Upper Swat a period of waiting has supervened. Naturally, there is much discussion in the camp as to future movements. A reconnaissance has displayed the whole of the Boner Valley, a valley containing large numbers of rebellious tribesmen – and naturally everyone has been eager to invade so promising a country. But from Simla an order has arrived that the Bonerwals are to be spared. Great disappointment has been succeeded by trenchant criticism. Forbearance is construed by the natives as fear, and Boner's successful defiance of the Government will ring along the frontier, and find an echo in every bazaar in India. The 'home authorities', generally called 'politicians', the House of Commons, the Secretary of State, are successively arraigned. 'Is India,' it is indignantly asked, 'to be governed for its own good or to harmonise with party politics in England?' And the reply that the British public, having acquired by luck and pluck a valuable property in the East, intend to manage it as they please meets with no approval.

In so vexed a controversy I do not venture to express a decided opinion, but it is possible to compromise. India has a right to be governed for its own good. Great Britain has a right to govern India as it sees fit. The only solution which will reconcile these two statements is to instil into the minds of the British people correct ideas on the subject, and then duty and inclination will combine to produce a wise and salutary policy.

Meanwhile rumours run through the camp of movements here and marches there, all ultimately pointing to a move against the Mohmands, It should be remembered that this powerful tribe deliberately made an unprovoked attack on a British post, and, without cause or warning, committed a violation of the Imperial territory. I rejoice to be able to end this letter with the news that such audacity is no longer to remain unchastised, and that movements are now contemplated which indicate the adoption of a policy agreeable to expert opinion and suited to the dignity of the Empire. Of the progress of these movements, of the resistance that may be encountered, of the incidents that occur, I hope to give some account in my subsequent letters, and, if possible, to draw for the everyday reader, at his breakfast-table in 'comfortable England', something of a picture of the vivid open-air scenes which are presented by the war in the Indian Highlands.

THE WAR IN THE INDIAN HIGHLANDS
By a Young Officer [Churchill]
16 November 1897

We have entered upon a period of comparative peace. The Mohmands have expressed a wish to sue for terms, and negotiations are now going on between the political officers and the tribal jirgahs. The khans of Jar and Khar, who have been, from interested motives, very loyal and useful to the British Government during the stay of the brigades in this valley, are also endeavouring to promote a settlement. It would be rash to predict what the outcome will be. The peculiar position of this tribe – astride the frontier line – enables them to assume a very different attitude towards the Sirkar than could be maintained by tribes of equal strength otherwise situated: Not only do they receive assistance from Afghanistan in arms and men, but it is a refuge to which they can withdraw, and in which they have already placed their families, their flocks and herds. The independent demeanour which they display takes the form during the negotiations of shooting at our grass cutters and foraging parties, and of firing into camp from time to time. The troops, of course, feel it incumbent on them to reply, so that I am justified in qualifying the peace we are enjoying by the epithet 'comparative'.

A second convoy of sick and wounded leaves the camp tomorrow, and, travelling slowly down the line of communications, should reach Nowshera in about a week. There the hospital is, I hear, full, but room for the latest arrivals will be made by drafting the less serious cases to the large new base for wounded which has been established at Rawal Pindi, and which contains accommodation for 500 men. It is a long and a tedious journey for invalids, and they will be very weary of the jolting doolies before the comfortable beds of Nowshera are reached. The cheeriness and patience of the wounded men exceeds belief. Perhaps it is due to a realisation of the proximity in which they have stood to Death; perhaps partly to that feeling of relief with which a man turns for a spell from war to peace. In any case, it is remarkable. A poor fellow – a private in the Buffs – was hit at Zagai, and had his arm amputated at the shoulder. I expressed my sympathy, and he replied, philosophically, 'You can't make omelettes without breaking eggs', and, after a pause, added, with much satisfaction, 'The regiment did well that day'. He came of a fighting stock, but I could not help speculating on the possible future which awaited him. Discharge from the service as medically unfit, some miserable pension insufficient to command any pleasures in life except those of drink, a loafer's life and a pauper's death. Perhaps 'the regiment' – the officers, that is to say – would succeed in getting him work, and would, from their own resources, supplement his pension. But what a poor system it is by which the richest people in the world neglects the soldiers who have served it well, and which leaves to newspaper philanthropy, to local institutions and to private charity a burden which ought to be proudly borne by the nation.

Most of the officers and men wounded in this valley have been hit by bullets from Martini-Henry rifles, and it may be of some interest to consider the sources from which the tribesmen have obtained these arms. The perpetual state of intestine war in which they live creates a naturally keen demand for deadly weapons. A good Martini-Henry rifle will always command a price in these parts of Rs400, or about £25. As the actual value of such a rifle does not exceed Rs50, it is evident that a very large margin of profit would accrue to the enterprising trader. All along the frontier, and from far down into India, rifles are stolen by expert and cunning thieves. One tribe – the Ut Khels – who live in the Khyber Pass, have made the traffic in arms their especial business. Their thieves are the most daring. Their agents are the most remote. Some of their methods are highly ingenious. One story, which may not yet have reached the English Press, is worth repeating. A coffin was presented for railway transport. The relatives of the deceased accompanied it. The dead man, they said, had desired to be buried across the frontier. The smell proclaimed the corpse to be in an advanced state of decomposition. The railway officials afforded every facility to the passage of so unpleasant an object. No one impeded its progress. It was unapproachable. It was only when coffin and mourners were safe across the frontier that the police were informed that a dozen rifles had been concealed in the coffin, and that the body was represented by a piece of well-hung beef.

I regret to have to state that theft is not the only means by which the frontier tribes obtain weapons. At the camp near Manda I had an opportunity of inspecting a hundred rifles which had been surrendered by the local tribesmen. Of these rifles nearly a third were condemned Government Martinis, and displayed the Government stamp. Now no such rifles are supposed to exist. As soon as they are condemned, the Arsenal authorities are responsible that they are destroyed, and this is in every case carried out under European supervision. The fact that such rifles are not destroyed and are found in the possession of trans-frontier tribesmen points to a very grave instance of dishonest and illegal traffic which is being carried on by some person or persons connected with the Arsenal. It need hardly be said that a searching inquiry has been instituted.

Another point connected with these rifles is that even when

they have been officially destroyed – by cutting them in three pieces – the fractions have a marketable value. Several were shown me which had been rejoined and mended by the tribesmen. These were, of course, very dangerous weapons indeed. The rest of the hundred had strange tales to tell. Two or three were Russian military rifles, stolen probably from the distant posts in Central Asia. One was a Snider – taken at Maiwand – and bearing the number of the ill-fated regiment to whom it had belonged. Some had come from Europe, perhaps through Persia; others from the arms factory at Cabul. It was a strange instance of the tireless efforts of supply to meet demand.

We have now been nearly a month in the Mohmand Valley, and every spur and re-entrant of the mountains that surround it have acquired significance and importance from the numerous actions and reconnaissances. It now appears that the end is in sight, and that this episode in the story of the Malakand Field Force is soon to be concluded. At such a time it may not be inappropriate to consider the question of profit and loss. The tribesmen are reduced to submission. Their villages have been punished. Their grain and fodder have been requisitioned. The towers and forts from which they carry on their feuds and wars have been blown up by dynamite and are now in ruins. A severe lesson has been given. An example has been made. The power of the Empire has been asserted. But the cost has been heavy. Twenty-three officers and 245 men have been killed and wounded.

The whole question of the armament of the frontier tribes is of the greatest importance. The natives of these hills display a surprising aptitude with the rifle. Whatever frontier policy be pursued it is well that it should be pursued rapidly. The difficulties of dealing with these tribesmen will naturally increase as they obtain possession of more and better weapons. In this country transport is the life and soul of any force. At night it is necessary to pack the animals into the small area of an entrenched camp. A night attack by long-range fire on such a target must inevitably be attended with many casualties among the mules and camels. At Markhanai, on 14 September, eighty were killed, and in the severe attack on Sir Bindon Blood's camp at Nawagai, on 20 September, no fewer than a hundred and twenty were destroyed. Such losses would soon impair the mobility of any brigade. Nor is there any way by which in such a country they can be prevented. It is impossible to find camping grounds which are not commanded by some hill or assailable from some nullah. The more general adoption of such tactics as I have alluded to would soon paralyse military operations in these valleys, and reduce to immobility any force that might be employed. And so by this road I have come to the old conclusion that whatever is to be done on the frontier should be done quickly and completely.

It must seem strange to many people in England that the casualties in this valley should be in so different a proportion to those which have occurred elsewhere. While other generals have been gaining comparatively bloodless victories in various quarters, it has fallen to the lot of a single brigade to meet with stubborn and severe resistance and to sustain losses which exceed the accumulated losses of all the great armies now mobilised on the Indian frontier. The main cause is, as I have already stated, the proximity of the Afghan border. But it would be unjust to deny to the people of the Mohmand Valley the reputation for courage, tactical skill and marksmanship which they have so well deserved. During uncounted years they have brawled and fought in the unpenetrated gloom of barbarism. At length they struck a blow at civilisation, and civilisation, though compelled to record the odious vices that the fierce light of scientific war has exposed, will yet ungrudgingly admit that they are a brave and warlike race. Their name will live in the minds of all men for some months, even in this busy century, and there are many families in England who will never forget it. The valley and its people have become historic. But perhaps they do not realise all this, or if they do it may not filter the regret they feel for having tried conclusions with the British Raj. Their game has cost them dear. Indeed, as we have already been told, 'Nothing is so expensive as glory.'

ARMOURED TRAIN ATTACKED
11 December 1899

The event of the week has been the attack upon the armoured train. On Wednesday morning it was ordered out at five a.m. to proceed carefully from point to point to Frere. Under Captain Haldane, of the Gordon Highlanders, who for the time was attached to the Dublin Fusiliers, seventy-two non-commissioned officers and men of that battalion, with Lieutenant Frankland, forty-five non-commissioned officers and men of the Durban Light Infantry, under Captain Wylie and Lieutenant Alexander, and five bluejackets from Her Majesty's ship *Tartar*, under a petty officer, manned the train. Besides these were the engine hands and about seven platelayers to repair damages. Mr Winston Churchill, of the *Morning Post*, also rode upon the train. Correspondents were wont to proceed in rotation upon the trips, but that morning others whose turn it was, either too sleepy or indifferent, did not embark. A Scotch or Glasgow telegraphist in the Natal Government employ also accompanied the troops, so as to wire back any information either from the stations or by hitching on to the telegraph lines en route. The train stopped for a few minutes at Ennersdale, the first station, and about seven miles north. From there a message was sent back that the line was clear, and, receiving authority, the train proceeded onward to Frere, the next station. There another brief stoppage was made, and the police patrol, being interrogated, stated that they had seen no Boers, although it was known that a few of the enemy had occupied a farm but four miles off the previous night. A wire was sent in to headquarters from Frere that all was clear, and, without waiting for any reply, the train ran on to Chieveley. On the way several natives tried to warn the train back. At Chieveley Station about 300 Boers were seen upon both sides of the line, but some distance away, riding furiously towards Frere, as if to intercept the return of the train. It consisted of, in front, an open, flat truck, upon which was a seven-pounder, manned by the bluejackets. Next it was an armoured truck with some of the Dublins. Behind that was the engine and tender, and again came two armoured trucks and an open flat truck with railway plant. In the rear armoured trucks were a few of the Dublins, the Durbans, and the railway staff.

Three miles nearer Frere, rounding a curve and under the slope of a hill, the Boers poured volleys at the train, and at the same moment a repeating three-pounder Maxim-Nordenfeldt cannon began blaring at them. Two similar guns also opened fire on the devoted train. Suddenly, in a moment, and without warning, as the train was steaming rapidly back – it is a single line – a point was reached where the Boers had removed the fish-plates and propped up one side of the lines with stones. Instantly the flat rear truck – then in front, as the engine was backing – jumped the metals, followed by the next two trucks.

They ran, bumping, for a little distance; then the flat truck and the armoured truck next turned over, throwing all the occupants into the field. The flat truck turned over, wheels uppermost, whilst the top-heavy armoured carriage almost turned a complete somersault. Luckily the engine and tender and the other trucks kept the metals. A platelayer was killed outright, being pinned under the wagon, but most of the others miraculously escaped with a shaking and slight bruises. Then it was that the Boers began firing shells and bullets, faster than ever, at those struggling upon the ground, striving to free themselves from the wreckage. With magnificent intrepidity, although being shot at from three sides, the Dublins and Volunteers began returning the enemy's fire, taking what little shelter they could alongside the line. Mr Winston Churchill and Lieutenant Frankland clambered out of the truck next to the gun, and, proceeding to the detailed wagons, called for volunteers to assist in clearing the line. A score of willing hands responded, Captain Wylie and others of the Durban Light Infantry assisting. Amid a hail of bullets and bursting three-pounders the flat truck was tilted over, and a few men released. Then they tried to push away the armoured truck, but it was too heavy for their united efforts. Churchill and the others encouraged the men, rallying them again and again.

Meanwhile the Dublins, Durbans and a few others were pouring volleys into the almost unseen Boers hidden behind the rocks, about 1,000 yards away. Independent firing was also being kept up at them, and the bluejackets, bravely commanded by their petty officer – who was the incarnation of coolness – got their seven-pounder into action. They sent in two, if not three, well-aimed shells at the Boers, several hundred of whom lined the hills. But just then, a shot from the enemy's three-pounder or field gun hit the small naval seven-pounder, knocked gun and carriage on to the veldt, and wounded several of the seamen. But the men were not a whit beaten. Sergeant E. Bassett, of the Dublins, standing up, shouted his orders to the men, giving them the direction and ranges in the coolest manner. Nearly everybody had clambered out of the armoured trucks, which were being pelted with the enemy's shells. The 'character' of the Dublins, Private Kavanagh – that day one of the stretcher-bearers – chaffed and encouraged his comrades, telling them the Boer shells could hit nothing. He it was who at Dundee, after the long day's battle, on being asked if he was hungry and did not wish for something to eat, said, 'No. How can I with my mouth full?' 'Full!' said his officer – 'what do you mean?' 'Why, my heart's been in it all day, sir,' replied Kavanagh, with a grin. And so the 'hard case' of his battalion shouted and joked, walked about amid a tempest of bullets, and stirred the gallant, glorious Dublins to shoot well and true.

The trucks could not be man-handled, so engine-driver Wegner and his mates uncoupled the wagons that had been in front, ran them down the line a little way, and commenced to butt and smash a road through the overturned wagons. By dint of pulling back with chains and smashing forward, the engine and tender won past the wreckage. Then they tried to return and pick up the other two wagons, the armoured and flat trucks, but they were baulked by one of the others having swung round across the line, and finding the coupling chains smashed. Captain Wylie, who had been shot through the leg early in the action, got Sergeant Tod, of the Durbans, to place some stones to protect his head as he lay upon the ground. Scarcely had Tod done so and turned to help the other wounded when a shell knocked Captain Wylie's little parapet away, and Tod was himself thrown up by a kick from a piece of the projectile which hit him severely. All the wounded, with the help and direction of Churchill, were placed upon the tender. Meanwhile, the engine was struck in several places by shells. The feed-injector was broken. A shell passed through a corner of the tender, killing one of the wounded men and maiming others as they lay prone upon the coal-sacks, whilst another missile struck the smoke-box, and missed penetrating the boiler by the merest shave, but it started a leak or two. Wegner, the driver, also was hit and stunned by a piece of shell. Then, there being no more to be done, the engine and tender, with its freight of fully a score wounded and well – there were a dozen injured – steamed on to Ennersdale and then to Frere, to summon assistance.

Those left behind spread out along the line were still blazing away at the Boers, fighting as a forlorn hope whilst the train drew off. Several of the Durbans and Dublins followed it a little way on foot, shooting at the enemy as they slowly retired. At Frere it was found that the station hands and police had gone and taken the telegraph instruments with them. Those McArthur took out with him had been broken in the action, and there being no other way out of it, with their mangled freight of dead and wounded, engine and tender steamed back into Estcourt.

Mr Churchill, however, after handing in his revolver and field-glasses, said he was going back to the scene to assist the wounded, and stand by the men. The last seen of him was as he trudged alone away down into the arena of battle, where the shot and shell were still screaming, splintering rocks and ploughing the ground. A few of the luckier fugitives passed him on the way, but failed to turn him back from his purpose. A small body of mounted Volunteers who rode out from Estcourt and Frere got upon the right flank of the Boers, and inflicted some loss upon the enemy before they were compelled to retire before superior numbers.

The news of the disaster to the train caused a shock to the little garrison, all of whom were anxious to be led out to their comrades' rescue. But it could not be; larger interests held the commander's hands no doubt, and the firing which we had all heard went on for some little time longer, and then ceased. Subsequently an ambulance tram was sent out, under Surgeon-Captain Briscoe, to bring in the wounded. The Boers met him, but declined to give any information or return a man until General Joubert had been communicated with. The officer was told to return next day, when an answer would be given him. He did so, taking as before medicines and stretchers with him, but the answer was the wounded and prisoners would be sent to Pretoria. Incidentally, Surgeon-Captain Briscoe learned that, according to the Boers, three of our men had been killed and twelve wounded. That does not include the killed and wounded brought in by the engine and tender. The exact number missing are – Dublin Fusiliers, two officers (Captain Haldane and Lieutenant Falkland) and forty-five non-commissioned officers and men; Durban Light Infantry, twenty-four non-commissioned officers and men missing. During the afternoon and evening several of the men straggled back, including a platelayer or two. There are four platelayers missing, and Mr Winston Churchill, about whom the Boers would give no information beyond saying that the list and report of the affair would appear in the Pretoria newspapers.

In periods of great excitement small matters become lost to the recollection. Of those I interrogated very few agreed as to various details of the disaster. The telegraphist, Mr. R.T. McArthur, furnished, perhaps, the clearest and most succinct account. He said:

'We left Estcourt at 5.30 a.m., and ran on to Ennersdale, and reported by wire, "All clear". Shortly before reaching Frere we met and spoke to some of the Natal Police, who had been bivouacking upon the kopjes. They told us the Boers had all gone back the previous night. Then we went to Frere, where we wired the General, "All well", and without waiting for a reply ran on to Chieveley. Shortly before entering that station we saw fifty Boers going west at a canter with some wagons, as we thought. We waited a few minutes at Chieveley, and then started back. About three miles out, or two miles north of Frere, we noticed several hundred Boers about 800 yards off, on the west side. Then we saw more on the east of the line. They began firing at us, first with rifles and then with Maxim-Nordenfeldt cannon. One of their shots made a big dent in the rear armoured truck, but did not enter.

'Their guns were behind the kopje – at least two repeating-cannon, which shot a steady flame, and a heavier piece that threw shrapnel at us. But a few yards on our rear then the front truck ran off the line, shaking and jolting terribly, and ours, the next or armoured one, followed suit, and soon all three left the rails. The next thing I knew we were all upset, and, strangely, only one man was killed. We all scrambled out. Sitting down, the soldiers began firing volleys at the Boers, who responded by peppering us with more shot and shell. In about five minutes Mr Churchill came from what had been the front of the train, took charge, and asked for volunteers to shift the trucks. About fifteen men helped to do so, but the wagons were too heavy to move. Then the engine managed to smash through, breaking them up and getting knocked about in doing so. All this was done under heavy fire. We tried to couple up the trucks that had been in front, but could not, the line being blocked. Then, picking up all the wounded we could see, we started for Frere to get assistance. My instruments were smashed, and we found those at Frere had been carried off by the police for safe-keeping. From there we pushed ahead to Ennersdale, whence I wired to the General, giving him a few details. We had several men shot down whilst we were putting the wounded on the tender, although our troops did their best to cover the operation by firing volleys. Several of the shells struck the telegraph wires and poles, cutting and knocking down the line.'

Wednesday was a sad, weary night in Estcourt. The rain fell continually, and the troops were soaked and covered with mud. An order was issued for the women and children to leave the town, and there were preparations made for the troops to retire upon Mooi River. Finally sterner and wiser counsels prevailed, and a rallying position was chosen, as I have said, upon Fort Durnford, or the kopje that stands over it, and which commands the railway station and bridges. The next day (Thursday) we heard the Boers were coming on, but they perhaps, like ourselves, were busy trying to dry their clothes and other belongings, for the day turned out, in its earlier part, light and warm. Happily, too, further reinforcements arrived in the shape of two battalions, and more were hourly expected.

THE WAR
15 December 1899

Mr Winston Churchill has escaped from Pretoria. The Boer source from which we derive this information does not say whether he has fled. He will no doubt turn up in good time. It will be remembered that he was captured with nearly 100 men who had gone out once too often with an armoured train from Estcourt without any protecting or scouting force.

A servant of the adventurous War Correspondent of the *Morning Post,* writing to Lady Randolph Churchill, told the circumstances of his master's capture in a letter worth reprinting: 'I came down in the armoured train,' says the writer, 'with the driver, who is wounded in the head with a shell. He told me all about Mr Winston. He says there is not a braver gentleman in the Army. The driver was one of the first wounded, and he said to Mr Winston, "I am finished." So Mr Winston said to him, "Buck up a bit; I will stick to you", and he threw off his revolver and field-glasses and helped the driver pick twenty wounded up and put them on the tender of the engine. Every officer in Estcourt thinks Mr C. and the engine driver will get the VC. It took them two hours to clear the road. They had to knock the iron tracks off the road by running into them with the engine. The shells had knocked them all to pieces. How the engine escaped being blown up I don't know; it was a total wreck. The engine, with Mr C. on it, got back to Frere Station safe, and then Mr C. would get off and back to look after Captain Haldane. Mr C. left his field-glasses and revolver on the engine and the driver says he had lost his hat. It was a frightful morning, too. It had been raining for about twenty-four hours, and it rained in torrents all the day, so he must have been very wet; he had a good mackintosh on, though. The driver says he was as cool as anything, and worked very hard, and how he escaped he doesn't know, as about fifty shells hit the engine.'

If Mr Churchill is caught the Boers won't let him have the privileges of a prisoner of war again. He cannot be shot unless he uses arms to resist capture, but he may be subjected to confinement rigorous enough to control the innate daring and resourcefulness of which he inherits his full share.

Chapter 2

Churchill as an Author

Churchill developed his writing skills early on. His war correspondence for the *Telegraph* formed the basis of his first book, *The Story of the Malakand Field Force: An Episode of Frontier War*. In fact Churchill's writing helped him make a name for himself. As an author he wrote books on his war experiences and adventures, biographies on his father and ancestor John Churchill, histories of the 'English-Speaking Peoples' as well as his famous war memoirs from the First and Second World Wars. Churchill's journalism and writing became a staple of his life. He often said that he lived 'from pen to mouth'. In 1953, Churchill was even awarded the Nobel Prize for Literature in recognition of 'his mastery of historical and biographical description as well as for brilliant oratory in defending exalted human values'.

THE MALAKAND FIELD FORCE
14 March 1898

We do not pretend to take up this bright and valuable volume in any absolutely impartial spirit. It was the privilege of this journal during the recent frontier war in India to present to the public from time to time some of the few glimpses of the actual marching and fighting which were permitted to appear. After the first one or two of these letters had been printed the country learned to expect with interest the subsequent lively and graphic sketches which brought home almost the only complete information about the costly and anxiously watched campaign. The letters, it will now be known, were contributed to our columns by Lieutenant Winston Spencer Churchill, of the 4th Queen's Own Hussars, the son of the late Lord Randolph Churchill. In the present volume, which is inscribed to Major-General Sir Bindon Blood, KCB, whose portrait graces the front page, Mr Spencer Churchill expands his letters to the *Daily Telegraph* into an ample and very interesting story of the Malakand Field Force, calling it an 'Episode of the Frontier War', and working in such particulars and developments as were necessary to round off the tale. The first chapter of the book is devoted to a picturesque and striking description of the tribes on the border, which will be read with all the more attention now since we have learned what tough customers they are to deal with. As a specimen of Lieutenant Churchill's vivid style we may quote the following passage:

> Every man is a soldier. Either he is the retainer of some Khan, the man-at-arms of some feudal baron, as it were, or he is a unit in the armed force of his village, the burgher of medieval history. In such surroundings we may, without difficulty, trace the rise and fall of an ambitious Pathan. At first he toils with zeal and thrift as an agriculturist on that plot of ground which his family have held since they expelled some former possessor. He accumulates in secret a sum of money. With this he buys a rifle from some daring

thief who has risked his life to snatch it from a frontier guard-house. He becomes a man to be feared. Then he builds a tower to his house and overawes those around him in the village. Gradually they submit to his authority. He might now rule the village, but he aspires still higher. He persuades or compels his neighbours to join with him in an attack on the castle of a local Khan. The attack succeeds. The Khan flies or is killed, the castle is captured, the retainers make terms with the conqueror. The land tenure is feudal. In return for their acres they follow their new chief to war. Were he to treat them worse than other Khans treated their servants they would sell their strong arms elsewhere. He treats them well. Others resort to him. He buys more rifles. He conquers two or three neighbouring Khans. He has now become a power. This state of continual tumult has produced a habit of mind which recks little of injuries, holds life cheap and embarks on war with careless levity. The tribesmen of the Afghan border afford the spectacle of a people who fight without passion and kill one another without loss of temper. Such a disposition, combined with an absolute lack of reverence for all forms of law and authority, and a complete assurance of equality, is the cause of their frequent quarrels with the British power. A trifle rouses their animosity. They make a sudden attack on some frontier post. They are repulsed. From their point of view the incident is closed. There has been a fair fight, in which they have had the worst fortune. What puzzles them is that 'the Sirkar' should regard so small an affair in a serious light. Thus the Mohmands cross the frontier, and the action of Shabkadr is fought. They are surprised and aggrieved that the Government are not content with the victory, but must needs invade their territories and impose punishment. Or, again, the Mohmands, because a village has been burnt, assail the camp of the Second Brigade by night. It is a drawn game. They are astounded that the troops do not take it in good part.

What follows this preliminary sketch is a long and most animated narrative of the events of the campaign, so far as they come within the purview of the gallant author. He leads us with a firm strong step from the Malakand camp through the stirring events of the defence and relief of Chakdara; next at the Gate of Swat we see the third brigade formed, and the action of Landakai waged; and he recounts, among many other incidents, that splendid exploit in which Lord Fincastle gained his Victoria Cross, the details of which are familiar to everyone. After his vivid description of the scene, he says:

> The extremes of fortune which befell Lord Fincastle and Lieutenant Greaves may well claim a moment's consideration. Neither officer was employed officially with the force. Both had travelled up at their own expense, evading and overcoming all obstacles in an endeavour to see something of war. Knights of the sword and pen, they had nothing to offer but their lives; no troops to lead, no duties to perform, no watchful commanding officer to report their conduct. They played for high stakes, and fortune, never so capricious as on the field of battle, dealt to one the greatest honour that a soldier can hope for, an honour, as some think, the greatest in the gift of the Crown, and to the other a glorious death.

After this, in Lieutenant Churchill's excellent company, we follow the advance against the Mohmands; we march up Janol Valley, we pass with Sir Bindon Blood to Nawagai, to watch the battles of Shahi Tangi, and of Bilot, and with the Mohmand field force we behold the Maharajah of Patiala and Sir Pertab Singh fighting bravely and loyally under the Queen's colours. Lieutenant Churchill has a theory about this same happy spectacle in connection with polo which we must quote. He says:

I could not help thinking that polo has had a good deal to do with strengthening the good relations of the Indian princes and the British officers. It may seem strange to speak of polo as an Imperial factor, but it would not be the first time in history that games have played a part in high politics. Polo has been the common ground on which English and Indian gentlemen have met on equal terms, and it is to that meeting that much mutual esteem and respect is due. Besides this, polo has been in some cases the salvation of our subalterns in India, and the young officer no longer, as heretofore, has a 'centre-piece' of brandy on his table night and day. The pony and polo-stick have drawn him from his bungalow and mess room to play a game which must improve his nerve, his judgment, and his temper. The author of 'Indian Polity' asserts that the day will come when British and native officers will serve together in ordinary seniority and on the same footing. I do not myself believe this is possible, but if it should ever come to pass the way will have been prepared on the polo ground.

In a series of spirited chapters the author thus brings us back to the frontier with the war more or less finished, and proceeds to enrich his book with some most interesting dissertations on the work of the cavalry, on the health of the troops, and on the troublesome business of 'sniping'. It would be worthwhile to give Lieutenant Churchill's picture of a sniping night (page 265) if our limits permitted, in which such strange things occur as that fifty bullets should fall into a camp 100 yards square, and hit nothing except a single mule in the tail. But we must close this notice of a very able and fascinating soldier's book with the recommendation that the last chapter, that upon 'The Riddle of the Frontier', should be carefully read. Loyally and dispassionately the author discusses the merits and demerits of the 'Forward Policy' to which he considers that we are now as good as committed. He recognises its perils and difficulties, but in a striking passage compares the situation to one of those dark defiles in the Afghan hills, which seem to have no outlet until suddenly the gap opens, and an easy way is disclosed to the quiet valley beyond.

THE RIVER WAR
8 November 1899

Many excellent books have been written about the loss and recapture of the Sudan. Each successive stage in the development of the tragic story has found its historian in either soldier or war correspondent who made the campaign, and it seemed as if there were hardly any room left for the tale to be told over again. Mr Winston Churchill, however, who was present at the Battle of Omdurman, has compiled two admirable volumes, which will, to a considerable extent, supersede much of what has previously appeared. He has taken his time in the production thereof, and, though the capture of the Khalifa is even yet a thing of the future, and another expedition is certain to be required, the main work is done. Our author describes in detail the operations on the Blue Nile, culminating in the fiercely fought actions of Gedaref and Rosaires, where only the splendid pluck of the British officers and 10th Sudanese prevented disaster, and the hazardous reconnaissance under Colonel Kitchener in the neighbourhood of Shirkela, where the column, which was sent out on the assumption that there were scarcely a thousand warriors with the Khalifa, suddenly found that he had eight or nine thousand, and that a speedy retreat was absolutely imperative. There were no war correspondents present on these occasions, and the country hardly realised what tough work was accomplished after the crowning event at Omdurman.

Mr Churchill is the master of a most fascinating style. His opening chapter, on the annual miracle of the Eternal Nile, is an effective piece of writing; his chapters on the rise of Mahdism and the early Sudan expeditions, on the responsibilities of the Gladstone Administration, and the tragedy at Khartoum, are, equally with his battle pictures, vivid and masterly. Yet there is one obvious and serious blot on the merit of these volumes. Outspoken criticism is a virtue, but Mr Churchill does not lose an opportunity of adversely criticising the Sirdar. He praises him for his military capacity, extols his clear-sightedness, admits that he stands out as a 'great and splendid figure', and yet more than once he leaves the impression that he is insinuating a personal dislike. Take, for example, the following passage:

The meaner historian owes something to truth. His wonderful industry, his undisturbed patience, his noble perseverance, are qualities too valuable for a man to enjoy in this imperfect world without complementary defects. The General, who never spared himself, cared little for others. He treated all men like machines – from the private soldiers, whose salutes he disdained, to the superior officers he rigidly controlled. The comrade who had served with him and under him for many years in peace and peril was flung aside incontinently as soon as he ceased to be of use. The Sirdar only looked to the soldiers who could march and fight. The wounded Egyptian, and latterly the wounded British soldier, did not excite his interest, and of all the departments of his army the one neglected was that concerned with the care of the sick and injured . . . The stern and unpitying spirit of the commander was communicated to his troops, and the victories which marked the progress of the River War were accompanied by acts of barbarity, not always justified by the harsh customs of savage conflicts or the fierce and treacherous nature of the Dervish.

Again he strongly denounces the destruction of the Mahdi's tomb – though Colonel Rhodes, who edits these two volumes, expressly dissociates himself from such criticism, while admitting that the manner in which it was destroyed left much to be desired – he attempts to whitewash the character of the Khalifa in the face of the evidence of Slatin and Ohrwalder and Noufeld, who lived for long desolate years in his clutches; he denies that the subject races of the Dervishes welcomed the invaders, though they freely enlisted on our side whenever they had a chance, and he makes the most of the few isolated cases in which British soldiers failed to govern their passion for revenge on the battlefield. On points such as these the evidence of men whose experience of Sudan campaigning is infinitely greater than Mr Churchill's is worthy of more implicit credence than his.

The great stage pictures of the Sudan are familiar by this time to every reader. Mr Churchill's rendering of them is admirable, but we will select our passages for quotation from other chapters than those dealing with the Atbara and Omdurman. Here, for example, the author pays a glowing tribute to the British officers in command of native regiments:

> There is one spirit which animates all the dealings of the British officer with the native soldier. It is not seen only in Egypt; it exists wherever Britain raises mercenary troops. The officer's military honour is the honour of his men. In many countries where the Empire has varying shades of responsibility and power the natives

are formed into regiments and squadrons. Some are cowardly and debased; others reckless and excitable. But whatever they are, or wherever they are, the officer who leads them believes in them and swears by them. The British officer of an active corps is never known – on duty or off duty, before or after dinner, by word or implication – to speak disparagingly of his own men. The captain who commands a squadron of Bengal Lancers boasts proudly of his stately Sikh sowars, and does not hesitate to declare that they are better all round than British cavalry, which is, of course, absurd. The officer of Guides prefers the long-limbed, hawk-eyed Afridi. The Gurkha subaltern's eyes glisten as he tells of those whom he believes would follow wherever he would dare to go. There is no exception.

In another place he philosophises on the little wars of the Empire and the remorseless fate which befalls those who withstand its might. We may consider how strange and varied are the diversions of an Imperial people. Year after year, and stretching back to an indefinite horizon, we see the figures of the odd and bizarre potentates against whom the British arms continually are turned. They pass in a long procession: The Akhund of Swat; Cetewayo, brandishing an assegai as naked as himself; Osman Digna, the Immortal and the Irretrievable; Theebaw, with his umbrella; Lobengula, gazing fondly at the pages of *Truth*; Kruger, singing a psalm of victory; Prempeh, abasing himself in the dust; the Mad Mullah, on his white ass; and, latest of all, the Khalifa, in his coach of state. It is like a pantomime scene at Drury Lane. These extraordinary foreign figures – each with his complete set of crimes, horrible customs, and 'minor peculiarities' – march one by one from the dark wings of barbarism up to the bright lights of civilisation. For a space their names are on the wires of the world and the tongues of men . . . And when the world-audience clap their hands, amused yet impatient, and the potentates and their trains pass on, some to exile, some to prison, some to death – for it is a grim jest to them – and their conquerors, taking their possessions, forget even their names. Nor will history record such trash.

President Kruger scarcely deserves to be placed in such a gallery, for history will certainly record his name as long as the British Empire remains. Another interesting passage is that in which Mr Churchill describes the movements of the Khalifa after the flower of his army had fallen on the plain outside Omdurman.

> He seems, if we may judge from the account of his personal servant, an Abyssinian boy, to have faced the disaster that had overtaken him with singular composure. He rested until two o'clock, when he ate some food. Thereafter he repaired to the Tomb, and in that ruined shrine, amid the wreckage of the shell-fire, the defeated sovereign appealed to the spirit of Mohammed Ahmed to help him in his sore distress. It was the last prayer ever offered over the Mahdi's grave. The celestial counsels seem to have been in accordance with the dictation of common-sense, and at four o'clock the Khalifa, hearing that the Sirdar was already entering the city, and that the English cavalry were on the parade-ground to the west, mounted a small donkey, and accompanied by his principal wife, a Greek nun as a hostage, and a few attendants, rode leisurely off towards the south.

It would, as Mr Churchill says, have been the easiest thing in the world to cut the tyrant's throat, but his Emirs were faithful to the last, and rallied again to his side. As for the Fashoda incident, the author gives us some personal details which, so far as we are aware, have not been published before.

Major Marchand, with a guard of honour, came to meet the General. They shook hands warmly. 'I congratulate you,' said the Sirdar, 'on all you have accomplished.' 'No,' replied the Frenchman, pointing to his troops, 'it is not I, but these soldiers who have done it.' And Kitchener, telling the story afterwards, remarked, 'Then I knew he was a gentleman.'

But though the Sirdar and the Major were on good terms, matters nearly came to an open rupture when the two leaders quitted Fashoda, and Captain Germain was left in charge of the French camp, while Marchand went down to Cairo to receive instructions from Paris. Germain began to be aggressive and defiant.

Colonel Jackson protested again and again. Germain sent haughty replies and persisted in his provoking policy. At last the British officer was compelled to declare that if any more patrols were sent into the Dinka country he would not allow them to return to the French post. Whereat Germain rejoined that he would meet force by force. All tempers were worn by fever, heat, discomfort and monotony. The situation became very difficult and the tact and patience alone of Colonel Jackson prevented a conflict which would have resounded in all parts of the world. He confined his troops strictly to their lines, and moved as far from the French camp as was possible. But there was one dark day when the French officers worked in their shirts with their faithful Senegalese to strengthen the entrenchments, and busily prepared for a desperate struggle. On the other side little activity was noticeable. The Egyptian garrison, though under arms, kept out of sight, but a wisp of steam above the funnels of the redoubtable gunboats showed that all was ready.

When Marchand returned he reproved his subordinate, expressed his regrets to Colonel Jackson, and when the tricolour was hauled down, and the French mission departed for home, they parted good friends amid mutual salutes. The extracts we have quoted will bear out the estimate we have given of Mr Churchill's book. Despite the blemish referred to it is the best account of the River War that has yet appeared, and will not only add to the author's literary reputation, but excite great hopes for his literary future.

RECENT LITERATURE
16 February 1900

Mr Winston Spencer Churchill in the short preface to this novel, *Savrola*, states that it was written in 1897, and that 'he submits it with considerable trepidation to the judgment or clemency of the public.' Yet crude as it undoubtedly is in certain important particulars and melodramatic in not a few passages, we have no doubt that it will be widely read and generally liked. Its faults are more than counterbalanced by its many good points. Mr Churchill has a stirring story to tell, and tells it in vigorous, straightforward English. His personages are real flesh and blood; his characters are drawn with a bold, free hand, and his incidents are full of life and vigour. He introduces us to an imaginary Republic of Laurania, on the shores of the Mediterranean, ruled by an able despot named Molara, who has suspended the Constitution and firmly gripped the reins of absolute power. The people are on the eve of a revolution, and their leader is Savrola, the hero of the novel, a young man self-centred and philosophical, and able to twist the mob to his will by his eloquence. Savrola is a sort of latter-day Rienzi, and his plans succeed. It is a curious plot. Molara has a beautiful wife, who, at her husband's bidding, tries to worm Savrola's secrets from him, and ends by falling in love with him; the army is disaffected, with the exception of the Republican Guard, and joins the popular side when an invader crosses the frontier and marches on the capital; the fleet, owing to foreign complications, is sent away by the Dictator just before the revolution breaks out, and is recalled post haste only to find the city in the hands of the rebels. The best chapters of the book are those which describe the progress of the insurrection, the fighting in the streets, the last stand of the tyrant, and the escape under fire of a young lieutenant along the telegraph wires – a sensational incident, which is dealt with in a masterly way. Then the fleet returns and bombards the city, and the last scene of all shows us the triumphant patriot deserted by his party in the hour of triumph and fleeing from the burning city in the company of the dead Molara's wife. Judged as a complete whole, the book everywhere bears traces of a first essay in novel-writing. The construction of the plot runs on the lines of an Adelphi drama. Yet the vigorous strokes with which the fighting episodes are narrated and the interesting observations on politics which are scattered through these pages amply redeem its imperfections. Its abundant cleverness is manifest throughout, and gives promise of admirable work to come when this talented young soldier author returns from his campaigns.

MR CHURCHILL'S BOOK: THE WORLD CRISIS

Reviewed by Lieutenant-Colonel Repington

30 October 1923

Mr Winston Churchill's new book, '*The World Crisis, 1915*', is mainly concerned with the Dardanelles and with the political, naval and military aspects of that great adventure. Other subjects come under review, such as the action of the Dogger Bank and the origin of the Tanks, but the Dardanelles makes such an absorbing story that everything else becomes subordinate to it.

The book is undoubtedly of very great interest. It is enriched and distinguished by the author's talent for writing, by uncanny gifts for special pleading, and by infinite incapacity to bore. It is packed full of pseudo-secret documents, private letters, and summaries of War Council meetings. The Official Secrets Act has no terrors for ex-Ministers, and the next person convicted under it will have cause for serious complaint. We are permitted to observe, as from a stage box, the play of personalities, passions and prejudices aroused by the not distant clash of arms. Among the personalities, the figures of Kitchener and Fisher may be among those whom history will account great, and there are scores of other personages involved whose conduct will interest posterity. We receive an impression that Mr Churchill was everything on the War Council, and his colleagues nothing. 'The Admiralty is actually carrying on the war,' he writes to Mr Asquith, and the Admiralty was Mr Churchill. Mr Asquith is not given the dominant position which, in common esteem, he occupied. He appears rather as taking a motherly, if languid, interest in the activities of his irrepressible First Lord, but there is fastened upon him full knowledge of and acquiescence in all that is done. Sir Edward Grey chiefly figures as the recipient of Churchillian homilies. Mr Lloyd George appears as a dark figure looming in the background of all these great occurrences, and scarcely emerging from it. It is all drawn from life, but strikes us as only lifelike in patches. Perhaps Mr Lloyd George will later have an Eastern epic devoted to him alone.

We find here, again, as we found in Mr Churchill's last book, that he interpreted with a liberty bordering on licence the Letters Patent and Orders in Council which regulate the high office which he held in 1915. He both asserted and assumed unlimited powers of suggestion and initiative over the whole field of war, particularly in relation to the higher strategy, with which he had but slight familiarity. He even admits that he drafted 'operational telegrams'. His rhapsodies and spread-eagle flights about the East and strategic flank attacks give us the measure of his judgment. He did most of the talking at the War Council on naval affairs while the great Admirals at his side remained mute – partly perhaps from stupefaction, and partly from a mistaken sense of duty. The War Council rarely, if ever, called upon them to speak, and never demanded from them an opinion upon the practicability or otherwise of action proposed by the First Lord. For this omission the whole of the War Council and the experts have been roundly and deservedly trounced by the Dardanelles Commissioners. Mr Churchill favoured the War Council with a succession of papers on strategy which should have been presented by his naval advisers. His statement that 'it was left to the War Council Members to write papers on the broad strategic view of the war' is disingenuous. Why were the competent authorities not asked to write them? His catching enthusiasm, his torrent of speech, and his aplomb seem to have carried the Council away and to have caused them to lose all sense of realities. At long last, what with the efflux of time, the boredom of perpetual listening, the disappointments and the failures, Mr Asquith one day asked Mr Churchill what he could do for him, and the Admiralty knew him no more. In this book he shows that others erred besides himself, but this does not help him very much. We are sensible all through – and it is almost comic relief in the tragic story – that the sailors are being dragged unwillingly to school by their domineering and vertiginous First Lord. We admire his infinite capacity for taking pains, but it would be an intolerable state of affairs were another First Lord, in another war, to be allowed to exercise the indefensible powers which Mr Churchill both claimed and exercised in 1915.

The proper Appendices to this book should be the conclusions of the two Reports of the Dardanelles Commissioners, for these would allow people to keep their heads cool in presence of the author's rhetorical seductions. Those Reports are authoritative. Mr Churchill rarely alludes to them directly, but he battles with them indirectly all the time. They brought out, amid much else, that in 1906 the General Staff, after consultation with the Admiralty, had expressly deprecated an attack upon the Straits by the Fleet alone, and had even thrown doubt upon the feasibility of a joint enterprise. The Defence Committee had concurred with this opinion on 28 February 1907, and had ruled that the adventure 'would involve great risks and should not be undertaken if other means of bringing pressure on Turkey were available'. We are certainly not compelled to tie down the War Council of 1915 to the academic opinion of 1907, but it is obvious that the War Council, with this proposal again before them, should have instituted a fresh and most searching conjoint inquiry and not have moved till they were satisfied that all the means were available and all the plans made to ensure success so far as human foresight can insure anything in war. That this was not done stands to the everlasting discredit of all concerned, and the only excuse for the War Council is the valour of their ignorance.

Mr Churchill was personally responsible for advocating the naval attack. As we read his account of the preparations we observe the prominence accorded to the Turkish forts and the subordinate interest taken in the mines, which were the main element of the defence in Turkish eyes. The Admiralty did not fit out Admiral de Robeck with the proper means for dealing with mines. All that he had on March 18 was twenty-one trawlers of a speed which did not permit them to sweep against the current, and they were manned by fishermen, unsupported by a trained and disciplined naval personnel. It happened that ten days before the attack the astute Turk sent out a little steamer by night to lay a line of moored contact mines in Eren Keui Bay, which was assumed by our people to be clear of mines on the day of the attack, because it had been frequently swept before. All the losses on March 18 were caused by these mines, and the disaster was so unexpected and unaccountable that it bewildered the assailants and induced them to withdraw. Mr Churchill resents Admiral de Robeck's ultimate decision to discontinue the naval attack. He declares that the Admiral was 'consternated'. But the truth about this newly laid line of mines was not known till after the war, and from the Admiral's letters at the time we see that he attributed his losses to floating mines or to torpedoes fired from the shore. It is on that basis that his decision should be judged, and not upon what we know now.

The ten Turkish lines of the regular Turkish minefields,

with their 300 to 400 mines, were still quite intact, and there was also this still inexplicable danger for which neither the Admiral nor anyone else could account. The minefields were covered by mobile batteries and lit up at night by searchlights, which combination was formidable for light craft to meet, while the forts were still largely intact and could oppose heavier ships sent to support the trawlers. The indirect fire of the *Queen Elizabeth* was unable to hit a single gun in two days' firing, though this was a primary feature of the Admiralty plan. Surely the point could have been cleared up by peace experiments? The power of ships to silence the forts by direct hits upon the guns had been found to be far less than naval opinion had expected. Unless all the Turkish organisation were destroyed, Admiral de Robeck, even supposing that he had forced his way through regardless of loss, could not have been followed by unarmoured ships bringing his shells, stores and supplies, and what he could have done with a few ships 'Duckworthed' in the Marmora is not easy to see. Let us admit, however much Mr Churchill may hate the decision not to persevere, that Admiral de Robeck's decision was an honest one and may have been right.

The 'case for perseverance and decision' is argued by Mr Churchill in a chapter of much interest. At a later stage, after the failure of the Suvla operation in August, Commodore Keyes made plans for a fresh naval attack, and urged the Admiralty, as did Admiral Wemyss, to carry it out. But this was not approved. When the admirals would attack the Admiralty was coy, and vice versa. The details of Commodore Keyes's plan are given, and are full of interest. The plan was novel and exceedingly audacious. We could almost wish that the victor of Zeebrugge had been given the run of his teeth, but it will remain for ever an open question whether he would have succeeded. From the Admiralty point of view, the question whether the losses to be expected would have been justified while the navies of the Central Powers were still more or less intact and the action of some neutrals uncertain is also a matter deserving of serious consideration, for we might, after a ding-dong fight by the main Fleets at sea, have had to fall back upon our older ships. The failure of the naval attack was mainly due to the wholly inadequate provision by the Admiralty of mine-sweeping flotillas and to the misconception of the efficacy of direct and indirect fire by ships' guns against forts.

Mr Churchill takes us through the glorious story of the land attack without adding substantially to our knowledge of it. His account of the prowess of our submarine officers in the Marmora is first-rate. His acid criticisms of the French GQG for not pulling us out of the mire would require a long answer. It is sufficient to recall that it was not the French GQG, but the French Government, which sent the two French divisions to the Dardanelles. The French GQG, as the *Revue Militaire Française* has recently explained, regarded 'la fâcheuse expédition des Dardanelles' as a series of costly improvisations and bloody mistakes on sea and land. They considered the decision to launch the expedition as 'insufficiently matured by the British Government', and they stigmatise the improvised French collaboration, the failure to adapt the means to the ends pursued, and the discordance of efforts. 'Such are,' says the *Revue*, 'the principal characteristics of the Dardanelles adventure, which was based upon an idea which was eminently correct, but wherein we find concentrated almost all the errors arising from the total absence of centralised direction in the war operations of a coalition.' With France invaded, her fair provinces overrun, and the mass of the German armies still confronting the French, how could the GQG feel any joy in an expedition so improvidently launched which threatened to withdraw, and was withdrawing, important Allied forces from the decisive theatre of war? That the French, by substituting Salonika for the Dardanelles, repeated our error at a later stage, and deserved Mr Churchill's criticisms, most of us admit. But the GQG kept out of it until a political decision in Paris forced their hand, and it is not for our English pot, to call the French kettle black.

Naturally, Mr Churchill resents the decision to evacuate Gallipoli. He caustically and bitterly attacks General Sir Charles Monro for recommending it. Before attacking General Monro he should, in bare justice, have quoted that General's telegram of 31 October, giving the reasons for his opinion, which were solid, well weighed and convincing. Monro showed that, except for the Anzacs, the troops were not equal to a sustained effort, owing to inexperienced officers, the want of training of the men, and the depleted condition of many units. He showed how we only held the fringe of the shore and were confronted by the Turks, growing in strength, in formidable entrenchments, with all the advantages of position, and power to observe our movements. He reported that the beaches were exposed to observed artillery fire and that we could no longer count upon any action by surprise. Only a frontal attack was possible, and no room remained on the beaches for the landing and deployment of artillery, which would have acted under the greatest disadvantages. An attack on the Turks appeared to him to offer no hope of success. These opinions were fortified by the state of health of the troops, who were much enfeebled by diseases and were losing a very high percentage of their numbers per month from these causes alone. Mr Churchill's authority for saying in one place that General Monro estimated the loss on withdrawal at 30,000 and in another place at 40,000 should be stated. The Dardanelles Commissioners reported that Sir Charles Monro, in his telegram of 31 October, stated 'that he was unable at that moment to give any definite estimate of the losses that would be incurred'. It only remains to add that Mr Bonar Law, in his memorandum of 4 December, stated that 'every military authority, without a single exception, whom we have consulted has reported in favour of evacuation'. These truthful pictures of the real state of affairs are omitted from Mr Churchill's book, and he does not give us Lord Curzon's memoranda of 25 and 30 November in which the case for and against evacuation is stated.

There is nothing in this book to cause me to alter the judgment which I gave in my article of 17 October, on the evidence of the *Times* abridgment, upon the broader aspects of this question. Everyone admits that Constantinople was a correct objective for us provided that the means, the trained men and the munitions had been available, which they were not. In this book Mr Churchill is preaching a deadly heresy throughout, the heresy of the Easterners, who pusillanimously averted their gaze from the hard but unavoidable task of overcoming the main German armies in the decisive theatre, and sought, by the exercise of their imagination, to win the war by legerdemain. Without adequate plans or means they disseminated our armies all over the earth in chase of chimeras, and by wasting our resources they became the prime architects of our defeat of March 1918 in France. Not until we are given Sir Maurice Hankey's paper of 28 December 1914, and Mr Lloyd George's of 1 January 1915, shall we be able to trace the origin of these errors and to fix a date upon which the perversion of the War Council was accomplished. But meanwhile it is enough to know that the author of this book was the most vocal preacher of the Eastern heresy in 1915. To him and to the Eastern school we owe the greatest defeat in the history of the Army, and whatever our regard may be for him personally, we can no more make a compromise with him on this subject than John Knox could with the Mass.

MR CHURCHILL'S HISTORY OF THE SECOND WORLD WAR

By Harold Nicolson

4 October 1948

Readers of the *Daily Telegraph* have already been given a rich foretaste of Mr Churchill's history of the Second World War. The first volume of this gigantic work is published today under the title *The Gathering Storm*. Those who derived pleasure and profit from reading the extracts published in this newspaper will find the full volume just as entrancing and even more impressive. The details are ingenious and well devised; the decoration harmonious; but it is the architectural mass of the completed structure which compels our admiration.

The book is in fact incomparable, since it combines three elements which, in such proportions, have never been combined before. It is the history of a tremendous epoch recorded by one of the main protagonists. It is an autobiography which provides a self-portrait of a singular character. And it is a work of literature.

Other men have written records of the events with which they were concerned. Caesar's account of the Gallic War is certainly literature, but it is too untruthful and too impersonal to be described either as history or autobiography. Napoleon's *Memorial* which he dictated at St Helena is discreditably personal, but makes small claim either to veracity, or form, or style. The memoirs of Frederick the Great, although written in clean French prose, are not of literary value, and as history and autobiography they are weak indeed.

The memoirs of Churchill stand by themselves. As history they are accurate and objective; as autobiography they rank with the many great self-portraits which the English genius for intimacy for composition has produced; as literature they are models of composition, virility and style.

No man, of course, can become the complete historian of his own epoch. However scrupulous he may be in admitting his errors of prescience of decision; however generously he may strive to appreciate the motives, characters and actions of his opponents; he is forced by the compelling factors of space and time to adopt an egocentric, or more precisely concentric, attitude of mind. He observes and records the whirl of circumstance, the orbits of events which wheel around him. However strong may be his powers of detachment, he cannot transport himself into the infinite or analyse these vast revolutions from outside.

Mr Churchill's powers of detachment are in themselves astonishing. Unlike his great predecessors, he has no need of self-justification; his record stands unassailable for all to learn. But he does have personal cause for bitterness; only in one passage (which I regret) does he allow that righteous resentment to pierce the covering of his dignity and reserve.

For eleven years his warnings and authority were discarded; for five years he held supreme power and saved his country; he was rejected by his countrymen when the danger had passed. Such experiences might well strain the philosophy of the firmest stoic. Mr Churchill's philosophy has not been strained; he preserves throughout his equanimity.

His purpose to this first volume is to show how easily the Second World War might have been prevented; how 'the malice of the wicked was reinforced by the weakness of the virtuous'; and how, when the battle came, we found ourselves spiritually encumbered and physically unprepared.

Calmly he recites the long series of errors, hesitations and optimisms which brought us to the brink of disaster. He leads us back along the Via Dolorosa of appeasement, marked as it is by the shattered monuments of our mistakes – Stresa, the Naval Agreement, Abyssinia, the Rhineland, Spain, the rejection of Roosevelt, the rejection of the Grand Alliance, the rejection of Russia, Munich.

At every stage (even at the last stage) of this disastrous pilgrimage a halt could have been called and catastrophe avoided. Calmly is this shameful catalogue related, and the volume ends with the flames of retribution and tragedy of the Norwegian campaign.

Tempting it is for any historian to give acumen to his narrative, and to oversimplify the tangle of motives, by attributing misfortunes solely to the timidity, optimism and conceit of individuals. Mr Churchill has made and watched and written and read so much history that he knows that such personal attributions are too facile to be wholly true. He knows that the hesitation of statesmen to proclaim, or even perhaps to face, a danger is due not always to personal cowardice or self-satisfaction, but often to the existing climate of opinion.

When the people are both apathetic and apprehensive, both ignorant and suspicious, it takes a very overt crisis to render them receptive of disagreeable truths. It is indeed a noble thing to be allowed to lead a great people by promising blood, sweat and tears; but it needs the impending menace of a foreign invasion for such realism to become generally acceptable. In times of imagined safety a statesman who insists too much upon the danger of a situation may lose his audience and be rejected as the prophet of a nightmare.

Politics is the art of the possible; the glory of a two-party system is that it enables the Opposition to express with a sense of responsibility those apprehensions which the Government share whole-heartedly but would rightly think it indiscreet and dangerous to proclaim. The real indictment of those in power before the 1938 crisis is that they actually believed the nonsense that they wrote and talked; Churchill is too generous to rub this vinegar into their wounds.

Mr Churchill is not a didactic man, but the implications of his teaching stand manifest to all. You cannot avoid war by proclaiming how much you dislike it; the precision of evil men is always more potent, at first, than the amicable uncertainty of the good. Those who believe that violence must be restrained by force can be called 'warmongers' only by the interested and the inane; you cannot check violence by dispersed benevolence; conciliation must be based upon concentrated and united strength.

As a history, therefore, Mr Churchill's book is something more than a record of events and motives; it is a formidable cautionary tale. It is also the self-portrait of a most remarkable man. He is not seeking in these volumes to write his auto-biography; but his personality is so intense that the whole character of the man is divulged.

Courage in the First Place: not merely the manliness which can affront disaster unperturbed; but that sensitive, sympathetic courage which can be quickened by heroism in others, even by the heroism of one's enemies. Energy again, such as can derive renewed zest from the prospect, as one tops the crest, of new mountains of labour to be traversed.

An excellence of patriotism, which desires not the dominance of one's own country but the triumph of the principles and customs which one has grown to admire and to love. A deep philosophy, not founded upon academic conceptions but upon the fruits of profoundly meditated experience. A brave imagination, which can see beyond the expediency or perplexities of the present towards the dim requirements of the future. A power of will at once dogged and flexible.

A strain of mysticism which sees in the chain of circumstance something more than the play of destiny, something more than the intrusion of chance, and can feel the best of 'invisible wings'. And that generosity of temperament which softens the edges of pugnacity by forgiving, not the fallen only but those whose timidity occasioned the very disasters which they strove with trembling fingers to avert. Without desiring to do so, Mr Churchill in his history has painted a portrait of himself, more accurate and more vivid than any which his predecessors have dared to limn.

Mr Churchill's book is in the third place a work of literary art. It is said that it is his practice to dictate at least the first draft of his books and thereafter to revise from proofs; if this be so, there is not a vestige in his style of the lax compositions, the prolix irrelevancies, which afflict the ordinary author who dictates.

The architecture of the first volume – the proportion of masses, the relation between form and content, between the uniform and the varied – is a model of literary construction. He is aware that in a theme of such solidity, in a work of such sober magnitude, the colour, the decoration and the details must be rendered subordinate to the simplicity of the general design.

Such passages of delicate decoration as occur are not purple passages; they are lapidary; they adorn the façades and porticos of his immense edifice with all the solemnity of Roman inscriptions. He is aware that the drama of his story is by itself so compelling that he must reduce to the minimum all personal dramatics. Yet he is also aware that the vast frontage which he has to cover must be relieved now and then by a few well-placed apertures, by certain emblems of relaxation.

The attention is thus revived at carefully selected intervals by some intimate reflection, a momentary glimpse into the human and domestic, a sally of irony or humour, a piece of vivid portraiture or analysis, a sudden stirring story, a splash of sentiment or romance, a phrase of understatement, or one of those startling interpretative words (homely and yet unfamiliar) of which he holds a store in his vocabulary. The style of Mr Churchill is as unflaunting, cool and as Saxon as the English landscape combines an infinite variety of surprise with a uniform atmosphere of equability; it has a perfect tone.

Mr Churchill is not among those men who regard life or death as meaningless. His history inspires fortitude, his character emulation; and his literary power leaves one with that elation of spirit which comes from the contemplation of a deliberate and successful work of art.

Chapter 3:

Churchill as a Politician

Winston Churchill had an extraordinarily long life in politics. His parliamentary career lasted the better part of a century. He served thirteen Prime Ministers and represented five constituencies from Oldham, his first, to Manchester, Dundee, Epping and Woodford. Remarkably, he campaigned in twenty-one elections, winning sixteen of them. His time in parliament was not boring either. Churchill had little use for toeing a party line. In 1904, he left the Conservatives to join the Liberal Party, earning him the nickname 'the Blenheim Rat'. In 1924 he 're-ratted' to the Conservatives, but during the 1930s he was often at loggerheads with Conservative foreign policy, especially concerning the appeasement policy of the Chamberlain Government.

SOCIALISM AND TRADE
19 March 1908

Lord Brassey, President of the Association of Chambers of Commerce, took the chair at the annual banquet of that body, held last night at the Whitehall Rooms, Hôtel Métropole.

Mr Winston Churchill, MP, replying to the toast of 'His Majesty's Ministers', observed that the benefits of the Patent Law were already being realised in many parts of the country. He would, however, say that he distrusted profoundly the positive intervention of Governments – particularly party Governments – in the delicate and intricate worldwide operation of trade. They did not understand it. He rejected as impractical the insane Socialistic idea that we could have a system whereby the whole national production of the country, with all its infinite ramifications, innumerable transactions, its rebates from day to day, the whole productive energy of the country, should be organised and directed by a permanent official, however able, from some central office. The idea was not only impossible, but unthinkable. (Cheers.) If it were even attempted, it would produce a most terrible shrinkage and destruction in productive energy. So he was drawn to the conclusion that the intervention of Government in regard to trade must be mainly of a liberating character – of a negative character in that sense. (Cheers.) But, even so, there were very considerable spheres into which they might, without risk of peril, advance. They might try to set the taxpayer free from the burden of debt which pressed upon him, they might set the canals free – (cheers) – and they might attempt to set railways free from internecine competition, which, though it might have been all right in the early days, had for a long time ceased to be economical, and had lately become wasteful and injurious. Best of all, Governments could try to set nations free from the hideous terrors of war which hung over us.

HOME RULE
1 May 1912

The Second Reading debate of the Home Rule Bill began yesterday – and began very well indeed. The opening speeches of Mr Churchill and Mr Walter Long were remarkable efforts, absolutely different in style and purpose, but both alike worthy of a great occasion.

The First Lord of the Admiralty brought with him to the House his speech in manuscript, though, like his father before him, he knew it by heart, and there was no suggestion of any lack of spontaneity in its utterance. The phrasing was admirable. Mr Churchill loves a neat, clean antithesis, and has a pretty oratorical trick of producing them in strings. He had polished his gems with unusual care, and their sparkle repaid his pains. Nevertheless, the speech was more in the nature of an essay. He might have called it 'Thoughts on Home Rule'. It had no special reference to the bill before the House. It might have been written a year ago, or five years ago for that matter, save for allusions to one or two contemporary happenings. As a brief for Home Rule in the abstract it was excellent, but so far as it threw light on the actual proposals of the Government it was absolutely naught.

But it was highly original. Mr Churchill got away from the beaten track, and escaped to a surprising degree from the ordinary round of party politics, with the result that while it was an added pleasure to listen to him, the cheers were remarkably few. No one could have imagined a few months since that Mr Churchill would make a non-provocative speech in moving the second reading of a Home Rule Bill. But so it was. He deprecated wrath. He curbed his natural propensity to sarcasm. He anticipated hostile demonstrations with a deprecatory smile. It was quite a new manner for Mr Churchill. He brimmed over with appeals – appeals to the Opposition and appeals to Ulster – for a settlement by consent. He did not seem desirous of scoring a personal triumph. It was as if he were really anxious to be on the side of impartial truth.

Decidedly, therefore, this was a remarkable utterance. Mr Churchill was anxious to minimise the importance of Home Rule. It was no longer, he said, as big a question as it once was.

Compared with the two tremendous groups of questions, the one internal and the other external, with which the country was faced, the Irish question was really a small one. He laboured this point with manifest earnestness, and then, passing on to discuss the question whether our military and naval security would be affected by the grant of Home Rule to Ireland, he stated his emphatic conclusion that while an Irish Parliament could help England much it could harm her little, even if it had the will to do so. But this, of course, he denied. There would no longer be divergence of interests, but identity. It would be 'the first interest of Ireland' to keep on good terms with British Governments, and he defied anyone to picture any conceivable conditions in which the ruin of England would not also be the ruin of Ireland.

Then he dealt with the other phase of the Home Rule problem, as it affected Nationalists and Orangemen in Ireland itself. For them he admitted that it was 'a question of life and death', and that being so, it was the duty of Great Britain to try and appease Irish hatreds, and not set the two cocks fighting. In the only part of his speech where he came near provoking party feeling he spoke bitterly of the 'insulting condition of inferiority' to which, as he said, Unionists relegated the Irish members at Westminster, while in their own land they repressed them with a powerful constabulary. There could be no peace, he added, echoing a phrase of Mr Healy's, until we had 'comforted the soul of Ireland', and that could never be done by trying to buy off national sentiment with benefits. 'What shall a nation have in exchange for its soul?' he cried. 'A tax on imported butter!' It was one of the rare flashes of the old manner. The House laughed to recognise that the old Adam was not quite extinct in Mr Churchill after all.

And so, by easy transition, to Ulster – the Ulster which bars the way, and is the 'only serious obstacle to a thoroughly satisfactory settlement'. Mr Churchill was vastly polite to Ulster. He spoke most respectfully of Ulster. Heaven forbid that he should under-rate the power of Ulster! Of course, Ulster had 'the right – nay, the duty – to resist oppression!' The House listened with grave attention to this unexpected turn. What did it mean? It meant, clearly enough, that the Government are afraid of Ulster, and that Mr Churchill's bland inquiries as to whether Ulster claimed, and would be content with, 'special treatment' for herself covered a really serious desire to know whether she was ready to do a deal. 'We contemplate no violence to Ulster,' he said. 'We seek no quarrel with Ulster!' Yet, only a few weeks ago, the mere mention of the word sufficed to throw the whole Coalition into fits of contemptuous laughter. Ulster's duty, he said, was to stand by the ship of Ireland and bring it safely into port. Ulstermen could earn undying fame if they led united Ireland home! But he contributed not a single practical suggestion as to how it might be done.

Then it was Mr Walter Long's turn. There was, at least, nothing new in his manner. He stands where he stood, and that is by the side of the friends whom Mr Churchill had appealed to him to desert. He hotly attacked the bill before the House. He condemned the financial proposals as being not only unsound, but dishonest. He showed how, instead of imposing new taxes on Ireland, the Irish Government would instruct the Irish members at Westminster to squeeze the British taxpayer through the Imperial Parliament. He drew from the reluctant lips of the surly Mr Birrell the acknowledgment that while Land Purchase was reserved for the Imperial Parliament, the duty of fixing the judicial rents would be left to the Irish Parliament, and he pictured what will happen if and when a new rent-lowering campaign is entered upon. And then he exposed the miserable imposture that this bill is intended to lead to Federalism, as Mr Churchill and Mr Asquith had maintained. Finally, replying to Mr Churchill's references to Ulster, he quoted words used by the late Duke of Devonshire in 1893, and warned the Government that even if they contrived to get their cranky vessel into port, they would probably find it impossible to unload her cargo. It was a good fighting, no-surrender speech. Mr Long is the very last man on the Front Opposition bench whom it is any good for Ministers to approach with suggestions of compromise.

MR CHURCHILL ON THE ABUSE OF THE 'DOLE' (I)

By the Rt Hon. Winston Churchill, MP

26 March 1930

Few spectacles have been more remarkable, even in these late eventful years, than that of Great Britain tormenting herself with the problem of unemployment. This grievous, but at the same time limited, evil has been artificially raised and emphasised out of all proportion to its real part in our national life and economy.

Unemployment exists in all industrial countries; it has always existed in Great Britain; it often exists in other countries at a higher level than in Great Britain. It has first of all been fictitiously inflated, by processes which I shall presently describe, and thereafter has been used by party politicians as a means of discrediting the Government of the day, or even the foundations of our present civilisation. The weekly figures are eagerly scanned by interested partisans throughout the country, and blatantly proclaimed to the world as proof that Britain is 'going to the dogs', that she is a 'down-and-out' nation, and that the capitalist system of society has failed.

The frequent general elections which so greatly hamper British trade revival are nearly all fought upon the numbers of the unemployed. Governments are condemned because they have failed to cure the evil. Oppositions easily succumb to the temptation to gain votes by declaring that they can. Good, worthy people of the soft-hearted, soft-headed type turn indignantly from any party, or any public man, who is not glibly ready to recite his list of positive and infallible proposals.

And if anyone were to say that the surest remedy is hard work, thrift, faithful co-operation and goodwill among all classes and in all relationships, strict social discipline for slackness or inefficiency, persevering application of science and intelligence to industry, he would be condemned.

Unemployment is a modern disease, in the sense that the doctors have only recently begun collecting statistics about it and trying to collect fees for curing it. It is not the only modern disease, nor even perhaps the most violent about which statistics are being collected. For instance, since the beginning of the century a disease called 'motor-cars' has reached a point where it kills ten thousand and mutilates a quarter-million of our fellow-countrymen every year. However, nobody worries about that. We adopt what was called in the war the philosophy of the optimist: 'He did not mind what happened so long as it did not happen to him.'

But unemployment is a political theme. It is a disease which has become an obsession to the average Briton. Every week he feels his unemployment pulse. Watch in hand, feverishly, he counts the beats. 'Ah, faster this week! I'm getting worse. There – I dropped a beat. I'm breaking up. At any moment my heart may stop. How can I go down to the office today or concentrate on my work at the factory? I may die at any moment. I must go back to the doctor.

'But which doctor? I sacked my old family physician last year, but this new man, who promised me a certain cure, has only made me worse. My pulse is up five beats since I went to him. I will go to another man. I'll go to Lloyd George. What do I care if they call him a quack! He says work on the roads will cure me. There are his words, quite clear: "Lay aside every other form of activity and work at road-making; all will be well, you will feel a new man No more of these palpitations!"

'You say I tried him before? Well, where am I to go? I must find somebody who will tell me something. I must go somewhere! There is my heart beating so oddly and irregularly that I cannot think of anything else. I must find some prophet with a message, or even some charlatan with a patent pill.

'There it is again! Up another 200,000 after the Christmas holidays! This cannot go on! Abandon every well-tried principle, repudiate the slowly gathered teachings of experience. Get a move on. Squander the public treasure; never mind about Egypt, India, or the Navy. Overturn the mighty structure of your trade and commerce; smash up your social system. What do I care about those who have got work?

'Show me how to cure this unemployment. Don't talk to me about 300,000 more employed now than there were last year. Don't talk to me about the country getting richer every year, and every class of people enjoying more solid benefits. "England," say the newspapers, "will tolerate no statesman, no party that has not got a cure for unemployment."'

At the last election the Socialists and the Liberals vied with each other in lashing the Government for not having cured unemployment. 'Socialism,' said the former – 'That will put it all right. Nationalise all the means of production, distribution and exchange, and you will see everyone fully employed, at good wages and short hours – as they are in Russia.'

'No,' cried the Liberals. 'Borrow money on a gigantic scale, use the credit of the State to the full. What is it for, but to be used? What are any savings for, but to be spent? Spend your money, dissipate your credit in making artificial work, and save the nation at the public expense.'

At the next election the roles may well be reversed. I remember with what sorrow I watched the weekly totals of unemployment when I was Chancellor of the Exchequer, knowing well the vile advantage that would be taken of every increase or stubborn maintenance of the level. Now, at any rate, I see another set of poor wretches tortured in the same way. 'Serve them right!' may well be said when one remembers their promises and their boasts, when one remembers the more than ordinary political unfairness with which distorted facts and figures were used.

Thus we see what we thought was John Bull, prototype of phlegm throughout the world, yielding himself to a mood of insane hysteria, grovelling in the poverty complex, while all the time the general economic well-being of every class of the population advances steadily, while we still sustain the heaviest burdens in the world, while we still raise a revenue of £800,000,000 sterling and pay £355,000,000 to the interest and amortisation of debt, while we still have the highest standard of real wages of any country in Europe, while we still export a far higher value per head of manufactured articles than any other nation, and built last year half the world's ships.

The attention of Britain is riveted upon the weekly totals of unemployment, but foreign observation is concentrated on the moral and sociological aspects of what is called the 'dole'. All through my journey across Canada and back by the United States quiet, serious men accosted me upon this subject. These men were the friends of England, many were her sons, but everywhere they asked the same question: 'What about the dole? Is the old country really finished? Has her stamina gone?'

These were the days when the new Labour Government by their vigorous demeanour at The Hague and their broad acceptance of responsibility for the general business of the State had excited great hopes in the hearts of Britons or friends of Britain all over the New World. So I was asked continually: 'Do you think this new Government will have the courage to abolish the "dole" and save the Old Country?'

And then I had to explain a lot about the 'dole', and how that word applied only to a minority of those who drew the benefits of unemployment insurance. But I did not then have to say what I should have to say now, that the new Government, specially cognisant, as it ought to be, of the real conditions of manual labour and all the weaknesses of human nature in the trade-union sphere, so far from purging unemployment insurance from the odious taint of being a 'dole', had only taken every step to confirm and, in part, justify the prejudice.

Let us look more closely at this Live Register of unemployment, according to which, we are told, the life and fortunes of Britain are to be measured. Twenty years ago there was set on foot a system of unemployment insurance for a certain number of selected trades which were specially subject to seasonal and cyclical variations. This scheme involved contributions from the workmen, contributions from the employer (which orthodox economists would probably argue were also deductions from real wages), encouraged by substantial equal contributions from the State, in order to build up in these variable trades a system of wage-spreading over the year.

By this system it was hoped to prevent disaster to a thrifty and industrious workman by having the home and furniture which he had laboriously acquired pulled down about his ears because of some temporary gap produced by world economics in the regularity of his employment. Upon this modest foundation a national system of universal unemployment insurance has been established by law, which covers practically all persons aged sixteen to sixty-four in wage-earning employment with the important exceptions of agriculture and domestic service. The employer is liable for payment of the whole contribution each week, but he may recover the amount of the employed person's contribution by deduction from wages or otherwise. The State now pays one-third of the total contribution. Prior to April 1929, the State paid two-sevenths only.

Undoubtedly this system of unemployment insurance constitutes the finest example of wage spreading both as regards the individual and for industries that has ever been brought into existence. Unquestionably it affords a bulwark to the solid, trustworthy workman – outnumbering as he does the others by more than ten to one – against the inevitable fluctuations in modern industrial employment. Secondly, more than half the balance who draw the 'dole' at any time have paid for every penny they receive and are as much entitled to their benefits as any man who has insured his house against fire, and having punctually paid the premiums to a company, recovers his ascertained loss.

So far everything is sound. But now we come in contact with a new factor, namely, the punctilious use by an ever-increasing number of insured persons of the actuarial rights which they enjoy under the system. All the insured workpeople in England pay their weekly contribution of 7d to the unemployment insurance fund. But probably one-third of these 12,000,000 never need or never care to touch a penny of the benefits. Even if they are out of work for a few weeks, it is their pride not to 'go on the burroo'.

But the habit of using an undoubted legal right acquired by previous payments whenever occasion arises has become yearly much more general. 'I am out this month; I shall be in the next. I have never drawn my benefit before, but I have paid for it three or four times over. My mates are drawing it; all the loafers are drawing it; it is my own; I have saved it up. Why should I not go and draw it, even if I'm only out a fortnight?' No one can gainsay this. But the tendency for substantial efficient persons to utilise to the full their legal rights, devised for the rescue and mitigation of genuine and grave misfortune, is a new factor in the finance and statistics of unemployment insurance.

The minor vicissitudes of labouring men, such as an occasional month out of work between satisfactory jobs, are borne in almost every other country in the world in silence.

They may cause some embarrassment or even distress to the individual, but they do not emerge as a problem of State. It is my belief that there were many years before the war which were deemed prosperous years, and yet in which there was as much distress as there is today, without any remedial measures. But now every case of unemployment, even for short periods, is recorded in the National Register, and the benefit is increasingly applied for, even by those not in actual want, as a matter of course and as an addition to the income of not unprosperous families, and as a contribution toward what may be little more than a needed holiday.

Many British employers, particularly in the textile trades, have lent themselves to an abuse of the system of unemployment insurance. Suffering from trade depression and working short time, they systematically arrange to give their workers just that amount of employment as will enable them to qualify for the benefit. Masters and men are found habitually and deliberately co-operating on the basis of, say, two weeks of work – then two on the dole.

It is significant that after every public holiday, Christmas, Easter, Whitsuntide, there is a very large addition to the unemployment total, which falls off again a few weeks later. Obviously thousands of employers, when their business is inactive, say to their workmen, 'You had better prolong your holiday for a fortnight and draw the benefit to which you are entitled.' Thus both parties are equally convenienced. In these cases the unemployment benefit, paid for mainly by the industrious and successful workmen in other trades, has really become a subvention in aid of wages. Whatever else may or may not be said about such an arrangement, it is certainly not the use to which the insurance fund should be put.

Next on the live register come the women. There are a quarter of a million of them. No one dares mention them, because they have all been given the vote, and it is supposed they will use their votes against any public man or party which does not adopt a super-feminist attitude. All the same, I will venture to say that unless a woman is solitary, or the breadwinner of a family, her position in industrial insurance is entirely different from that of the average man. The woman living with her father or her husband, who has acquired some time ago the qualification as an industrial worker, and has now found out she can put in a claim for 'the dole', certainly does not belong to the class of unfortunate citizens for whom the system was called into being.

When we have dealt with those who have paid for every penny of their benefit, and the women, we have covered nearly three-fourths of the British live register of unemployed persons. Three-fifths of the men are only receiving what they have paid for, by State organisation and personal thrift. Almost another quarter consists of women, most of whom are living in men-supported homes, and many of whom can find a ready opening in domestic service.

Up to this point there is nothing which should cause serious concern. On the contrary, a system is at work which, were it purged from these minor abuses – in so far as they are abuses – would be sound and healthy, making alike for popular contentment and good housekeeping. I have no hesitation in saying that none of these figures, covering as they do three-fourths of the British total of unemployment, ought to be included in the weekly returns.

MR CHURCHILL ON THE ABUSE OF THE 'DOLE' (II)

By the Rt Hon. Winston Churchill, MP

27 March 1930

The average number of unemployed assumed last autumn by the Socialist Government as likely to be maintained during the next two or three years has been stated at 1,200,000. The total has now suddenly risen to nearly 1,600,000. That is due first to a temporary wave of worldwide trade depression; secondly, to lack of confidence in the business world during the advent of the Socialist Budget; and, thirdly, to the scandalous relaxation of the administration of the Insurance Fund.

These conditions are either passing or removable. For the basis of this discussion it is necessary to adopt the average 'pre-relaxation' figure of 1,200,000. Of these 600,000 at least, at any given moment, have paid for all they get. Another 250,000 are the women, whose unemployment certainly does not constitute a grievous social evil. There remain 350,000 to be accounted for. Let us examine these.

In the hard years following the war, with all the stringency caused by necessary deflation, with all the dislocation arising from politically fanned labour troubles, large numbers of workmen became unemployed who had exhausted all the benefit for which they had paid and which the fund could provide.

The Coalition Government of Mr Lloyd George, oppressed by unparalleled difficulties, yielded itself to what we can now see to have been a weak and dangerous expedient. It allowed these workmen who had run out of the benefits for which they had paid – or, in the case of certain trades that were first brought into insurance just after the war, who had not had time to qualify – to continue to receive as if they were members of the insurance fund benefits for which they had not paid and never could pay on the basis of one week's benefit for each six contributory.

This breach in the principle that benefit should be paid strictly in proportion to contributions was, it must be admitted, widened by the legislation of the late Conservative Government in 1927, based on the recommendation of the Blanesburgh Committee. That committee recommended a new principle, namely, that benefit should be paid subject simply to the condition that thirty contributions had been paid in the previous two years. Subject to this condition there was to be no limit, under a permanent scheme, to the period for which benefit could be drawn. Of course, when a claimant reached the point when he could no longer show thirty contributions in the past two years, benefit would cease. This condition was further relaxed to allow benefit to be paid to those persons mainly in the depressed areas, who could not satisfy even this lenient test. At a recent date there were 120,000 such persons claiming benefit.

The consequences were disastrous not only to the finance of the fund, which was the least part of the trouble, but to the character of the insurance system. No distinction was drawn between 'covenanted' and 'uncovenanted' benefits, and the uncovenanted beneficiaries were treated on the same footing and through the same organisation as the covenanted. This vitiated the whole principle of unemployment insurance and perverted its objects.

It classed the self-supporting workman with those who had, in fact, become indigent. It disparaged the whole principle of contributory insurance. It lumped together in one indiscriminate mass pauperism, saving-forethought and mutual aid. It cast the insulting aspersions of the dole over an enormous number of workmen, in fact the large majority, who, by previous self-denial and State organisation, had provided against temporary misfortunes. It presented to the whole world a distorted picture of British national life. It falsely advertised to every country more than a tenth of our whole working-class population as if they were living in a state of pauperism. It provided a weekly means of crying down British credit. It caused all our friends abroad a bewilderment and regret, and all our enemies a jubilation, both of which were at least three parts unfounded.

And this is still going merrily on. Indeed, it has been further aggravated to an amazing extent by the new forms of demoralisation introduced by the Socialist Government. The assertion by Parliament that a man need no longer be 'genuinely seeking work' to obtain 'uncovenanted' benefit, marks the nadir of unemployment insurance. If we had looked about to find the worst and dullest thing that could be done, morally, politically and financially, here it is clothed in the form of the 'dole'.

But now we have to look at the unemployment totals from a different angle. Among the many fallacies and wilful mis-representations which have gathered round the unemployment problem, none is more erroneous or more frequently encountered than the statement that 'there is a standing army of a million and a quarter unemployed'. No term could, in fact, be more inapplicable than that of a 'standing army'. It is not a 'standing army', but a dreary militia that we must contemplate. The million and a quarter or million and a half who figure on the register are not individuals permanently unemployed, but only the representatives on any given day of a far larger number who use or have used the insurance fund and draw covenanted or uncovenanted benefits.

If we analyse this alarming total on any day we should find that more than half had been or would be employed within a month; that three-quarters would not be out of work for three months; and that even if the remaining quarter, composed as it necessarily is of the least efficient, trusty and active members of the community, the stragglers from life's battle, the weaker brethren, not excluding the inevitable admixture of shirkers and impostors, even in this last melancholy quarter only a small proportion had not found work within six months.

Such facts have only to be stated to show the folly of all plans of marching off the unemployed in gangs and battalions to artificially fomented public works, and professing thereby to remedy unemployment. There is, indeed, a small proportion, for whom some disciplinary control in labour colonies might well be appropriate, but the vast majority must look only to reabsorption in the normal or natural industries.

I ought not to quit this question without running the risk of making some positive proposals. What would England do about it now, if she were wise? What would she do if a Government existed strong enough to rise above the over-bearing and overweening currents and tides of electioneering? Her first step should be to purge her system of unemployment insurance of every vestige of uncovenanted benefit, and thus to draw a hard, clear, unmistakable line between insurance and relief. No one who has not paid his full actuarial contribution should receive a farthing from National Insurance, or be associated in any way with its finance and economy.

The reports of the working of insurance should be presented once a year. The total of the 'uncovenanted' unemployed should be an entirely separate publication. They must be provided for. They cannot be left to starve – no one is ever allowed to starve in England – but they must be decisively divorced from insurance. Whether the totals relating to them should be published every week, or every month, or every quarter is a matter for discussion. In view of the base use which has been made of these figures in a recent past, it would be necessary to continue for some time the usual statistics, so as to provide a comparable basis.

But in my view the total of uninsured employed – the real unemployed, not those who by admirable precautions have spread the wages of ten or eleven months over twelve, but the definitely non-self-supporting element – should be published quarterly, and with them should also be published a general review of the state of the Poor Law and other forms of pauperism. This by a sabre stroke would free Great Britain from the many misconceptions and disparagements which flow from the present muddled, misleading figures.

It would be seen, for instance, that apart from women employed in industry (theirs is a special branch of the problem), the number of persons declaring themselves unemployed who have not paid their proper contributions vary from 300,000 to 600,000, according to the season of the year or exceptional circumstances.

In a population of 45,000,000 such a fact demands the earnest attention of Parliament and the public departments concerned with social welfare. But it affords no foundation for the hateful processes of national self-depreciation which are now in progress, and lends no countenance to those who incubate pessimism from interested motives. Once this step has been taken the unemployment problem would be reduced to its true proportions, and serious though these proportions be, they would afford no opportunity for party and political manoeuvres at home, and would no longer decry our country abroad.

In analysing and exposing the fictitious and misleading character of our unemployment statistics, I do not wish to minimise the gravities and poignancies of the post-war unemployment problem. There are not only among 'uncovenanted' but 'covenanted' beneficiaries unquestionable cases of grievous unemployment. There is acute distress among miners and workers in heavy trades, the world-demand for whose services has diminished, or are increasingly thrown upon the labour market through the process of rationalisation.

Among a great body of oldish men – fifty-five and onwards – who in a more buoyant market would get employment again, but who nowadays, once they lose their hold on industry, do not get back at all, there is a wide field of grievous social and moral distress. The treatment of this unfortunate body of citizens should be varied according to their numerous categories, and this is the proper study for the present House of Commons. It must vary from generous measures of public aid at one end of the scale, to quite strict methods of toning up at the other.

There is no real difficulty in this discrimination. In the old trade union days before the State concerned itself with unemployment, very practical and salutary methods were adopted by the workmen themselves for dividing the sheep from the goats. There is not one of the real Labour Ministers of the present Government – I exclude the careerists and the Liberal renegades – who is not conscious of this fact. I suspect that every one of them, whatever they may say, will be grateful to me for proclaiming it with some roughness: Separation once effected – for the sheep, compassion; for the goats, discipline.

It is contrary to our conceptions that any person should be, otherwise than through his own fault, in utter destitution, and our arrangements are in this respect more complete than those of any other people in the world. But if the ne'er-do-well, or the confirmed sturdy loafer, or the Bolshevik misfit, or other members of the tribes of tired Tims and weary Willies – alas! I must add manoeuvring Marthas – seek in their dire straits the aid of the community, then they should receive that aid in forms which will do them good, even if these do not give them satisfaction.

I have surveyed with what I expect will be unpalatable candour some of the prominent features of the British unemployment problems which have been brought home to me by my responsible duties during the last twenty years. The first conclusion to which I seek to guide the reader is the monstrous exaggerations of the scale and importance of unemployment in the real economic life of our country. The advance made by the British people during the present tumultuous century in social life and comfort has been enormous. The houses they live in, the clothes they wear, the food they eat, the amusements and leisure they enjoy, the education they possess, the culture and contentment which they have acquired, have separated them widely from the conditions which their fathers remember and their grandfathers can never forget.

Yet in some moods we seek to represent ourselves as a decayed and disconsolate community, morbidly obsessed with one particular puzzle of modern life, and ready to quit the paths of sanity and progress in the hopes of unravelling it. The more unemployment is exploited by party politicians the worse it will become. The more we bite on the sore tooth the more surely we shall induce an abscess at its root. The robust and clear-sighted relegation of unemployment to its appropriate place in national affairs is rapidly becoming a matter of national safety. The exploitation of it for party purposes has already become a national scandal.

Not the least of the evils which these follies are bringing in their train is the general discredit in which the marvellous social institutions and bulwarks against individual misfortune which we have built up are now increasingly involved. During the whole of the twentieth century the British people have been building up these great insurance systems. They are unexampled in the world. There is contributory insurance on a compulsory and nationwide basis against sickness, invalidity, accident, old age, widowhood and unemployment. We have brought the magic of averages to the rescue of the millions.

Those who have not studied the actuarial qualities of these schemes will be astounded if they merely contrast the few pence paid a week by every industrial worker with the massive benefits resulting therefrom. Once everyone is compelled to contribute, insurance enters upon a new domain. No longer is it the pack-horse of all bad risks; it has the full life of the nation to draw upon. Thus the percentage of misfortunes which afflict individuals is easily carried on the shoulders of the whole mass.

A British workman dying at thirty-five and leaving a wife and four children has a virtual power of bequest to his family equal to £600 sterling, a sum utterly beyond the power of ninety-nine men out of a hundred to save from weekly wages in Europe by a lifetime of thrift and work. Old people at sixty-five have £25 a year. This they obtain without prejudice and as a supplement to any private savings they have made.

The poorer members of the bourgeoisie look with envy upon these vast schemes in which the artisan and the labourer are compulsorily comprised. They would gladly pay three or four times the contribution to have the same reward as a nucleus of their individual thrift.

A future generation will have to judge whether all this policy of national insurance – in which, next to Mr Lloyd George, I have been more directly concerned than almost anyone else – will have made for the enduring strength and vigour of the British race. Personally, my faith is firm. It would be quite impossible for our anciently built-up society, with its inevitable deposits of old, weak and poor people, to adopt the rigorous and almost ruthless individualism which young nations in vast regions are still able to assert.

Within their sphere the actuaries are able to explore the future. Their statistics unroll blandly and inexorably before our eyes. As we study the population charts of Great Britain we can see our history written with cold, dispassionate knowledge. Here is the great expansion in our numbers which attended and followed the industrial revolution of Victorian days. Here is the impingement which the teachings of Bradlaugh and Mrs Besant began to make upon it from the 1880s onward. Here is the horrid gash of the slaughter of the Great War. Here are the old-age pensioners arriving in such unwelcome, increasing numbers, sixty-five and seventy years after the mid-Victorian expansion of the birth-rate.

We may lift the veil of the future. We know the rate at which the population were born; we have the tables of mortality; and we can see the consequences of the greater care of old age, better hygiene, better conditions of life and labour, and their interplay with the modern teachings of birth-control. We can now forecast the kind of British nation which will inhabit England, let us say, in 1970. We know that the population then will not be much larger than it is now.

We know that it will contain an ever-increasing proportion of old and feeble people and of no longer productive elements of society. It is only by means of all these immense insurance funds started far in advance that we can gather the strength with which the new life of the nation will be able to carry the dead-weight of the old.

I do not sympathise with those who think that this process of compulsory mass saving will sap the virility and self-reliance of our race. There will be quite enough grindstone in human life to keep us keen. We need not worry about that. But certainly the British social legislation in the twentieth century has already evolved a far more sociable, urbane and instructed people than we have known before.

CONSERVATIVE CONFERENCE AND NATION'S VITAL PROBLEMS
29 March 1934

Mr Churchill, who had a good reception, said that he did not wish in any way to mar the friendliness of the meeting. 'Not only are we met as friends, but as friends who within two years will be united in a desperate struggle against all subversive forces in this country, roused up by every form of prejudice.

'I agree that we should make a solid front of all the strong forces which we can get together, forces of the sort which pulled this country through the war and broke the General Strike. Such forces should be led against the Socialist menace, and that is our prime and foremost duty.'

He denied the suggestion that the Indian problem was 'a sectional job'. 'We are bound to press our views on India,' he said. 'We have had a very hard fight and a very long one, but we are making progress. If we had had this gagging a year ago, should we have had this wonderful statement from the leader of the party that the party should be consulted before action is taken on a report of the Select Committee?'

Some of them with whom the Council were angry had put up a fight, for they felt that they had to put their point of view, and 'We shall continue to do it,' said Mr Churchill.

Mr Churchill said that now, according to the resolution, the matter should be taken out of further consideration for what might prove to be a very long time. He urged that the meeting should secure to the National Union its full liberty. The resolution was not one involving a matter of confidence in the Government. 'It has been made plain that this resolution has not any official inspiration,' he added, amid laughter.

'We got a third of the vote at Birmingham, and if we get more than a third today the forces in India which are holding up the landslide will be strengthened.' (Hear, hear.)

Chapter 4

Churchill, the Navy and the First World War

Churchill had a deep connection with the British Navy as he was twice the First Lord of the Admiralty. He was first appointed to the position in 1911 and held it until 1915. During his tenure the British Navy underwent several reforms including switching from coal-fuelled ships to oil-fuelled ships, in order to boost speed and efficiency. Churchill's innovation did not stop there. While at the Admiralty, he championed the use of flight in the Committee of Imperial Defence, which led to the establishment of the Royal Naval Air Service in 1914. He also established the Landships Committee, which eventually developed the tank for use in the First World War.

However, Churchill also suffered some major defeats during his tenure at the Admiralty. As the German Navy laid siege to the city in 1914, Churchill mounted a defence of Antwerp that was a failure and which did little to change the outcome of the siege, though some historians have theorised that Churchill's strategy actually extended the resistance for an additional week, effectively saving Calais and Dunkirk. But one of Churchill's greatest defeats, the failure to force the

Dardanelles, resulted in the disastrous Gallipoli campaign which ultimately cost Churchill the position and a place in the War Cabinet.

Disgraced, Churchill was demoted to the position of Chancellor of the Duchy of Lancaster; he quickly decided his talents were not being utilised so he re-enlisted in the military. Though he wanted to command a brigade, General Douglas Haig refused to offer the command until Churchill had proved himself capable of leading. Churchill settled on commanding a battalion of 6th Royal Scots Fusiliers, which were stationed near Ploegsteert in Belgium. While he was there he saw action on the Western Front and was allowed to return to Government as Minister of Munitions, largely owing to the benevolence of Lloyd George. After the war, Churchill published several articles in the *Telegraph* on his view of the causes and consequences of the First World War. This chapter contains a rarely seen collection of articles Churchill wrote for the *Telegraph* entitled 'The U-boat War', which focuses on the naval aspects of the First World War.

ONE MILLION MEN IN THE FIELD
12 September 1914

At a meeting in Dundee last night addressed by Earl Curzon the following message was read from Mr Winston Churchill:

'The only sure way of winning this war is for the British Empire to put on the Continent and maintain in the field an army of at least a million men. The Army under Sir John French must be reinforced steadily and continuously until, within eight or nine months, the British Commander-in-Chief is at the head of twenty-five Army Corps composed entirely of men who have gone voluntarily because they know what is at stake, not only for Britain, but for civilisation.

'This is quite practicable. And that army so formed will be in character, in natural energy and in martial initiative, without its equal in the world. When formed, this army must be continually built up to and maintained at full strength, in spite of all losses.

'Such a sword, thrown into the scale at a time when our enemies have exhausted all reserves of manhood, will decide the issues in our favour, irrespective, so long as we keep on fighting, of what may happen in the interval.

'This is the only prudent course to pursue. If victory comes earlier, so much the better. Let us not count on fortune, but build now on a sure foundation the means of securing, under Providence, the ultimate success of our cause. Lord Curzon's visit to Dundee offers an occasion for the more effective concentration of all the moral and patriotic energies which are now awake in Scotland upon that simple obvious duty by doing what we can to rid the world of this present carnage, and take good securities against its repetition. I wish I could be with you all, but my duty keeps me here.'

GERMANY'S DESPERATE U-BOAT DECISION

By the Rt Hon. Winston Churchill, MP

16 November 1931

The fifth and final volume upon the Naval Operations of the

War has in due course appeared. It covers the whole of the Navy's work in the last two years of the war.

There it is at last – the story of all that the Navy did. But the epic that lies therein is frozen. The book is not an inspiring book. It repels not only by its mass of technical detail, but by the fact that it is the work of composite hands.

The able historian has evidently had to submit his chapters to authorities and departments, and important personages in the story have clearly applied their pruning-knives and ink-erasers with no timid hand. The result is a sort of official amalgam which seems to be neither a plain, fearless narrative nor a fair and searching analytical examination of the great disputes.

Nevertheless, so grim and startling are its abundant materials, so vast and costly the tremendous engines of war moving through its pages, so deadly the issues at stake, that this carefully jumbled mass of incident and detail is a veritable treasure-house of information upon the last two most gigantic years of the naval war.

To understand the main issues of this final volume, it is necessary to bear in mind the earlier phases of the war. The years 1914 and 1915 had vindicated Admiralty strategy. The vastness of the unseen task performed by the Fleets was not fully appreciated in those days of stress and strain.

The whole of the enemy trade had been swept off the outer seas, and all avenues of victualment and reinforcement were held for the sole use of the Allies. In April 1915, England enjoyed a supremacy at sea the like of which had never been seen even in the days of Nelson. Security was so complete as to pass almost unnoticed. There remained to Germany in all the oceans only a couple of fugitive cruisers, the *Dresden* lurking stealthily beneath the glaciers of Tierra del Fuego, and the *Koenigsberg* lying helpless and imprisoned in the steamy recesses of a South African lagoon.

It was accepted as a matter of course that the seas were safe for all the Allies, and an insurance of less than 1 per cent was sufficient to cover merchant ships putting to sea in time of war unguarded and unrestricted in every direction from every port.

The guarantee for all this marvellous immunity was the Grand Fleet lying almost motionless in its remote northern harbour at Scapa Flow. It ruled the seas as they have never been ruled in our history. The whole of the war ultimately hinged upon this silent, sedulously guarded and rarely visible pivot. But for the Grand Fleet, Germany would at once have attacked and severed all the Allied communications at sea, and have threatened the coast of France at every point.

But for the Grand Fleet, the German cruisers and other ships of war, ranging the Atlantic and the Channel at will, would have accomplished in a few weeks that entire suspension of ocean traffic, that remorseless blockade from which no relief was possible and for which her U-boats were afterwards to struggle for two bitter years, and to struggle in vain.

But for the Grand Fleet in the first phases, the whole war-structure of the Allies must have collapsed. It was upon the seas the 'sure shield' behind which France defended herself, and under which twenty-two million men from first to last were finally carried or recarried to and from the Allied fighting lines.

The strategic effect of placing the Grand Fleet at Scapa Flow before the declaration of war had been alike complete and instantaneous. When at the end of August 1914 the prestige of the Royal Navy was proved by the brilliant and lucky dash into the Heligoland Bight, the Kaiser, all his inferiority complexes confirmed by the sinkings of his cruisers on their very war parade-ground – accepted the triumph of British naval power on the surface of the seas.

The thoughts of the German Admirals, thus foiled, turned inevitably to the submarine. Here was a wonderful and terrible new weapon, whose power and endurance had never been tested by any country till war came. Yet it was not until February 1915 that Germany resolved to employ this weapon against commerce, and Von Pohl was allowed to proclaim the first German blockade of the British Isles.

This was an enormous decision. But though the world looked with horror and indignation at the sinking of merchant ships without a thought for the safety of passengers and crews, the British Admiralty felt no serious alarm. We knew that the Germans had only some twenty-five U-boats, and that not more than one-third of them could be on the prowl at once.

On hundreds of ships proceeding weekly in and out of scores of harbours, this handful of marauders could make no serious impression. It was like hundreds of rabbits running across a ride, with only two or three one-eyed poachers to shoot them. Nearly all the rabbits got across every time, and the poachers themselves were harassed by the gamekeepers.

We actually announced in 1915 that we would publish all the sailings and sinkings every week, and Admiralty confidence was swiftly justified by events. No substantial or even noticeable injury was wrought upon British commerce by the first German submarine campaign.

Upon the other hand, grave difficulties loomed up for the German Government. The torpedoes that sank neutral ships destroyed the goodwill of the neutral world. Finally, the sinking of the *Lusitania* roused a storm of wrath, and a Note from America which brought the campaign in British waters to a close.

The first U-boat attack ceased in June 1915, and thereafter for more than a year – nearly two years in all – from the declarations of war, the British command of the seas was absolute and unchallenged. Outside the land-locked waters of the Baltic and the Black Sea, not a single hostile vessel cleft salt water. Had the war ended in 1915 or 1916, history would have recorded – in spite of the broken-off encounter of the fleets at Jutland – that the domination of the British Navy had been undisturbed.

Within this halcyon period there was one, and only one, great naval opportunity of ending the war both by land and sea. That opportunity was lost for ever in April 1915, when the Navy desisted finally from all attempts to force the passage of the Dardanelles. But even after all the misfortunes of the Allied armies in 1915 the naval calm continued, and a decisive victory of the British, French and Russian armies in 1916 would have brought peace, with British naval power unquestioned and seemingly unquestionable.

All this time the Germans were building U-boats, and the German Admiralty staff clamoured unceasingly to be allowed to use them.

The conflict between the Civil Power, terrified of bringing the United States and other neutrals into the war against them, and the German Admirals, sure that they had it in their power to free the Fatherland and its dependents from the stranglehold of the British blockade, is a long, cold, intense drama. Desperation alone turned the scale.

In 1916 the miscarriage at Verdun, the strain of the Somme, the surprise of Brusilov's offensive and, finally, the Rumanian declaration of war, constituted for Germany the second climacteric of the war. The men of dire decision were summoned to supreme control.

Hindenburg and Ludendorff were given the helm. They threw their whole weight upon the side of the Admirals. The Chancellor and Foreign Secretary were borne down by a new strong heave of the wheel. Their warnings that the United States would surely be drawn in to the hostile ranks fell upon unheeding ears of ruthless, violent men fighting for national survival.

From October 1916 onwards German submarine activities had been increasing, and sinkings had begun to rise sharply.

On 9 January 1917, in conference with the Kaiser at Pless, the civilians abandoned their opposition to the extremist measures. A hundred submarines lay ready to proceed on fateful missions. The Admirals marshalled facts and figures to prove that unrestricted U-boat warfare would certainly yield a sinkage of 600,000 tons a month, and that five months of this would bring Great Britain, the arch-enemy and soul of the hostile co-operation, to her knees.

The Kaiser ratified the decision of his servants. The orders were issued; the declarations were made; unrestricted warfare began on 1 February, and the United States became a mortal enemy.

These prodigious stakes would never have been played if any of those who gathered at Pless had known that a few months later Russia would collapse, and that a new prospect of victory on land would open. It was their destiny to take the plunge just before they would have learned that far less grievous hazards offered safety.

The first phase of the naval war was the tacit submission of the German seagoing fleets to the superior strength of Britain. There supervened upon this from October 1916, with ever-growing intensity, the second phase, namely the life and death struggle of the Royal Navy with the German U-boats.

It was a warfare hitherto undreamed of among men, a warfare at once more merciless and complicated than had ever been conceived. All the known sciences, every adaptation of mechanics, optics and acoustics that could play a part were pressed into its service.

It was a war of charts and calculations, of dials and switches, of experts who were also heroes, of tense, patient thought interrupted by explosions and death; of crews hunted and choked in the depth of the waters, and great ships foundering far from port without aid or mercy.

And upon the workings of this grisly process turned the history of the world.

POLITICIANS WERE RIGHT AND ADMIRALS WRONG

By the Rt Hon. Winston Churchill, MP

18 November 1931

November and December 1916 had seen a tentative revival of the sinkings, but the public, and even the Government, had grown so confident of the security of our commerce that it was some time before they began to feel serious anxiety. This new attack would no doubt be speedily dealt with.

To those concerned in the rising art of propaganda it was even pleasing, because of the effect on neutral and United States opinion. But the attack went on. The sinkings mounted month by month.

On 3 February 1917, following the German declaration of unrestricted warfare, the American Ambassador left Berlin.

But it was not until 6 April that the United States entered the war. So enormous an accession of strength seemed to make victory certain.

How could the Teutonic Empires, already hard-pressed, withstand this new surge of 120 millions against them?

But supposing the American armies could not get across the Atlantic; nay, supposing the seas were barred to war materials, oil, and even food, what would happen to an island – the mainspring of the war – with 40 million mouths to feed, and often scarcely three weeks' supply in hand?

Hitherto British sea-power had been so unchallenged that its existence had been as unnoticed as the air we breathe. Then suddenly the air began to get horribly rarefied. The cannonade thundered on in Flanders, but in all the wide circles of the British Government a new preoccupation possessed men's minds.

The sinking of British, Allied and Neutral merchant shipping by submarines alone had crept up in October and November to nearly 300,000 tons a month. In January this total was still 284,000 tons. With the opening of unrestricted warfare in February the dial mounted sharply to nearly 470,000 tons. The German Naval Staff had calculated that England, after providing for her own and Allied military needs, had about 10½ million tons of shipping for her supplies. She could not manage with less than 7½ million tons.

If the promised 600,000 tons could be sunk monthly, the fatal 7½ million tons limit would be reached in five months, and by the plain logic of figures Germany's most formidable opponent must give in. The danger was mortal and near. No talk now of decisive battles at sea, or of the Dardanelles, or landings in the Baltic, or attacks on Heligoland. A blow was being aimed at the heart and a stranglehold was tightening round the throat. Would it succeed, or would it fail? This was the question that stood staring Whitehall in the face.

April saw another tremendous rise, and the fateful finger moving remorselessly up. It was pointing to 837,000 tons of British, Allied and Neutral sinkings, of which 516,000 tons were of British sinkings. It was, in fact, had we known it, only one-fifth short of the promised German Naval Staff figure! Every other aspect of the war declined and grew thin and pale before the U-boat menace.

This last volume of the Naval History describes its impact on the War Cabinet, the Admiralty and Navy, and the measures taken to cope with the danger. The methods of defence fell into three categories. The first was mechanical. The preparations and counter-measures set on foot during the first abortive submarine attack by the Board of Admiralty in 1915 had not been neglected by their successors. A great volume of small craft was built or building. The dodges and devices of 1915 had been elaborated and multiplied.

Depth charges to explode at set depths, hydrophones to detect the slightest sound of submarine engines; flotilla-hunting manoeuvres, explosive paravanes for towing under water; nets with tell-tale buoys, decoy ships, zigzagging – all these were in full activity.

The second category comprised the reorganisation of the Naval Staff and the creation of an anti-submarine department. But it was the adoption of the tactics of convoy that alone decided the fate of nations.

No story of the Great War is more remarkable or more full of guidance for the future than this. It was a long, intense, violent struggle between the amateur politicians, thrown by democratic Parliamentary institutions to the head of affairs, on the one hand, and the competent, trained, experienced experts of the Admiralty and their great sea officers on the other. The astonishing fact is that the politicians were right, and that the Admiralty authorities were wrong.

The politicians were right upon a technical, professional question ostensibly quite outside their sphere, and the Admiralty authorities were wrong upon what was, after all, the heart and centre of their own peculiar job.

The second fact is not less noteworthy. The politicians, representing Civil Power at bay and fighting for the life of the State, overcame and pierced the mountains of prejudice and false argument which the Admiralty raised and backed with the highest naval authority. In no other country could such a thing have happened.

In Germany, for instance, the Kaiser and his Ministers had to accept the facts, figures and opinions of the naval experts as final. When Admiral Holtzendorff declared that unrestricted warfare would sink 600,000 tons of British shipping per month, and that five months would ruin England's war-making power; when he put that forward on his honour and conscience as the head of the German Naval Staff, there was no means of disputing him.

Hindenburg and Ludendorff endorsed in professional loyalty the opinions of their naval colleagues, and the Civil Power, dumb before mysterious assertion, saw itself if it did not adopt the technical advice accused of timidity or weakness which might deprive Germany of victory and even life. Naturally they yielded, and all went forward to disaster.

But the British politicians – we apologise for their existence – were powerful people, feeling they owed their positions to no man's favour. They asked all kinds of questions. They did not always take 'No' for an answer. They did not accept the facts and figures put before them by their experts as necessarily unshakable. They were not under moral awe of professional authority, if it did not seem reasonable to the lay mind. They were not above obtaining secretly the opinions of the junior naval officers concerned with the problem, and of using these views to cross-examine and confute the naval chiefs.

The sleuth-hound of politicians was Sir Maurice Hankey, Secretary of the Committee of Imperial Defence and Secretary to the War Cabinet. He had a lawful foot in every camp – naval, military, professional, political – and under every form of official correctitude he sought ruthlessly 'the way out'.

Above him stood Mr Lloyd George, with Mr Bonar Law at his side. Both these men had keen, searching minds for facts and figures. Neither of them was a stickler for professional etiquette. Neither was unduly impressed by gold-laced personages. Mr Lloyd George in particular had grasped power by a strange combination of force and intrigue. He was sure he would be hanged if we did not win the war, and was quite ready to accept the responsibility on such terms.

Both these Ministers, as early as November 1916, when the sinkings began to rise, had suggested that the Admiralty should use convoys for merchant ships. There was nothing novel about the proposal. Convoy had been a usual method in former wars. It had been used at the beginning of the Great War to protect troop-ships against German cruisers, and had been completely successful. Not a single vessel had been sunk. The Grand Fleet or detached squadrons of battleships were invariably convoyed and protected against U-boats by escorts of destroyers.

Now let us see the mountain of objections which the Board of Admiralty and the heads of its expert departments built up against this proposal. The Admiralty argued that a convoy would be no protection against submarine attack. First of all, it was not physically practicable. Merchant ships could not keep their stations in a convoy. They would certainly not be able to zigzag in company. Their different speeds would make their pace that of the slowest. Time would be lost, danger increased, and tonnage capacity wasted.

They would be readily thrown into confusion on a sudden attack. A submarine in the midst of a convoy might make tremendous havoc. We should be putting too many eggs in one basket. No fewer than 2,500 merchant ships, said the Admiralty, entered or left British ports every week. No convoy would be safe if it contained more than three or four merchantmen to every escorting warship.

Where were the destroyers and small craft for this prodigious task? We had not got them. After the safety of the fighting fleets and the patrols of the Dover Straits and narrow seas had been provided, the destroyers left over would be hopelessly inadequate.

Such, in outline, was the monumental case which the Admiralty raised against the adoption of a convoy system against unrestricted U-boat attacks. It must be admitted that few stronger arguments were ever set forth on paper. And when these were backed by the sincere deep-rooted convictions of able and experienced sailors who had spent their lives upon the sea, and understood all the difficulties and mysteries of which landsmen are necessarily ignorant, it is amazing that any force should have been found within the organism of the British State capable of overriding it by command and overturning it by experiment.

Yet this is what happened; and unless it had happened America would have been cut from Europe, England would have been starved into submission, and Germany would have won the war.

JELLICOE'S DRAMATIC DECISION AT ADMIRALTY

By the Rt Hon. Winston Churchill, MP

23 November 1931

No part of the Official History is written with more circum-spection than the account of the conflict between the War Cabinet and the Admiralty upon the adoption of the convoy system.

A layman might read these pages attentively and remain quite unconscious of its intensity, or indeed of what actually happened. All the main essential facts are stated, but they are stated with such a studied absence of emphasis, and often in so inverted a sequence, that the conclusion to which they remorselessly point is hidden. It is only when we decipher the cryptogram by the key of chronology that the truth – to many the unwelcome truth – emerges.

At the discussions on 2 November 1916 in the War Cabinet (Mr Asquith being still Prime Minister), Mr Lloyd George had asked the Commander-in-Chief, Sir John Jellicoe, whether he had any plan against German submarines working upon our trade routes. The Commander-in-Chief admitted that he had not. Mr Bonar Law then asked why they could not use the system of convoy. He was answered by the Chief of the Naval Staff that it did not do to lend more than one ship at a time under escort. The First Sea Lord, for his part, added that merchant ships would never be able to keep sufficiently together to enable a few destroyers to screen them.

The weight of adverse authority was for the time being decisive. As the losses from sinkings grew continually, anxiety deepened, but the increasing apprehension in no way altered the Admiralty view.

The arrival of Sir John Jellicoe as First Sea Lord confirmed it. The Admiralty staff massed all their opinions and authority in a memorandum in January which condemned the convoy system with elaborately marshalled reasons. There is no doubt; we are told that this memorandum recorded the collective opinion of the Admiralty, 'for the minutes of those high officials who were more particularly concerned with the defence of trade are all expressive of the same, or nearly the same, view'.

On 1 February 1917, the unrestricted U-boat campaign began, and immediately the sinkings rose to an alarming pitch. It was at this point that Sir Maurice Hankey wrote his celebrated memorandum challenging all the main objections to the convoy system, and armed with this Mr Lloyd George (now Prime Minister), on 13 February, reopened the whole question with the Admiralty authorities. This masterly paper and the pointed manner in which it was pressed upon the Admiralty by the new head of the Government, left the dominant and senior naval opinion unchanged.

There can, of course, be no doubt that many of the facts and arguments upon which it had been built were those of the junior members of the Admiralty Staff departments dealing with the U-boat problem. In the Naval Service the discipline of opinion was so severe that had not the channel, or safety valve, of the Committee of Imperial Defence been in existence, these opinions might never have borne fruit.

The firmly inculcated doctrine that an admiral's opinion was more likely to be right than a captain's, and that a captain's opinion was superior to that of a commander, did not hold good when questions entirely novel in character, requiring keen and bold minds unhampered by long routine, were under debate.

Argument, however, was reinforced by practical experience. Ships engaged in the coal trade with France had suffered heavy losses in the closing months of 1916. The French immediately suggested convoy, and on 7 February the Admiralty deferred to their wishes. The colliers were despatched in company and under escort. The new system was immediately effective. Out of 1,200 colliers convoyed to and fro in March, only three were lost.

Still the Admiralty staff continued obdurate. But one cannot wonder at their tenacity considering the data upon which their reasoning was based.

In the early part of the war when we were publishing our losses from U-boats compared to our incoming and outgoing traffic, the number of ships arriving at or leaving British ports within a week had been magniloquently stated to amount to 2,500. How was it physically possible for the sixty or seventy destroyers which were at most available, supplemented by armed trawlers and other small craft, to deal with this vast inflow and outflow of thousands of ships?

However, this damning figure of 2,500 was now itself attacked. A junior officer, Cmdr R.G. Henderson, working in the anti-submarine department and in close contact with the Ministry of Shipping, broke up this monstrous and long tamely accepted obstacle. It was shown that the 2,500 voyages included all the repeated calls of coasters and short-sea traders of 300 tons and upwards. But these were not the ships upon which our life depended. It was the ocean-going traffic to and from all parts of the world that alone was vital.

In the early days of April it was proved by Cmdr Henderson that the minimum arrivals and departures of ocean-going ships of 1,600 tons and upwards upon which everything hung did not exceed between 120 and 140 a week. The whole edifice of logical argument collapsed when the utterly unsound foundation of 2,500 was shorn away.

April saw a terrible intensity of the submarine war, and in every direction the secret graphs of the Cabinet showed the time limits which were closing in upon the food supplies of the central island and the war supplies of its armies and of the Allied armies in the various theatres. Still the Admiralty in the ruins of their previous arguments resisted convoy. It may be that a dread of becoming responsible not only for the warships of the Navy, but of the safety of every merchant ship that sailed, lay heavy upon their minds. Whatever the root reason, they remained inflexible.

On 10 April 1917, the United States having entered the war, Admiral Sims conferred with the First Sea Lord. The grim facts of the submarine campaign were put before the American sailor, and he was urged to procure all possible assistance in small craft. At the same time, he was induced to accept the Admiralty view that convoy was impossible. He conveyed this opinion to his own Government as the most authoritative expression of British naval science.

To all this cumulative pressure of events and reasons there were now added the conclusions of a committee of officers from the Grand Fleet, who had sat for some weeks at Longhope, in the Orkneys, on the question of the sinkings on the Scandinavian trade route. They unanimously recommended convoy. Nevertheless, the First Sea Lord, while agreeing to an experiment on this particular route, would only report to the War Cabinet that the question of its general use was still 'under consideration'.

Awful months had thus passed without relief. But now

matters had reached a climax. On 23 April the War Cabinet debated the whole issue with their naval advisers. The results of the discussion were wholly unsatisfactory. On the 25th, therefore, the War Cabinet, sitting alone, resolved upon decisive action.

It was agreed that the Prime Minister should himself visit the Admiralty 'to investigate all the means at present used in anti-submarine warfare, on the ground that recent inquiries had made it clear that there was not sufficient co-ordination in the present efforts to deal with the campaign'.

The menace implied in this procedure was unmistakable. No greater shock could be administered to a responsible department or military profession. The naval authorities realised that it was a case of 'act or go'.

On the 26th the head of the anti-submarine department minuted to Admiral Jellicoe: 'It seems to me evident that the time has arrived when we must be ready to introduce a comprehensive scheme of convoy at any moment.' On the 27th Admiral Jellicoe approved the policy. When Mr Lloyd George visited the Admiralty on 30 April in accordance with the Cabinet's decision, he was presented with a complete acceptance of the demand of the Civil Power. He was able to report to his colleagues:

'As the views of the Admiralty are now in complete accord with the views of the War Cabinet on this question, and as convoys have just come into operation on some routes and are being organised on others, further comment is unnecessary . . .'

Says the 'Official Naval History': 'Admiral Jellicoe's decision stands out clearly, even dramatically, as one of the most important of the war.'

TRIUMPH OF THE CONVOY SYSTEM

By the Rt Hon. Winston Churchill, MP

25 November 1931

Of course, as everyone knows, the adoption of the convoy system at sea defeated the German U-boat attack. By July 1917 it was in working order. Five months of unrestricted submarine warfare had passed, and Great Britain had not been brought to her knees.

In September the clouds began to break. Monthly sinkings had fallen from 800,000 to 300,000 tons. In February 1918 the curve of building output crossed the sinkage curve. By October 1918, 1,782 great ships had been convoyed across the seas with a loss of only 167.

The war effort of the Allies had never slackened. The American armies had been carried safely across the seas, and the doom of Germany had for some months been only a matter of time.

This remarkable story had two suggestive sequels. When the Admiralty took their famous decision to adopt the convoy system, the First Sea Lord demanded in return from the War Cabinet that the naval task should be lightened by the abandonment of the Salonica operation and the withdrawal of the Allied armies from the Balkan theatre. He proved conclusively that 400,000 tons of shipping would be saved by this curtailment.

Salonica and the Balkan campaign was Mr Lloyd George's pet scheme. So relieved was he to obtain the Admiralty's consent to the adoption of convoy that he agreed on 30 April 1917 to sacrifice it. The French were also compelled to agree.

However, a subordinate Minister, Sir Leo Chiozza Money,

working in the Foreign Trade department, produced a paper, endorsed by the Ministry of Shipping, showing that this 400,000 tons' saving could be effected by drawing the whole of the Allied supplies from the American continent instead of from all parts of the world; and that the supplies would be forthcoming. The scheme was adopted and the Salonican armies were therefore permitted to continue their campaign.

As we all know now it was the surrender of Bulgaria in October 1918 which produced the final collapse of the Teutonic Empires. But for this, the German armies would have effected their retreat to the Meuse or the Rhine, and another bloody year might have dawned upon the world involving the killing and wounding of another two or three millions of men and the consumption of ten or twelve thousand millions of our dwindling wealth.

The second incident is much smaller. Early in May 1917, the Admiralty, having accepted the War Cabinet's decision in favour of convoy, asked the Navy Department at Washington to adopt it also. But the American naval authorities knew from Admiral Sims's reports that the convoy system had been forced upon the British sailors against their better judgment by political interference. They therefore refused to risk their ships upon what they knew was inexpert and unprofessional advice.

It was some months before the vast and patent triumph of convoy removed their deep misgivings. The reluctance of all the naval chiefs in every Allied country to adopt convoy finds its counterpart only in the reluctance of the military chiefs of all the armies, Allied and enemy, to comprehend the significance of the tank. In both cases these means of salvation were forced upon them from outside and from below.

A submarine going round by the Orkneys took nearly a

week to reach its hunting grounds in the Channel or its approaches. If it ran the gauntlet of the Dover Straits, it took only a single day. It thus saved seven days of the fortnight that it could stay out.

If the smaller U-boats could pass safely through the Dover Straits, the number which Germany possessed was for practical purpose almost doubled. The closure of the Straits and of the Belgian ports abutting on the Straits was therefore cardinal.

The need to close the Straits against all enemy vessels had from the beginning of the war made Dover an important command. Admiral Bacon had come there in 1915, and in 1916 had laid a net barrage right across the Straits from the Goodwins to the Belgian sands.

Great results were expected from this barrage, and its reputation was established by a curious coincidence. On the very day that it was laid, 24 April 1916, Admiral Scheer, the German Commander-in-Chief, had been ordered to restrict submarine warfare. The German Government had decided that merchantmen were to be boarded before being sunk. In protest Scheer had called off his U-boats.

None, therefore, passed the Straits for some months, and the cessation of their attempts gave rise at Dover to the idea that they had been stopped by the new net barrage.

A false confidence in this device was established in many able minds upon strong foundations.

Admiral Bacon was the victim of the illusion that his net barrage could stop the U-boats. He was an able officer with a chequered history. The bent of his mind was technical. He was a brilliant formulator and exponent of complicated designs. His bombardments of the Belgian coast were embodiments of higher mathematics. He had made a 15-inch howitzer in an incredibly short time at the beginning of the war. In everything that concerned machinery, invention, organisation, precision, he had few professional superiors. He was a fine instrumentalist.

In the autumn of 1917 the newly formed Plans Division of the Admiralty War Staff were quite sure that U-boats were habitually passing through the Dover barrage, and that it was neither an obstacle nor a deterrent. Rear-Admiral Keyes, in charge of this Division, began to press upon his superiors at the Admiralty first the reality of the evil, and secondly a number of remedial measures. The defence had originally consisted of a line of nets buoyed upon the surface, occasionally patrolled, and supported by elaborate minefields.

Critics of our pre-war naval arrangements have justly censured the Admiralty mine. Lord Fisher, in his earlier peacetime administration, had been hostile to mines. The sub-department concerned had dwelt in a highly secret and secluded nook, defended on every side by abstruse technicalities. There is no doubt that it had produced at the beginning of the war a mine which would rarely keep its depth and very often not explode on being bumped. Even these defective instruments were not very numerous. The main strategy of the Admiralty had not contemplated elaborate minings and counter-minings.

But now the war had gone on for nearly three years, and in the absence of any coherent scheme of a naval offensive, live mines played an ever-increasing part. By the middle of 1917 new and thoroughly effective mines were flowing out from the factories, and in November fresh deep minefields were laid in the Dover Straits.

ELEVEN U-BOATS DESTROYED IN DOVER MINEFIELDS

By the Rt Hon. Winston Churchill, MP

30 November 1931

A great dispute arose in the winter of 1917 between the Plans Division of the Admiralty and the Dover Command. Admiral Keyes asserted that Admiral Bacon's existing arrangements were not stopping U-boat penetration.

He declared that the minefields must be not only watched by trawlers and drifters with all available small craft patrolling above the mines, but that they must be brightly illuminated and actively defended.

The movement of a U-boat, groping its way forward on the surface, ready to dive at any moment, would thus be detected. An alarm would be given, a hurroosh would be raised, cannon would fire, the submarine would dive and make its exit from the world by bumping into one of our good live mines.

Admiral Bacon, on the other hand, contended that the lights would warn the submarines, and teach them to avoid the minefields, and that if destroyers continually patrolled the Dover Straits it was only a question of time before the Germans sent out a strong force to devour the patrols. He argued, besides, that it was not true that submarines were passing the Dover Straits.

Anyone will see that the controversy thus outlined was well posed. Strong evidence was furnished by the Naval Intelligence that the Plans Division was right. A U-boat (UC 44) sunk in shoal water had been fished up, and her captain's log revealed the exact dates on which each of a continuous stream of U-boats had passed the Straits and, indeed, their whole timetable and fortunes. In fact, the U-boat commanders were told in their instructions that they could dive under or go over the Dover barrage at will.

It was possible, however, to be sceptical of the German figures, and though the Plans Division was convinced of their accuracy, the Dover Command continued obdurate and complacent.

When in the late autumn of 1917 the Plans Division began to criticise the efficacy of the Dover barrage, and avowed that German submarines were passing freely through Admiral Bacon's command, the admiral was neither pleased nor polite. Many coldly stated differences passed to and fro in official papers. The climax was reached upon the blunt issue of whether the minefields should be illuminated or not. The brightly lighted picture of these large areas picketed by almost defence-less trawlers manned by fishermen seemed a most unwarlike proposition. One might almost have said that common sense repelled such a remedy. But on this point the Admiralty Staff were right, and the Admiral on the spot was wrong. The simple truth emerged that the barrage and minefields were no use unless they were vigorously defended from above water.

Admiral Jellicoe (now First Sea Lord) had sided at the outset with Admiral Bacon. But at length he became convinced that the Plans Division was right. On 18 December 1917, with the cordial approval of the First Lord, Sir Eric Geddes, he ordered Bacon to institute the 'Plans' Patrol system. By good luck it drew blood the very first night it was tried. On 19 December a German U-boat was destroyed.

Admiral Jellicoe, who was greatly exhausted by the strain of his prolonged and valiant exertions in charge of the Fleet and later of the Admiralty, was relieved of his post. Admiral

Wemyss, his deputy, an officer not greatly known, but of robust temper, and who was reputed to be willing to make full use of a Staff, was appointed in his stead. Admiral Bacon was dismissed from the Dover Command, and Keyes, the head of the Plans Division, hitherto the chief critic, was sent to see if he could do the job.

Here again the results of the change, even though perhaps favoured by fortune, were amazing. In the next six months eleven identified submarines perished in the Dover minefields or their approaches. The sinkings in the Channel, influenced also by convoy, rapidly declined. The German voyage through the Dover Straits became one of intolerable peril.

In 1918 a Zeebrugge submarine could count on not more than six voyages before she met her inevitable doom. By the summer all attempts of U-boats to pass the Dover barrage had ceased.

The Official History is delicately careful not to emphasise the facts. But nevertheless all the salient facts are there. We see another clash between the new and somewhat irreverent junior brains of the Navy and august, old honourable authority. Such cases reproduce themselves in civil life and in political affairs. We see them in the management of great businesses and in the structure and fortunes of Governments. But certainly the story of the Dover barrage forms a corroborating sequel to the story of the convoy system. It was the Prime Minister, the War Cabinet and the First Lord who asserted the freedom of the new professional thought over embattled seniority. In both cases the Civil Power leaned, pressed, and finally thrust in the right direction.

There was, however, a bad moment for the new command at Dover. The patrolling of the illuminated minefields offered an obvious target to German attacks. The fishing craft on duty were vulnerable in the last degree. About a hundred little vessels of no military quality – trawlers burning flares, drifters, motor launches, paddle mine-sweepers, old coal-burning destroyers, P-boats, with a monitor in their midst – all lay in the glare of the searchlights. The area was as bright as Piccadilly; and its occupants scarcely better armed. Some miles to the eastward five patrolling divisions of destroyers offered their only possible protection. But if these were evaded by a raiding enemy, a massacre seemed inevitable. The acceptance of this hideous liability was the essence of Keyes' conception.

All the chances being balanced, this was the least bad to risk. But it was very bad.

On 14 February 1918, the Germans brought their best flotilla commander from the Heligoland Bight with their four latest and largest destroyers, and fell upon the trawlers of the Dover barrage with cruel execution.

By a muddle in the darkness of mistaken signals, and what not, the six British destroyers on patrol inexcusably mistook them for friends and they escaped in triumph to the north. The fishermen were deeply angered. They thought the Royal Navy had failed to give them the protection which it had guaranteed, and which they deserved. They saw themselves exposed on any night to merciless attacks. For a while they lost confidence in the new Dover Command, and, indeed, in the Royal Navy.

Admiral Bacon, who had predicted this very event, saw his arguments justified. He felt himself entitled to say, 'I told you so.' Keyes's reputation hung on a thread. Luckily, resolute new-minded men more or less banded together upon a common scheme of thought had now got grip of the Admiralty machine. Keyes survived the disaster, and the immortal epic of Zeebrugge on St George's Day restored alike the confidence of the

Admiralty in their officer and the faith of the fishermen in their chief.

It also gained the plaudits of the public and very favourable references in the newspapers, neither of which, even in their excess, will be disputed by history,

Chapter 5

Churchill as a Painter

Churchill first became interested in painting in June 1915. After having been dismissed from the Admiralty, he became inconsolably depressed owing largely to 'unwonted leisure time in which to contemplate the unfolding of the War'. However, one afternoon at Hoe Farm in Southampton, he happened to notice his sister-in-law, Gwendoline, sketching in watercolours and asked if he might try it. From that moment, Churchill knew he had found a passion. He enjoyed it so much he wrote an essay about it in 1921–22 for *Strand* magazine called 'Painting as a Pastime'. He even solicited help from famous artists John Lavery and William Nicholson. Churchill continued to paint for the rest of his life. His paintings have been displayed in the Royal Academy and fetched considerable prices, even when sold anonymously.

MR CHURCHILL ON ART
28 July 1937

Mr Winston Churchill, who was First Lord of the Admiralty

from 1911 to 1915, yesterday opened the 'Sea Power' exhibition at the New Burlington Gallery.

'It is when you come to the great issue of power over the sea,' he said, 'that you feel you are in contact with the immemorial past of Britain, and you feel the romance of the story which has led us from a barbaric and subjected island to our present still respectable position.' (Laughter.)

'There is a question of whether this exhibition is to be characterised under the heading of art or propaganda,' he continued. 'I cannot at all see why the two should not be combined, although they are not always combined.

'I noticed the other day in the newspapers that across the North Sea or German Ocean, a very great man [Herr Hitler], who is certainly a master of propaganda, favoured us with his views on art.

'They were very drastic and formidable pronouncements of which he delivered himself. Apparently, if you put too much green in your sky you are liable to be handed over to the Minister for Sterilisation. Whether there is any mitigation for the punishment if it is only performed in watercolours, I do not know.

'If you should make the mistake of putting too much purple in the sea, you are liable to be handed over to the Minister of the Interior to be put in a concentration camp.

'Now, looking round these walls, we have a deeper realisation of all that the British Navy shields us from.' (Laughter.)

Mr Churchill remarked that he wondered whether modern ships gave the artist the same chance as the tall galleons and frigates which for hundreds of years ruled the waves – or disputed the waves.

The function of art, it had been said, was to draw the spark of beauty from the most unprepossessing objects.

'If that be so it presents our modern painters with an almost inexhaustible theme,' he went on. 'For instance, the present garments of our modern age seem to offer to the Rembrandt of the present time or the future an opportunity of finding beauty in ugliness, a task at least as inspiring as that of the eminent scientist of Laputa, who was engaged in extracting sunbeams from cucumbers.'

Of all the countries in the world Britain was the one which should attract the attention of painters to the sea and to the great ships that sailed upon it. In the endless interpretations of those changing forms they would find a source of inspiration and of culture which ought to contribute to the general movement of our island life.

SIR WINSTON DISCUSSES MODERN ART
1 May 1953

Sir Winston Churchill gave Royal Academicians an insight into his views of the controversial sculpture of the 'Unknown Political Prisoner' exhibited at the Tate Gallery when he attended the Coronation dinner of the Royal Academy of Arts at Burlington House last night.

He was the principal guest, and for the first time in public since he was made a Knight of the Garter by the Queen at Windsor last week he wore the star and dark blue sash of the Order.

'This afternoon,' he said, 'I visited the Tate Gallery and I looked particularly at the "Unknown Political Prisoner". I understand that it is to be erected, or some suggested that it is to be erected, 300 feet high on the cliffs of Dover.

'I am not going to attempt, even as an honorary member extraordinary of the Royal Academy, to pronounce upon the artistic merits or otherwise of this work.

'But if it is to be erected 300 feet high on the cliffs of Dover, I feel that my duties as Lord Warden of the Cinque Ports might well force me to give it a very direct measure of attention.' (Laughter and applause.)

Although he is an Honorary Academician Extraordinary, and has five pictures in this year's exhibition, Sir Winston attended in his capacity as Prime Minister.

Before going in to dinner, in accordance with tradition he inspected a detachment of the 21st Special Air Service (Artists) TA, successors to the Artists Rifles. Although it was raining at the time, Sir Winston, in overcoat and top hat, walked round the ranks, which were drawn up in the courtyard of Burlington House.

A big crowd, some of whom had waited for more than an hour in the rain, gave him three hearty cheers as he walked into the Academy to be greeted by the President, Sir Gerald Kelly.

It was the fourth annual dinner since the war. There was not one last year because of the King's death.

When Sir Winston rose to reply to the toast of 'Her Majesty's Ministers', he was given an ovation and the company of more than 200 guests, all men, stood up.

He said that it would be disastrous if the control of the Royal Academy fell into any particular school of artistic thought which 'like a dog in a manger would have little pleasure itself and exclude all others'.

The function of such an institution as the Academy was to hold a middle course between tradition and innovation.

'Without tradition art is a flock of sheep without a shepherd. Without innovation it is a corpse.'

It was not the function of the RA to run wildly after every curious novelty. 'There are many opportunities and many places for experimental artists to try their wings.

'It is not until the results of their experiments have won that measure of acceptance from the general agreement of qualified judges that the RA can be expected to give its countenance.'

Art and politics have two things in common. 'The first is the controversial differences of opinion between those who are engaged in them. These are very lively and the controversies in the field of art are at least as vigorous as those in politics.'

The second element was the search for truth. In that they had only so far been partially successful. Although he would not discuss the political aspects, he said: 'About these novel forms of art, I have a feeling that people who go in for novel, unexpected supra-original, if I can coin that word, forms of art, ought to have credentials.'

They should have a thorough grounding in the profession of painting or sculpture, and prove themselves masters of line and colour 'before they have a bona fide claim to lay down the law to us about what we should admire'. (Laughter and applause.)

Churchill instanced Picasso as a 'master of the art of painting'. If a man had been through all that and had those credentials at his disposal, 'I certainly receive with respect and attention, even though I may lack comprehension, any later manifestations of his accumulated knowledge and experience with which he may favour us.'

With a foundation of that kind one must be respectful. 'But one does view with some suspicion, perhaps surliness even, people who have had no sort of artistic training, no comprehension of the enormous basis of professional training, perseverance, or knowledge that is required, and yet go in for the most extraordinary performances or manifestations in the hope that the result will obtain notoriety, and even profit from their exercise.'

CHURCHILL ART 'DAMN GOOD'
1 February 1958

Mr Truman, former United States President, spent forty minutes at Sir Winston Churchill's one-man art show at Kansas City, Missouri, and pronounced the paintings 'damn good'.

'At least you can tell what they are and that is more than you can say for a lot of these modern painters,' he declared. 'Ham-and-eggers, I call them. They just throw an egg at the canvas and mix in a little ham.'

But he still rated Sir Winston a better statesman than an artist. When a reporter appended the remark 'for an amateur' to his praise of the paintings, he snapped: 'What are you talking about? They are damn good.'

Mr Truman, who is seventy-three, grinned broadly at a still life showing a dozen or so bottles of liquor on a table. It was called 'Bottlescape'.

He said he had visited some of the scenes depicted by Sir Winston's brush, and had seen his 'entire collection of three or four hundred paintings', one of which he took away as a gift.

'I wish the old man were here to see this,' he added.

Chapter 6

Churchill's Letters from the Wilderness

During 1938 Churchill asked Lord Camrose, then the proprietor of the *Telegraph*, if he might publish a column of fortnightly articles on foreign policy and defence. Churchill had been writing for the *Evening Standard* but they cancelled his column because, according to Churchill, his 'views are not in accordance with the policy of the paper'. Lord Camrose jumped at the idea and Churchill began regularly writing for the *Telegraph* as he had done when he was a junior officer on the frontiers of British India.

These articles form a large part of Churchill's book *Step by Step* (1939), which was published almost on the eve of the Second World War. They illustrate the slow process by which war was becoming inevitable in Europe and also clearly demonstrate the prophetic nature of Churchill's words.

FRANCE'S NEW GOVERNMENT
By the Rt Hon. Winston Churchill, MP
14 April 1938

If France broke, everything would break, and the Nazi domination of Europe, and potentially of a large part of the world, would seem to be inevitable. It is therefore with keen and somewhat strained attention that all countries – especially friendly countries, great and small – have watched the prolonged deadlock in French Parliamentary affairs.

One stop-gap Government has succeeded another. The many interesting personalities involved, the intricate warfare of the various groups and parties, the vivid, indeed hectic, collective life of the Chamber provide all the elements of a most thrilling political game – if only this was the time to play one.

The Deputies and the Chamber have, as anyone can see, a very jolly time. They are perpetually making and unmaking Governments. Thirty or forty distinguished and astonishingly able men take it in turns to be Prime Minister, Foreign Secretary, Finance Minister, etc. They have a much more amusing time than their opposite numbers in Great Britain or the United States.

In both these English-speaking democracies when a man's in, he's in; and when he's out, he's out for a good long time. But the accomplished players at the French musical chairs monopolise with their own fads and prejudices, their own airs and graces, their own personal egotisms or party-isms, an altogether undue part of the life of France, and thus of the life of the free democracies.

What splendid attitudes they are able to take – and how

often! How they strut and pose! Here is a good man capable of giving the necessary directions, but if he moves one inch this way he loses the Left, or one inch that way and he loses the Right. Shuffle the cards again; shake the kaleidoscope; bring forth another highly competent personage and let him have a chance!

Ministers of State pass through their departments like weekend guests at Le Touquet. The experienced hard-bitten Chef de Cabinet has hardly time to make their acquaintance, offer the usual compliments and good wishes to a new Minister taking office, before the highly competent visitor has departed and another equally able successor is knocking at the door.

In England we only have a Cabinet crisis once in a blue moon, and when it happens it is both serious and exciting. Its consequences last for years. But in Paris Cabinet-making is a perpetual sport.

The question which has now arisen is whether this kind of sport is one which the French people 'risen against tyrants' can afford to enjoy so frequently. After all one can have too much of a good thing. A joke is a joke; but it palls with repetition.

I have for a generation taken the view that British fortunes are linked in many vital matters with those of France. For the first time since the war I have seen a real advance in British public opinion and in the declarations of his Majesty's Government towards a close, rigorous defensive alliance with the French Republic. No Englishman would presume to have a preference about the particular Ministers or the party groupings upon which any French Government depends. But Mr Chamberlain said the other day that we would fight in defence of France and Belgium. Therefore we naturally feel that we should like to know who are the men with whom we are to deal and whether they are likely to stay for any length of time in their present jobs. It seems to me that this is a reasonable request.

I wonder whether the French people realise how bitter and persistent is the pro-German propaganda in this island? The strongest point, repeatedly made, is that France is on the verge of collapse. She is portrayed as about to go down the same bloody sewer as Spain has done. All the 'Heil Hitler' brigade in London society exploit and gloat over what they are pleased to call 'the Parliamentary impotence of the French democracy'. Thus the amusing game in which French politicians rejoice is turned in deadly fashion to their detriment – and to our common danger. There surely ought to be an effort to put this right.

It is upon this footing that we come to the events of the hour. They are important. A very capable and sincere man has been chosen in M. Daladier. He has for nearly two years been identified with the French army and the defence of France. He cannot command the pledged allegiance of either the Right or the Left; but he has formed a small Inner Cabinet which has been welcomed by the almost unanimous vote of the buzzing Chamber; and he asks for power to give them a brief holiday while he and this small group govern the country.

The French finances are in great disorder. There is a nasty row about money. The urban working class, in acute and natural distress about the massacre of the Spanish Republic through Nazi and Fascist intervention, and otherwise angered by the rise in prices, has yielded itself to an epidemic of strikes.

On Tuesday 150,000 men were said to have ceased work. Some sulked in their homes; others occupied the factories. The production of munitions, especially aeroplane engines, the most tardy and necessary of all, was for the moment arrested.

The well-meant forty-hour week has produced an inefficiency and slowing-down in painful contrast with the vast iron-driven German munitions supply. Competition in such circumstances would be unequal. The awful sentence may be pronounced: 'Thou art weighed in the balance and found wanting.' Unless Nazi rule is to spread throughout Europe, these superficial yet vicious and morbid disharmonies must be brought to a speedy end. The agreement now reached is doubly welcome.

Those who know France well, or have long worked with French statesmen and generals, realise the immense latent strength of France. They see what is not apparent to the casual observer. They see the French army always on the watch.

Part of it mans the ramparts round the country. The rest constitutes the most perfectly trained and faithful mobile force in Europe. The French army means to France what the Monarchy means to Britain. It is above all parties. It serves all parties. It is cherished by all parties.

Never interfering in politics, though by no means unobservant of them, the officers and men of the French army discharge their professional duties and keep their vigil upon the frontiers of the land. Behind them lies the solid peasantry of millions of families rooted in the soil they own. Behind them stands this agitated intellectualism which presents so perfectly and expresses so volubly the vital ideas. There is also the inspiration in the soul of a people who feel themselves in a marked degree, and at this particular moment with intensity, the trustees of freedom throughout Europe.

We in Britain wish all success to the Daladier Government; and we hope it will last long enough to afford a solid foundation upon which the necessary arrangements for mutual security can be made.

M. Daladier has had disappointments in the formation of his Ministry. He has had to express upon a narrow front needs that deserve a much broader basis. But he has one important political force in reserve. M. Blum will not fail the cause of European freedom. His influence with the Socialist party is commanding. He will certainly give loyal aid.

WOULD PEACE OR WAR BETTER SERVE MUSSOLINI'S INTERESTS?

By the Rt Hon. Winston Churchill, MP

13 April 1939

Speculation has been rife in many countries about whether Signor Mussolini will carry Italy into a world war on the German side. Most people think that after what has happened in the last fortnight this question has already been decided. The Anglo-Italian Agreement has been violated in the most barefaced manner. There is not one single point upon which faith has been kept.

Italy promised to reduce her army in Libya by 30,000 men. She has taken them away and then sent them back. Italy promised to withdraw her troops from Spain, at any rate when the civil war was over. The war is over and the troops are still there.

She promised not to change the status quo in the Mediterranean, which included, and was understood to include, the Adriatic. She has now laid violent hands upon Albanian independence. She promised that all major troop movements would be notified beforehand to the other high contracting party. All this has been contemptuously torn in pieces.

As an additional piece of deceit, precise assurances were given by Count Ciano to the British Ambassador that no movement upon Albania was in contemplation. At this very moment the ships and troops were about to move upon their victim.

It is not possible to have a more complete instance of perjured faith and dishonesty than has been shown. One may well ask whether a Government who have thus flouted and spurned a solemn agreement, newly contracted with a friendly Power, have not already made up their mind to carry their hostility to that Power to all lengths as occasion may require.

Nevertheless, though faith may be broken, interest remains. It was a maxim of the eighteenth century, mentioned by the great Duke of Marlborough – 'Interest never lies'. And certainly Italian interests would be grievously injured in a war against Great Britain and France in the Mediterranean.

There never was a country more completely sprawled than Italy at the present moment. Four separate Italian armies have left her shores and would be hopelessly cut off if the Italian Navy were beaten by the Anglo-French fleets. These fleets are incomparably more powerful than the Italian Navy. Even if the Italian warships were all manned by Mussolinis, it is difficult to believe that they could keep the sea against the very heavy odds to which they would be exposed.

Nothing that happened in the war and nothing we have learned since leads us to believe that man for man the Italian sailors are twice or three times as good as the British, and French. Modesty compels resort to understatements of this character.

If a world war should be forced upon us all this year it might well be that the earliest decisions would be reached in the Mediterranean, and these decisions would bring consequential disasters upon the Italian armies in Abyssinia, Libya, Spain and Albania.

There is a school of British strategists who hold that in a world struggle with Nazidom it would be a positive advantage to have Italy as an enemy. In this long vulnerable peninsula, with its lack of raw materials, they observe a theatre in which important victories could be gained.

They declare that Germany would have to carry Italy as she carried Austria in the late war. German munitions and supplies would have to be poured southward. This process, indeed, has already begun. German troops – above all, German aviation – would become involved in the defence of Italy and so far as possible of Italy's overseas ventures.

This prospect cannot be at all pleasing to the Italian people. If the Nazi domination were successful in beating down the resistance of France and the British Empire, possibly assisted by the United States, there would, of course, be much loot to share. But Germany would be the tiger and Italy the minor attendant who had gone hunting with her. The Germans have a way, when they get into countries, of throwing their weight about. Even if the brightest hopes of the Berlin–Rome axis were realised, Italy would be in fact, if not in name, a dependency of the Nazi power.

But the fortunes of war might not take this course. The great nations of the West, whose existence would be at stake and whose allies in the East might gather under the pressure of events, might after all be successful. In that event Italy would not only have suffered and borne the brunt at the beginning, but at the end she would be upon the defeated side. Either way the Italian prospect does not seem inviting to any dispassionate eye.

There is every reason to believe that this is the view of the Italian people. The mass of them are not allowed to take any part in the shaping of their destinies. They are told only what it is thought good for them to hear. All free expression of opinion is sedulously prevented.

But we are told that even in the Fascist Grand Council stern words have been used against the policy of dragging Italy into a Mediterranean war with Great Britain and France. One important leader is said to have declared that Italy must not be drawn into a war 'against the wish of the Church, of the King and of the people'.

So far as we can tell, from the innumerable contacts which exist between British and Italian individuals, these sentiments are almost universal throughout Italy. It would be with genuine grief that the industrious and agreeable Italian population would find themselves condemned to a mortal struggle with the two democracies of the West. No doubt they are assured that the French and British are effete and decadent; that they are rotted with Bolshevism; that they are incapable of manly action. But this propaganda has not carried conviction with it, and to this moment it remains doubtful whether Signor Mussolini, if he had the will, would have the power to force the Italian people to this terrible plunge.

The breaking of agreements with Great Britain, which many people felt were not worth the paper on which they were written, is not necessarily a final test. The outrage upon Albania presents itself, like so many other episodes at these times, in an ambiguous guise.

It may be that it is the first move in a German–Italian drive upon the Balkans, which must lead inevitably to general war.

Certainly the movement of troops and munitions to Albania, far beyond what local needs require, would seem to support this sombre view.

On the other hand, one can imagine Mussolini explaining that his Albanian excursion is a mere local incident. He made, he might say, demands upon France which he considered just, but which were bluntly refused. No Tunis, no Corsica, no Nice, without war with the Western Powers. 'Where else,' he might exclaim, 'could I go but to this Albania, which gives me something to show my people, after all their hardships, without bringing them into direct conflict with England and France?'

Who will read the riddle? It would indeed be rash to pronounce. All that is contended for in this article is that no answer to it is yet forthcoming from the head of the Italian Government. But all must very soon become clear. The British and French Governments are believed to be about to give a guarantee to Greece and Turkey. Any attack upon the integrity or independence of Greece, which is nearest to danger, would precipitate the Mediterranean war and would no doubt be the signal for a far graver conflict in the north.

Although it is dangerous to prophesy in a positive sense, we may at least feel at the time of writing that the Berlin–Rome axis stands upon a no more sacred foundation than does the Anglo-Italian Pact.

Chapter 7

Churchill and the US: The Special Relationship

In many ways Winston Churchill embodied the 'special relationship' between the United States and Great Britain. His mother, Jennie Jerome, was American and his father, Lord Randolph Churchill, was British. Churchill saw the potential of a long-term relationship with the US even during the First World War, when he encouraged the intermingling of British and American troops to the War Cabinet on the grounds that it might have 'an immeasurable effect upon the future destiny of the English-speaking peoples'. At one stage he even considered a joint currency between the two powers. By the Second World War, Churchill's positive view of America had solidified because he knew that Britain and the US would have to work together to defeat Nazi Germany. Though the relationship was, at times, rocky, Churchill took a personal interest in advancing Anglo-American relations. He became fast friends with President Roosevelt, President Truman and General Eisenhower. In his second premiership, during the Cold War, Churchill continually sought foreign policies which would be compatible with

American aspirations, even when it was unpopular among his own colleagues. He continued to believe in the power of the special relationship, and in 1955 his parting words to his last Cabinet meeting were, 'Never be separated from the Americans.'

MR CHURCHILL BROADCASTS TO AMERICA
17 October 1938

Mr Winston Churchill, MP, dealt with the European crisis in a speech broadcast from London to America last night.

Mr Churchill said: 'I avail myself with relief of the opportunity of speaking to the people of the United States. I do not know how long such liberties will be allowed.

'The stations are closing down; the lights are going out; but there is still time for those to whom freedom and parliamentary government mean something to consult together. Let me then speak in truth and earnestness while time remains.

'The American people have, it seems to me, formed a true judgment upon the disaster which has befallen Europe. They realise, perhaps more clearly than the French and British publics have yet done, the far-reaching consequences of the abandonment and ruin of the Czechoslovak Republic.

'We must recognise that the parliamentary democracies and liberal, peaceful forces have everywhere sustained a defeat which leaves them weaker, morally and physically, to cope with dangers which have vastly grown.

'But the cause of freedom has in it a recuperative power

and virtue which can draw from misfortune new hope and new strength. If ever there was a time when men and women who cherish the ideals of the founders of the British and American Constitutions should take earnest counsel with one another, that time is now.

'All the world wishes for peace and security. Have we gained it by the sacrifice of the Czechoslovak Republic? Here was the model democratic State of Central Europe, a country where minorities were treated better than anywhere else. It has been deserted, destroyed and devoured. It is now being digested.

'The question which is of interest to a lot of ordinary people, common people, is whether this destruction of the Czechoslovak Republic will bring a blessing or a curse upon the world. We must all hope it will bring a blessing; that after we have averted our gaze for a while from the process of subjugation and liquidation, everyone will breathe more freely; that a load will be taken off our chests; we shall be able to say to ourselves, "Well, that's out of the way, anyhow. Now let's get on with our regular daily life."

'But are these hopes well founded, or are we merely making the best of what we had not the force and virtue to stop?

'There is another question which arises out of this: Can peace, goodwill and confidence be built upon submission to wrongdoing backed by force? One may put this question in the largest form: Has any benefit or progress ever been achieved by the human race by submission to organised and calculated violence?

'As we look back over the long story of the nations, we must see that, on the contrary, their glory has been founded upon the spirit of resistance to tyranny and injustice, especially when these evils seemed to be backed by heavier force.

'Since the dawn of the Christian era a certain way of life has slowly been shaping itself among the Western peoples, and certain standards of conduct and government have come to be esteemed. After many miseries and prolonged confusion there arose into the broad light of day the conception of the right of the individual; his right to be consulted in the government of his country; his right to invoke the law even against the State itself.

'Independent courts of justice were created to affirm and enforce this hard-won custom. Thus was assured throughout the English-speaking world, and in France by the stern lessons of the Revolution, what Kipling called "Leave to live by no man's leave underneath the law." Now in this resides all that makes existence precious to man and all that confers honour and health upon the State.

'We are confronted with another theme. It is not a new theme; it leaps out upon us from the Dark Ages – racial persecution, religious intolerance, deprivation of free speech, the conception of the citizen as a mere soulless fraction of the State.

'To this has been added the cult of war; children are to be taught in their earliest schooling the delights and profits of conquest and aggression. A whole mighty community has been drawn painfully, by severe privations, into a warlike frame.

'They are held in this condition, which they relish no more than we, by a party organisation several millions strong, who derive all kinds of profits, good and bad, from the upkeep of the regime.

'Like the Communists, the Nazis tolerate no opinion but their own; like the Communists, they feed on hatred; like the Communists, they must seek, from time to time, and always at shorter intervals, a new target, a new prize, a new victim.

'The dictator, in all his pride, is held in the grip of his party machine. He can go forward; he cannot go back. He must blood his hounds and show them sport, or else, like Acteon of old, be devoured by them.

'All-strong without, he is all-weak within. As Byron wrote 100 years ago: "These pagod things of sabre sway, with fronts of brass and feet of clay."

'No one must, however, underrate the power and efficiency of a totalitarian State. Where the whole population of a great country, amiable, good-hearted, peace-loving people, are gripped by the neck and by the hair by a Communist or a Nazi tyranny, for they are the same things spelt in different ways, the rulers for the time being can exercise a power for the purposes of war and external domination before which the ordinary free parliamentary societies are at a grievous practical disadvantage.

'We have to recognise this. But then on top of all comes this wonderful mastery of the air, which our century has discovered, but of which, alas, mankind has so far shown itself unworthy. Here is this air power, with its claim to torture and terrorise the women and children, the civil population, of neighbouring countries.

'This combination of medieval passion, a party caucus, the weapons of modern science, and the blackmailing power of air-bombing, is the most monstrous menace to peace, order and fertile progress that has appeared in the world since the Mongol invasions of the thirteenth century.

'The culminating question to which I have been leading is whether the world as we have known it, the great and hopeful world of before the war, the world of increasing hope and enjoyment for the common man, the world of honoured tradition and expanding science, should meet this menace by submission or by resistance?

'Let us see, then, whether the means of resistance remain to us today. We have sustained an immense disaster. The renown of France is dimmed. In spite of her brave, efficient army, her influence is profoundly diminished. No one has a right to say that Britain, for all her blundering, has broken her word; indeed, when it was too late, she was better than her word.

'Nevertheless, Europe lies at this moment abashed and distracted before the triumphant assertions of dictatorial power. In the Spanish Peninsula a purely Spanish quarrel has been carried by the intervention, or shall I say the "non-intervention", to quote the current jargon, of dictators into the region of a world cause.

'But it is not only in Europe that these oppressions prevail. China is being torn to pieces by a military clique in Japan; the poor, tormented Chinese people there are making a brave and stubborn defence.

'The ancient Empire of Ethiopia has been overrun. The Ethiopians were taught to look to the sanctity of public law, to the tribunal of many nations gathered in majestic union. But all failed; they were deceived, and now they are winning back their right to live by beginning again from the bottom a struggle on primordial lines.

'Even in South America the Nazi intrigue, diving under the Monroe doctrine, begins to undermine the fabric of Brazilian society.

'Far away, happily protected by the Atlantic and Pacific Oceans, you, the people of the United States, to whom I now have the chance to speak, are the spectators, and may I add the increasingly involved spectators, of these tragedies and crimes.

'We are left in no doubt where American conviction and sympathies lie; but will you wait until British freedom and independence has succumbed, and then take up the cause, when it is three-quarters ruined, yourselves alone?

'I hear that they are saying in the United States that because England and France have failed to do their duty therefore the American people can wash their hands of the whole business.

'This may be the passing mood of many people, but there is no sense in it. If things have got much worse, all the more must we try to cope with them.

'For after all, survey the remaining forces of civilisation: they are overwhelming. If only they were united in a common conception of right and duty, there would be no war.

'On the contrary, the German people, industrious, faithful, valiant, but, alas, lacking in the spirit of proper civic independence, liberated from their present nightmare, would take their honoured place in the vanguard of human society.

'Alexander the Great remarked that the people of Asia were slaves because they had not learned to pronounce the word "No". Let that not be the epitaph of the English-speaking peoples or of parliamentary democracy, or of France, or of the many surviving liberal States of Europe.

'There, in one single word, is the resolve which the forces of freedom and progress of tolerance and goodwill should take. It is not in the power of one nation, however formidably armed, still less is it in the power of a small group of men, violent, ruthless men, who have always to cast their eyes back over their shoulders, to cramp and fetter the forward march of human destiny.

'The preponderant world forces are upon our side; they have but to be united to be obeyed.

'We must arm. If, through an earnest desire for peace, we have placed ourselves at a disadvantage, we must make up for it by redoubled exertions, and, if necessary, by fortitude in suffering.

'We shall no doubt arm. Britain, casting away the habits of centuries, will decree national service upon her citizens. The British people will stand erect and will face whatever may be coming.

'But arms – instrumentalities, as President Wilson called them – are not sufficient by themselves. We must add to them the power of ideas.

'People say that we ought not to allow ourselves to be drawn into a theoretical antagonism between Nazidom and democracy; but the antagonism is here now. It is this very conflict of spiritual and moral ideas which gives the free countries a great part of their strength.

'You see these dictators on their pedestals, surrounded by the bayonets of their soldiers and the truncheons of their police. On all sides they are guarded by masses of armed men, cannons, airplanes, fortifications and the like – they boast and vaunt themselves before the world, yet in their hearts there is unspoken fear.

'They are afraid of words and thoughts; words spoken abroad, thoughts stirring at home – all the more powerful because forbidden – terrify them.

'A little mouse of thought appears in the room, and even the mightiest potentates are thrown into panic.

'They make frantic efforts to bar out thoughts and words; they are afraid of the workings of the human mind. Cannons, airplanes, they can manufacture in large quantities; but how are they to quell the natural promptings of human nature, which after all these centuries of trial and progress had inherited a whole armoury of potent and indestructible knowledge?

'Dictatorship – the fetish worship of one man – is a passing phase. A state of society where men may not speak their minds, where children denounce their parents to the police, where a businessman or small shopkeeper ruins his competitor by telling tales about his private opinions; such a state of society cannot long endure if brought in contact with the healthy outside world.

'The light of civilised progress, with its tolerances and co-operation, with its dignities and joys, has often in the past been blotted out.

'But I hold the belief that we have now at last got far enough ahead of barbarism to control it and to avert it, if only we realise what is afoot and make up our minds in time. We shall do it in the end. But how much harder our toil the longer the delay.

'Is this a call to war? I declare it to be the sole guarantee of peace. The swift and resolute gathering of forces to confront not only military but moral aggression; the resolute and sober acceptance of their duty by the English-speaking peoples and by all the nations, great and small, who wish to walk with them; their faithful and zealous comradeship would almost between night and morning clear the path of progress and banish from all our lives the fear which already darkens the sunlight to hundreds of millions of men.'

MR CHURCHILL AT SEVENTY – 'THE MOST ALIVE MAN WE KNOW'

By Lawrence Hunt

30 November 1944

Winston Churchill still remains a young man with a bright future. That is what many Americans believe. It is a belief partly based on a sure conviction – that of all the statesmen of the United Nations he can best lead the way to a more decent world.

We Americans know, of course, that Mr Churchill has already lived a life that would take many volumes to tell. It is also a fact that the number seventy has been mentioned in connection with him, but we fail to see any significance in it. He is the most alive man we know, as alive as a small boy going to a circus. It is futile to measure him by age. We think of him in terms of achievement, ability, purpose and, above all, character.

We like him and need him so much that we do not care particularly what the 'verdict of history' about him will be. We suspect that the verdict will vary somewhat, depending on the intellectual fads and fashions of the time and the philosophies and prejudices of historians.

The conservative may glumly decide that Mr Churchill moved too fast; the radical may pompously point out that he failed to lead a revolution. We, his contemporaries, know that he is beloved by most men who love freedom and we feel that, much as it might embarrass a man with such a strong sense of humour, there is almost a certainty that Winston Churchill will be revered by future generations of men whose freedom he has fought so hard to save.

Suffice it to say, here and now, that we Americans, who are alive with him and among whom he moves almost as one of us, regard him with gratitude and with hope as the greatest statesman of our age.

There are many reasons why Americans appreciate Winston Churchill. Let us mention a few of them at random. He has done so much. Soldier, war correspondent, historian, liberal reformer, orator, statesman, artist and bricklayer are some of his pursuits which are known to us. Moreover, Mr Churchill has bounce. There is nothing sluggish or half-hearted in the way he does the job in hand. He tackles it with gusto, and men enjoy watching the happy workman at his task.

He is human. We like his honest enjoyment of the minor luxuries of life, the gay moment and the hearty laugh. He looks sociable, though never commonplace. He is a good fellow, but vastly more. We feel him to be a man who really understands and likes other men because he, too, has made mistakes, suffered disappointment, met defeat, struggled against indifference, endured pain and sorrow.

In these days of plans and blueprints, charts and catalogues, graphs and indices, and all the paraphernalia of the bureaucratic way of life, it is reassuring that the world's greatest statesman does not think of his fellow beings as a bunch of digits.

Mr Churchill, we believe, would give his shirt to a friend in need, but we are glad that to England's enemies, wherever they are, he has made it clear that he will not be the dupe of his own generosity when Britain is concerned. We are glad because we, in America, are slowly, in some instances reluctantly, but for the most part surely, learning that a mighty British Empire is vital to the future security of the United States. Proud of his country's past, the supreme servant of its present need, unafraid of its future. Winston Churchill is the

Mr Greatheart of his own countrymen and of all the English-speaking world.

Americans admire and have cause to be supremely thankful for Winston Churchill's genius as a statesman and orator. There is nothing synthetic about that genius. There are no ghost writers lurking behind his speeches. Nor are his public utterances marred and stained by malice and vindictiveness.

The noblest attribute of an American or British statesman is magnanimity. It is the hallmark of authentic greatness. America's Lincoln had it. So has Britain's Churchill. Since he became Prime Minister we have not even heard him say 'I told you so.'

In short, Winston Churchill's brain and character are well mated and inseparable. That is why plain men and women know that he is truly great and not merely greatly clever. When we hear him speak we think of him, first, not as an orator but as a man. He has poured life and meaning into our greatest words and restored them to their ancient primacy in our language and in our hearts. Words like Truth, Justice, Freedom, Mercy and Humility, Faith and Fortitude, Prayer and Sacrifice, Love and Duty, Toil and Sweat. We know again what they mean – thanks to Mr Churchill. The nations are now approaching one of those supreme climaxes of human history when even wise and good men may falter and fail. Whatever the politicians and intellectuals may think and scheme, the plain folk want two things. First, a world in which peace will be maintained and enforced by every necessary means. Second, a fair and workable compromise between two deeply rooted but historically conflicting desires of humankind – freedom and security.

The price of freedom has always been high, and if we are not careful it might land us in the jungle of unrestrained competition; but, if we are not even more careful, the price of security might be freedom itself, and we should then find ourselves governed by soulless bureaucracies which have no time or thought for the dignity of the individual man.

It is too much to expect and, indeed, it is un-American and un-British and unhealthy to believe that any man, singlehanded, can achieve these things for us. There must also be enough virtue and wisdom in plain men and women. And yet, they need all the courage and the vision and the common sense of their leaders. That is why so many Americans and so many men of goodwill everywhere look to Mr Churchill and pray that he can do even more than he has done for the betterment of mankind.

In conclusion, Winston Churchill is a great man not only by reason of his personal achievements, but also because he is an Englishman who has absorbed into the very marrow of his bones the best traditions and qualities of his own people. The British had the good fortune to produce him; the wisdom, at the supremely important time, to understand him; the courage, in mankind's darkest hour, to follow him; and the grace, today, to appreciate him.

In paying tribute to Mr Churchill we Americans are gladly compelled to pay tribute to his fellow-countrymen, our comrades in war, and our brothers in the fairer world which, together and with God's help, we can surely make.

ROOSEVELT TRIED TO BAR CHURCHILL
18 June 1961

If President Roosevelt had had his way in 1943 he would have met Stalin at Teheran unaccompanied by Mr Churchill.

This is disclosed in State Department documents released today. The documents also disclose that there were three major breaches of security.

The first two in which the venue of the meeting 'leaked' caused friction between Britain and the United States. The third, a premature release of the conclusion of the meeting, caused the United States to be irritated with Russia instead.

At Teheran, for the first time Stalin ventured outside Russia's borders to hold a summit conference. Efforts to arrange it nearly fell through, first because of the difficulty of agreeing on the place and later because the news leaked out.

Mr Roosevelt was very keen to meet Stalin. Moreover, he wanted to meet him without Mr Churchill being present. He sent Mr Joseph Davies, former United States Ambassador in Moscow, with a personal letter dated 5 May 1943 proposing 'an informal and completely simple visit for a few days between you and me'. One problem Mr Roosevelt noted was where to hold it.

Africa would be too hot in summer. Iceland he did not like because 'it would make it, quite frankly, difficult not to invite Prime Minister Churchill at the same time'.

Mr Davies told Stalin Mr Roosevelt's preferred spot was Fairbanks, Alaska: Mr Davies found Stalin agreeable in principle to the meeting.

Stalin, in his reply, attached a condition. 'Much will depend on how speedy and active will be the Anglo-American military operations in Europe,' he wrote.

Meanwhile, Mr Churchill had heard about the proposed meeting and assumed that he would be present, too. He sent a telegram to Mr Roosevelt suggesting a meeting at Scapa Flow.

Mr Averell Harriman, then Ambassador in Moscow, was

given the task of telling Mr Churchill in London that the proposed meeting was to be between Mr Roosevelt and Stalin only. Mr Churchill sent a telegram to Mr Roosevelt dated 25 June.

Enemy propaganda would make good use of 'a meeting between the heads of Soviet Russia and the United States at this juncture with the British Commonwealth and Empire excluded,' he wrote.

In reply on 28 June Mr Roosevelt blandly assured Mr Churchill, 'I did not suggest to U.J. ("Uncle Joe") that we meet alone.' After this somewhat less than frank assertion, Mr Roosevelt stated, 'Of course you and I are completely frank in matters of this kind.'

Mr Churchill wanted a meeting in the Eastern Mediterranean with each leader aboard his own naval vessel and he referred Mr Roosevelt to St Matthew's Gospel, chapter 17, verse 4, in which St Peter proposed, 'Let us make here three tabernacles, one for thee, and one for Moses and one for Elijah.'

Mr Roosevelt finally agreed to Teheran. The proposed meeting was then jeopardised when a United Press message was passed in Cairo by the Anglo-Egyptian censors stating the Mena House Hotel was being closed and fumigated in anticipation of 'visits and consultations of great portent'.

As the message had been transmitted by radio, the Germans had certainly picked it up. The American Chiefs of Staff complained to the British chiefs of this 'flagrant violation of conference security'.

When the Cairo conference with Chiang Kai-shek had ended and Mr Roosevelt and Mr Churchill were on their way to Teheran, there was another security branch. A joint communiqué was issued twenty-four hours in advance of its publication date.

The censors passed a Reuters message on 30 November referring to the communiqué and stating that those attending the Cairo conference were 'now en route to somewhere in Persia to meet Stalin'. There were angry protests from American officials.

The conclusion of the Teheran conference was officially announced over Moscow radio. The Russians explained they felt it necessary to set all rumours at rest. This Russian action had one fortunate consequence. It diverted American irritation from the British to the Russians.

Chapter 8

Churchill as a War Leader

Churchill's role as the wartime premier (1940–45) was the most important one of his life. When he was asked by George VI to take the reins of power in May 1940, he later recalled that 'I felt as if I were walking with destiny, and that all my past life had been but a preparation for this hour and for this trial.' The two major components of Churchill's war leadership were his amazing oratory and his desire to be personally involved in the action. His words inspired the British people and indeed the people of all Allied countries. However, his desire to be directly involved could frustrate those around him and on a number of occasions led to serious disagreements. The *Telegraph* reported on major moments when Churchill left Whitehall to participate in diplomacy or in a little action against the Nazis.

MR CHURCHILL PILOTED ATLANTIC PLANE
19 January 1942

Mr Churchill himself piloted the giant flying-boat *Berwick* for a spell during one stage of his historic flight home across the Atlantic from the United States, it was disclosed last night.

It is now believed certain that the packs of U-boats operating recently off the American Atlantic coast were sent there with orders to seek out and sink the battleship in which the German Government expected Mr Churchill to return.

This plan was foiled by the Prime Minister's dramatic decision to fly, which was taken at the last minute and must be considered one of the best-kept secrets of the war. Axis attempts to discover Mr Churchill's exact whereabouts by putting out reports of his being seen in places as far apart as Cairo and the Far East failed conspicuously. The Prime Minister's return was in fact made in the same secrecy that marked the outward journey. Mr Churchill arrived in the United States on Monday, 22 December, when it was stated that he had gone 'to discuss with the President all questions relevant to a concerted war effort'.

How Mr Churchill, who flew a plane as long ago as 1913, took over the controls of the *Berwick* for a spell was disclosed by Captain C. Kelly Rogers, the flying-boat's fair-haired six-foot Irish pilot.

The Prime Minister, dressed in his siren suit, smiling happily and smoking a cigar, walked into the control deck after breakfast while the *Berwick* was high over the sea.

On the spur of the moment, Mr Churchill asked Captain Rogers if he might take over the controls.

Captain Rogers agreed. Mr Churchill, after settling himself comfortably in the pilot's seat and allowing himself a few moments to get the 'feel' of the controls, smiled broadly as he sent the £200,000 flying-boat into a couple of steep turns.

'We were about 8,000 feet up and above the clouds at the time,' Captain Rogers said.

'After he had taken over the Prime Minister remarked casually that the aircraft was very different from a plane he had flown in 1913.'

Describing the journey from the start Captain Rogers said:

'Dawn was just breaking off the coast of Norfolk, Virginia, when a naval launch bearing the party came out to the flying-boat, which was riding in the harbour. The Prime Minister shook hands with me and also with the crew as soon as he came on board.

'The flight to Bermuda then began, and it was during that part of the journey that Mr Churchill took over the controls.

'The Prime Minister occupied a private self-contained suite, the rest of the party being accommodated in the usual passenger compartment. Hot meals were served and hot and cold water provided.

'An escort of United States aircraft was sent out with the flying boat, and Mr Churchill listened in while I exchanged messages with the leader of the escorting aircraft on the radio telephone.

'On the way over we had no trouble at all and the journey was quite uneventful. Part of the time the party played cards and paid occasional visits to the control deck.

'The Prime Minister especially took the keenest interest in the operational technicalities. At his request I furnished him with reports on the progress of the flight from time to time.

'The trip from Bermuda to Plymouth took 17 hours 55 minutes, and we covered 3,330 miles, so our average speed was something like 190 miles an hour.'

Captain Rogers said that the Prime Minister and his party had spoken in appreciation of the success of the journey. Air Chief Marshal Sir Charles Portal, the Chief of the Air Staff, took some astronomical sights on the journey and showed great interest in navigation by the stars.

'He also proved very good at card tricks,' Captain Rogers added.

Captain Rogers, one of the senior pilots of the British Overseas Airways Corporation, who has been flying since he was a youth, was making his twenty-third trans-Atlantic trip.

Yesterday Captain Rogers had lunch with the Prime Minister at No. 10 Downing Street. Mrs Churchill and Miss Mary Churchill, their daughter, were also present.

On this latest flight Captain Rogers had Captain A.C. Loraine as his co-pilot and Captain J.S. Shakespeare as chief officer. All three are among the pilots who went to America early last year to fly home the *Berwick* and other Boeing aircraft then newly consigned to British Airways.

MR CHURCHILL RETURNS TO LONDON
By Alan Dick
20 September 1943

Mr Churchill arrived at Euston Station yesterday evening from his long visit across the Atlantic.

He had a victory smile. He was smoking a nine-inch cigar as he greeted his Cabinet colleagues, shook the grimy hands of the driver and fireman of the engine which drew his train, and gave his famous 'V' sign to a delighted crowd jammed behind the grilles of the platform gates.

It was the longest time he has yet been away: nearly six

weeks. He had arrived in Canada on 10 August. The crowd gave him a special welcome home.

He was accompanied by Mrs Churchill, their daughter, Subaltern Mary Churchill, in her ATS uniform, and Mr Bracken, the Minister of Information.

The train was the Prime Minister's special combination of coaches, having light panelling, green walls and curtains and green upholstered furniture. As the maroon-coloured coaches of the train were drawn into Platform 6 by the engine *Phoenix* there was the usual swaying indecision among the people who waited to welcome him.

Then it became evident that, unlike a previous occasion, the Prime Minister's coach would draw up at the correct spot on the platform marked by a chalked arrow. The station master, the only man on the platform wearing a top hat, made way for Mr Churchill's other daughters, Mrs Duncan Sandys and Mrs Oliver, to slip into the coach and be the first to greet their parents. Mrs Oliver was in the uniform of a WAAF officer.

We waited expectantly while the family reunion took place in the saloon coach. Every eye was focused on the exit door. Most of the Prime Minister's colleagues hung back until Mr and Mrs Churchill and Mary had finished saluting the family. But Mr Attlee decided to jump in and shake his leader's hand in the carriage.

Suddenly a cheer went up and an American voice said: 'Gee, there's the old man himself.' We had our first glimpse of Mr Churchill, the dent in the top of his black Homburg hat as he looked down at the carriage steps to make a safe 'two-point landing' on the platform.

A laugh went up at this comedy entrance, in which Mr Churchill joined.

Immediately his foot met the platform the hat jerked back and the familiar square features were revealed to London for the first time for what most of us have felt were very long weeks. He at once raised his hat with the curious forward movement we have all grown to expect.

Mrs Churchill was wearing her favourite form of headgear, a snood, this time of midnight blue tied with a bow on top. She wore a coat of the same colour, and a lighter blue frock beneath.

She accompanied her husband as he went among his colleagues and the Ambassadors, High Commissioners and Service chiefs who had come to greet him.

He had a word and a pat on the back for each of them.

Mr Eden, accompanied by his wife, was hatless and wore a light grey suit. He was in high spirits and joking with a railway policeman and a porter about their difficulty in keeping a barricade in order. He was still laughing when he rejoined Mrs Eden and Mr Vincent Massey, the Canadian High Commissioner.

In one group Sir Kingsley Wood craned upwards to talk to Lord Halifax. Viscount Simon and Lord Portal completed the foursome. In another group cigars were popular. Both Sir Stafford Cripps and Sir Archibald Sinclair smoked cigars of Churchillian proportions while they talked with Mr Winant. Mr Churchill immediately got into conversation with Mr Winant about America. Then he went to Mr Massey to discuss the other side of the 49th Parallel.

His eyes darted about and his expressive face lightened with emotions as he recognised one friend after another and threw a word at each. Everyone was in the greatest high spirits, infected by the Prime Minister's gaiety and exuberant fitness.

Mr Churchill made a sturdy figure in his flapping black

overcoat and wide-brimmed hat. He was carrying a walking stick. Mr Dalton, the President of the Board of Trade, would have approved his coat. It was a single-breasted Melton. He has worn it since the war began.

On his left shoulder was the button we used to remember in the days when he wore a gas mask and had the button sewn on to prevent it slipping off his shoulder. It was symbolic of this and his previous visits that the button was no longer necessary. Perhaps Mr Churchill keeps it there as a reminder of sterner moments.

The most characteristic part of his attire was his bow tie, of black silk with white polka dots.

Meanwhile Mrs Churchill was speaking to other members of the Cabinet, and Mr Bracken was taking a quiet back seat with a couple of friends.

When the smiles and handshakes were over, Mr Churchill stumped off down the platform, cracking the ferrule of his walking stick on the hard surface, to talk to the fireman and the driver of the *Phoenix* and to the guard.

The driver is Harry Lawson and the fireman Charlie Crockett, both Carlisle men.

They wiped their greasy hands with an oil rag as the Prime Minister came up. They were delighted and surprised when he pushed his white hand into theirs and gripped their blackened fingers.

As he shook hands with Harry Lawson, Mr Churchill said: 'Thank you, driver. It was a very comfortable ride.' Mr Churchill made for his car, past large crowds hemmed in by hastily constructed barricades. They had found out, somehow or other, that he was arriving. As he came to the first fringe of crowd he stopped, turned, and grinned, and gave the people the Churchill 'V' sign.

At one end of the barricade was a little girl in a blue coat and fair pigtails who was jumping with excitement. She was Mary Pope, the ten-year-old daughter of Major Frank Pope, chief commercial manager of the LMS. She had been allowed to stay up specially to have her first look at Mr Churchill.

A great roar greeted him as he ducked into his car and drove off to Downing Street.

None of the general public was in the vicinity of Downing Street when two cars with Mr Churchill's party arrived. The arrival was seen only by two policemen and two reporters.

On his arrival in this country high-ranking Service officers and others were present to greet Mr Churchill. Soldiers were quick to recognise the well-known figure, and the Prime Minister acknowledged their rousing cheers by raising his hat and giving the 'V' sign.

When Mr Churchill arrived in Canada Mrs Churchill, Subaltern Mary Churchill, Lord Leathers, Minister of War Transport, and the Chiefs of Staff were with him. Later the party was joined by Mr Eden and Mr Bracken.

During and after the Quebec conference Mr Churchill travelled to Washington for discussions with President Roosevelt. It was their sixth wartime meeting and the fifth time Mr Churchill had crossed the Atlantic since the war.

Five of the Churchill–Roosevelt meetings have taken place since the United States entered the war. The first, in August 1941 which resulted in the publication of the Atlantic Charter, took place while America was still neutral.

PREMIER FIRES SHELL AT NAZI GUNS IN ITALY
22 August 1944

Mr Churchill personally fired a shell at an enemy gun position during a visit to the Fifth Army on Saturday. It was a ranging shot and fell short. The gunnery officer corrected the elevation, and two rounds later both guns in the enemy target position were destroyed.

On this visit he was presented with the Union Jack that had been raised at the liberation of Rome. Earlier he had visited troops of the Eighth Army and had said this to a brigade of Canadians only a few miles behind the front line:

'I cannot predict an early end to the war. But I can give no guarantee that it will not end sooner than we have so far allowed ourselves to hope.'

The Battle of Normandy promised to bring the end of the war much nearer, he said.

After staying a night at General Alexander's advanced HQ, Mr Churchill proceeded to his visit to the Fifth Army.

There he made three speeches to the troops, one of which was an address to a parade that included troops of the recently arrived Brazilian Expeditionary Force.

In one short speech he said of Hitler's tyranny: 'That tyranny we shall break.

'We shall shatter the sources from which its evil powers are derived, and which will be so obliterated and blasted that for many hundreds of years, none will dare to do the like again.'

In another address he praised the part already played by the Fifth and Eighth Armies and said: 'But though you have done great deeds in the past, and may well be proud of what you have achieved, I come here today to tell you that greater ventures and greater achievements are now ahead of you. You will be playing a constantly and absolutely vital part in the long, hard struggle, for whose speedy end we all strike and for whose speedy end we all pray.'

'We have here in Italy one of the finest armies in the world. The combination of the Fifth Army and the British Eighth Army bind two veteran armies in a bond of brotherhood and comradeship of arms.

'No operation could have been more fruitful in this theatre than the work you have done in drawing away perhaps two dozen or more enemy divisions down into Italy, where they have been torn to pieces.

'You aided notably and most effectively the great battle now proceeding to a victorious climax on the fields of France.'

The Prime Minister was sunburnt from his voyage in the destroyer to France. His nose and chin were peeling from the effects. He arrived at the airfield in General Alexander's personal plane, and was met by General Clark and American, British and South African officers. He was dressed in the uniform of the Lord Warden of the Cinque Ports and wore a tan sun-helmet.

Accompanying him were Lord Moran, his personal physician, Commander Thompson, his ADC, and Inspector Hughes, of Scotland Yard. He drove in a jeep to the Fifth Army Command Post, but constantly stopped it on the way to talk to British and American troops.

Many times he climbed out with General Clark to 'troop the line'. The welcome accorded to Mr Churchill was remarkable. The Americans invariably saluted him; British soldiers cheered 'Hooray, Winnie', and Italian civilians crowded to the windows along the route or stood in the streets clapping and cheering as he drove past.

On arrival at the Command Post, Mr Churchill, with General Clark, reviewed a Guard of Honour. At Leghorn he went aboard a British motor-launch with Captain R. McKenzie, the naval officer in charge, and inspected the repairs to the port.

One of the final ceremonies was when General Clark presented Mr Churchill with the Union Jack which was raised in Rome on the night of its capture by the Fifth Army.

In a note accompanying the gift General Clark wrote:

'As this is the first Allied flag to fly in a captured enemy capital in the present war it has peculiar historical significance.' Smoking his inevitable cigar, Mr Churchill finally drove to the airport and wished 'Godspeed' to the Allied soldiers who crowded about him.

MPS CHEER PREMIER'S ADVICE TO GERMANS
19 January 1945

Mr Churchill in two hours today made his most cheering speech of the war. With verve and wit he reviewed every aspect of the world conflict and found high hope in every field.

The Prime Minister, who has never over-estimated the chances of quick success, said firmly: 'I have never at any time been able to present a more confident statement to the House of the ever-growing might and ascendancy of the United Nations, or of the military solidarity of the three great Allies.'

Mr Churchill was in his best form. Many MPs considered today's speech to be his best since the dark days of 1940.

Halfway through it they expressed their feelings in a full minute of cheering. Not for years has the House of Commons heard such a prolonged tribute.

The cheering occurred at a deceptively disingenuous remark about a newspaper 'time-honoured and responsible' but not named. But behind the ovation was the pent-up enthusiasm of members on both sides of the House.

Mr Churchill's speech, broken for an hour at lunch time, was achieved despite a thick cold. When Mr Greenwood, the Socialist spokesman, asked him if there would be any interruption of his speech he replied: 'I am unfortunately a victim of the prevalent misfortune of having a cold, and I should just like to see how I can get on.'

In fact he got on for well over an hour before he broke off. By then he had discussed exhaustively the situation in Greece and dealt scathingly with the Government's detractors.

The House was full when the Prime Minister took his seat towards the end of question time. A score of MPs sat on the cross-benches beyond the Bar.

Every gallery was packed. Mrs Churchill and her daughter, Mrs Duncan Sandys, looked down from their special place above the Government back benches. The American Ambassador, Mr Winant, and several United States Army and Navy men listened to the debate. Mr Winant leaned forward when Mr Churchill referred to 'power politics' and the resources of America.

Mr Churchill's cold did not affect his delivery. It even seemed to give added resonance to his voice. His oratory was as full of fire and sparkle as ever.

Sparks flew when Mr Gallacher, the only Communist MP, muttered inaudibly and checked Mr Churchill in his stride.

Grasping the despatch-box with both hands, and gazing pityingly at Mr Gallacher over his glasses, the Prime Minister said with deadly calm: 'Every two or three minutes the honourable member, who receives exceptional courtesy from this House, thinks it necessary to assert himself by making some half-inaudible and occasionally partially intelligible interruptions.'

The House laughed, while Mr Gallacher glowered uncomfortably. Then came the turn of certain sections of the Press. Mr Churchill said that one could not wonder at the hostile attitude of some newspapers in the United States when in this country had been witnessed 'such a melancholy exhibition as that provided by some of our most time-honoured and responsible journals'.

Mr Gallacher smiled, until Mr Churchill added: 'and others to which that epithet would hardly apply'. Then followed the most dramatic passages of the speech.

In these Mr Churchill openly accused Communist elements in Greece of accepting British arms and keeping them to seize power over the Greek State in Athens, and brought forward evidence of the murder and brutal treatment of hundreds of hostages in ELAS hands.

Mr Churchill spoke of the attempt to install 'naked triumphant Trotskyism'. He again discomfited Mr Gallacher by addressing to him this afterthought: 'I think Trotskyism is a better definition for Greek Communists and certain other sects than the normal word. It has the advantage of being equally hated in Russia.'

When Mr Churchill sat down he put a throat lozenge in his mouth, and MPs adjourned for lunch.

In his after-lunch review of the Western Front Mr Churchill described Field Marshal Montgomery and General Bradley as 'highly skilled commanders'. In speaking of the East he referred to 'the punctuality' of Marshal Stalin.

'Let us be of good cheer,' he said in this, the sixty-fifth month of war. 'For both in the East and the West overwhelming forces are ranged on our side.' He made two portentous references – one to 'unconditional surrender' and the other to possible new phases of the war. He advised:

The Germans to consider that their life after surrender might be far easier than life in 1945 under the blows of the Allies.

The British to keep an eye on jet-propelled aircraft, rocket bombs and U-boats.

Mr Churchill ended by causing a laugh and establishing a new phrase. The laugh arose from speculation on the next meeting of the Big Three. Turning to Mr Eden, he said that the two of them would be at the rendezvous. Pointing upwards, he quoted: 'When the roll is called up yonder we'll be there.'

Churchill concluded: 'The British nation and Commonwealth may rest assured that the Union Jack of freedom will forever fly from the white cliffs at Dover.'

Chapter 9

Churchill and the Cold War

It came as a surprise to Churchill that his party lost the 1945 general election, especially since the war was still raging in the Pacific. The close of the war saw the use of nuclear weapons, Germany occupied, Churchill in opposition and an uneasy state of affairs with the Soviet Union. Increasingly, Joseph Stalin started to see the Western powers as enemies. He sought to create buffer states around Russia which subscribed to Communist ideals. Meanwhile, the West saw Stalin and the Soviet Union as hostile to democracy. Churchill had long been an enemy of Communism and after the war he saw an opportunity to restrict its influence. When he gave his speech entitled 'The Sinews of Peace' at Fulton, Missouri, in 1946, he practically laid out the parameters of the Cold War. He called for unity in Europe and between Western powers. He used phrases such as 'the Iron Curtain' and first made reference to the 'Special Relationship'. This had a major effect on how the United States and Britain conceptualised the post-war world. It had a major impact on how the Soviets saw it too. Churchill's speech was denounced in Moscow as warmongering.

However, with the advent of ever more powerful nuclear

weapons Churchill began to push for a summit between the major powers to ensure that there would be peace between the United States and the Soviet Union. This became a hallmark of Churchill's foreign policy during his second premiership (1951–55).

MR CHURCHILL URGES ANGLO-US PACT
6 March 1946

Mr Churchill, speaking last night at Fulton, Missouri, made an appeal for an Anglo-American 'fraternal association', which could be extended also to the Dominions, as necessary for the preservation of peace.

This was, as he said, the crux of an impressive address which surveyed a world-wide field and contained a blunt warning on Russian and Communist activities. Mr Churchill opened his address at 9.45 GMT, and spoke for three-quarters of an hour. He was repeatedly interrupted by applause, and at the end received a tumultuous ovation. The whole audience rose to its feet.

The proposed association with the United States, he declared, would require the continuance of the intimate relations between our military advisers, and of 'the joint use of all naval and air force bases in the possession of either country all over the world'.

'The dark ages,' said Mr Churchill gravely, 'may return on the gleaming wings of science . . . Beware, I say. Time may be short. A shadow has fallen upon the scenes so lately lighted by the Allied victory. Nobody knows what Soviet Russia and its Communist International organisation intend to do in the immediate future or what are the limits, if any, to their expansive and proselytising tendencies.'

But in spite of these 'sombre facts', Mr Churchill 'repulsed' the idea that war was inevitable. Russia did not desire war, but there was nothing she admired so much as strength or for which she had less respect than military weakness. Peace depended upon a good understanding with Russia under the general authority of the United Nations supported by the strength of the English-speaking world.

Other points in Mr. Churchill's address were:

International Air Force: Each of the States in the United Nations should be invited to dedicate a certain number of air squadrons to the world organisation.

The Atomic Bomb: It would be wrong and imprudent to entrust its secrets to the world organisation yet.

STALIN ATTACKS MR CHURCHILL
14 March 1946

A reply by Marshal Stalin to the speech by Mr Churchill at Westminster College, Fulton, Missouri, on 5 March was broadcast by Moscow radio last night. It was given in the form of an interview accorded to *Pravda* 'a few days ago'. *Pravda* which, like all other Soviet newspapers, is an official organ and is often used for important announcements.

Marshal Stalin described Mr Churchill's speech as 'a call for war with the USSR'. He compared Mr Churchill with Hitler, and said the course he had outlined was incompatible with the existing treaty of alliance between Britain and the USSR.

The broadcast was repeated in full during English-language

transmissions intended for Britain and the United States, after having been given in all news bulletins. Later it was broadcast at dictation speed in the special Moscow radio service of items intended for publication in the provincial Soviet Press.

The questions put to Marshal Stalin and the latter's answers were as follows:

Q: How do you assess the last speech of Mr Churchill, which was made in the United States?

A: I assess it as a dangerous act calculated to sow the seeds of discord among Allied Governments and hamper their co-operation.

Q: Can one consider that the speech of Mr Churchill is prejudicial to the cause of peace and security?

A: Yes, unquestionably. To all intents and purposes, Mr Churchill now takes his stand among the warmongers. In this, Mr Churchill is not alone. He has friends not only in Britain, but in the United States as well.

A point to be noted is that, in this respect Mr Churchill and his friends bear a striking resemblance to Hitler and his friends. Hitler began his work of unleashing war by proclaiming a race theory, declaring that only German-speaking people constituted a fully-fledged nation.

Mr Churchill begins to set war loose also by a racial theory, maintaining that only nations speaking the English language are fully-fledged, called upon to decide the destinies of the entire world.

The German racial theory brought Hitler and his friends to the conclusion that the Germans, as the only fully-fledged nation, must rule over the other nations. The English racial theory brings Mr Churchill and his friends to the conclusion that nations speaking the English language, being the only fully-fledged nations, should rule over the remaining nations of the world.

It is, therefore, highly probable that the nations not speaking English and which, however, make up the enormous majority of the world's population, will not consent to go into new slavery. The tragedy of Mr Churchill lies in the fact that he, as a deep-rooted Tory, cannot understand this simple and obvious truth.

In substance, Mr Churchill and his friends in England and the United States present nations not speaking the English language with something like an ultimatum to recognise their domination voluntarily, and then all will be well. In the contrary case, war is inevitable.

But the nations have shed their blood during five years of cruel war for the sake of liberty and the independence of their countries, and not for the sake of exchanging the domination of Hitler for the domination of the Churchills.

There is no doubt that the standpoint of Mr Churchill is a standpoint for war, a call to war with the Soviet Union. It is also clear that such a standpoint by Mr Churchill is incompatible with the existing treaty of alliance between England and the USSR.

It is true that Mr Churchill, to confuse his readers, declares, in passing, that the length of the Anglo-Soviet treaty for mutual aid and co-operation could be easily extended to fifty years. But how can one reconcile such a statement by Mr Churchill with his standpoint for war against the Soviet Union, his preaching of war against the Soviet Union?

It is clear that these things can in no way be compatible. If Mr Churchill, calling for war against the Soviet Union, still considers it possible to extend the duration of the Anglo-Soviet Treaty to fifty years, then it means that he considers the Treaty as an empty piece of paper, to be used in order to conceal and disguise his anti-Soviet set-up.

On this account, one cannot consider seriously the false statement of Mr Churchill's friends in England about the extension of the Soviet-English Treaty to fifty years or more. The extension of the terms of the agreement has no sense if one of the parties violates the Treaty and turns it into an empty scrap of paper.

Q: How do you assess that part of Mr. Churchill's speech in which he attacks the democratic regime of the European countries which are our neighbours and in which he criticises the good neighbour mutual relations established between these countries and the Soviet Union?

A: This part of Mr Churchill's speech is a mixture of the elements of libel with elements of insolence and lack of tact. Mr Churchill maintains that Warsaw, Berlin, Prague, Vienna, Budapest, Belgrade, Bucharest, Sofia: all these famous cities and the populations of these areas, are within the Soviet sphere and are all subjected to Soviet influence and to the increasing control of Moscow.

Mr Churchill describes this as the boundless expansionist tendencies of the Soviet Union. It requires no special effort to show that Mr Churchill insolently and unpardonably libels not only Moscow but also the above-mentioned States neighbourly to the USSR.

To begin with, it is quite absurd to speak of the exclusive control of the USSR in Vienna and Berlin, where there are Allied Control Councils with representatives of four States, where the USSR has only one-fourth of the voices. It happens sometimes that certain people are incapable of not slandering, but they should still be able to know the limit.

Secondly, one cannot forget the following fact. The Germans carried out an invasion of the USSR through Finland,

Poland, Romania, Bulgaria and Hungary. The Germans were able to carry out invasion through these countries by reason of the fact that these countries had Governments hostile to the Soviet Union.

As a result of the German invasion, the Soviet Union has irrevocably lost in battles with the Germans, and also during the German occupation and through the expulsion of Soviet citizens to German slave labour, about 7,000,000 people.

In other words, the Soviet Union has lost in men several times more than Britain and the United States. It may be that some quarters are trying to push into oblivion these sacrifices of the Soviet people, which ensured the liberation of Europe from the Hitlerite yoke. But the Soviet Union cannot forget them.

One can ask, therefore, what can be surprising in the fact that the Soviet Union, in a desire to ensure its future security, tries to ensure that these countries, on her border, should have Governments whose relations to the Soviet Union are loyal? How can one, without having lost one's reason, qualify these peaceful aspirations of the Soviet Union as 'expansionist tendencies'?

Mr Churchill further maintains that the Polish Government, which is under Russian rule, is making enormous and wrongful claims on Germany. Here, every word is a rude and offensive libel. Democratic Poland is today led by outstanding men. They have shown in deeds that they know how to defend the interests and worth of their motherland, as their predecessors failed to do.

Q: What reason has Mr Churchill to maintain that the leaders of contemporary Poland are allowing in their country the domination of the representatives of any Government whatsoever? Does Mr Churchill here libel the Russians because he has the intention of sowing seeds of discord between Poland and the Soviet Union?

A: Mr Churchill is not pleased that Poland should have made her policy one of friendship and alliance towards the USSR. There was a time when in the mutual relations between Poland and the USSR there prevailed some conflict and contradiction. This gave the possibility to statesmen such as Mr Churchill of playing on these contradictions, of taking Poland in hand under the guise of protection from the Russians, of frightening Russia by spectres of a war between Poland and herself, and of taking for themselves the role of arbiters.

But this time is past. For enmity between Poland and Russia has given place to friendship. The present democratic Poland does not wish any longer to be a ball in the hands of foreigners. It seems to me that this is just what annoys Mr Churchill, and urges him to make rude, tactless outbursts against Poland.

After all, it is no laughing matter for him: he is not allowed to play for other people's stakes. As for Mr Churchill's attack on the Soviet Union in connection with the extending of the western frontiers of Poland, as compensation for territories seized by Germans in the past, then it seems to me he is quite blatantly cheating.

Frontiers of Poland were decided upon at the Berlin conference of the Three Powers on the basis of Poland's demands. The Soviet Union repeatedly declared that it considered Poland's demands just and correct. It may well be that Mr Churchill is not pleased with this decision.

But why does Mr Churchill, not sparing his darts against the Russians in the matter, conceal from his readers the fact that the decision was taken at the Berlin conference unanimously, that not only they voted for his decision but also the English and the Americans? Why did Mr Churchill have to delude people?

Mr Churchill further maintains that the Communist parties, which were very insignificant in all these Eastern European countries, reached exceptional strength, exceeding their numbers by far, and are attempting to establish totalitarian control everywhere; that police Government prevails in almost all these countries even up to now, with the exception of Czechoslovakia, and that there exists in them no real democracy.

As is known, in England one party at present rules the Government. It is the Labour Party. The opposition parties are deprived of the right of taking part in the Government of England. That, Mr Churchill calls true democracy.

In Poland, Rumania, Jugoslavia, Bulgaria and Hungary, government is by a bloc of several parties, from four to six. The opposition, if it is more or less loyal, is assured the right of taking part in the Government. That, Mr Churchill calls totalitarianism, tyranny, police method.

Why? On what grounds? Do not expect an answer from Mr Churchill. Mr Churchill dos not understand in what a funny situation he places himself by his screaming speeches about totalitarianism, tyranny and police method.

Mr Churchill would like to see Poland governed by Sosnkowski and Anders, Jugoslavia by Mihailovitch and Pavelitch, Rumania by Prince Barbu Stirbey, Hungary and Austria by some king of the Hapsburg House. Mr. Churchill wants to assure us that these gentlemen from the Fascists servants' hall can ensure true democracy. Such is the democracy of Mr Churchill.

Mr Churchill wanders around the truth when he speaks of the growth of the influence of the Communist parties in Eastern

Europe. It must he pointed out that he is not quite accurate.

The influence of the Communist parties grew not only in Eastern Europe, but in almost every country of Europe where Fascism had ruled before – Italy, Germany, Hungary, Bulgaria, Rumania, Finland and in the countries which had suffered German, Italian or Hungarian occupation – France, Belgium, Holland, Norway, Denmark, Poland, Czechoslovakia, Jugoslavia, Greece and the Soviet Union.

The influence of the Communists grew because, during the hard years of the triumph of Fascism in Europe, the Communists showed themselves reliable, daring, self-sacrificing, fighters against the Fascist regime for the liberty of the peoples.

Mr Churchill sometimes recalls in his speeches the common people from the small houses, patting them on the shoulder in a lordly manner and pretending to be their friend. But these people are not so simple-minded as it might appear at first.

The common people, too, have their opinions and their own politics. And they know how to stand up for themselves. It is they, millions of these common people, who voted Mr Churchill and his party out in England, giving their votes to the Labour Party. It is they, millions of these common people, who isolated the reactionaries in Europe, collaborators with Fascism, and gave preference to the Left-Democratic parties.

It is they, millions of these common people, having tried the Communists in the fire of the struggle and resistance to Fascism, who have decided that the Communists deserve the complete confidence of the people.

Thus grew the Communists' influence in Europe. Such is the law of historical development. Of course, Mr Churchill does not like such a development of events, and he raises the alarm, appealing to force. But he also did not like the appearance of the Soviet regime in Russia after the First World War.

Then, too, he raised the alarm and organised an armed expedition of fourteen States against Russia with the aim of turning back the wheel of history. But history turned out to be stronger than Churchill's intervention, and the quixotic antics of Churchill resulted in his complete defeat.

I do not know whether Mr Churchill and his friends will succeed in organising after the Second World War a new military expedition against Eastern Europe. But if they succeed in this, which is not very probable, since millions of common people stand on guard over peace then one can confidently say that they will be beaten, just as they were beaten twenty-six years ago.

AS AMERICANS SAW IT IN 1946
21 April 1958

Sir Winston Churchill's Fulton speech in 1946 caused a sharp controversy in the United States, both in Congress and in the Press. Some of the critical comments have an odd sound today:

Mrs Eleanor Roosevelt: Such a situation [an Anglo-American military alliance] would not differ very greatly from the old balance of power politics that has been going on in Europe for hundreds of years ... Almost invariably it led sooner or later to wars and more wars.'

Max Lerner in the now-defunct newspaper *PM*: 'It was an ideological declaration of war against Russia ... a call for America to join Britain in an anti-Comintern pact.'

New York Post: 'Churchill's call to English-speaking unity is actually a call to world disunity and war. It is a proposal to split the world in two and carry the division into the United Nations organisation, with destructive effect.

But many spoke up strongly on the other side:

New York Sun: 'This address should be a rallying cry, not to sentimentality and emotion, but to a reasoned examination of the grave issues of peace, which at times seem harder to cope with than war.'

Dorothy Thompson: 'While one may have reservations regarding some parts of Mr Churchill's speech, his main thesis is correct.'

New York Times: 'The American people have long since realised that the United States and Britain are governed by a common destiny ... Sharing Churchill's anxiety about the future, they will give sympathetic hearing to his proposals for averting a new catastrophe.'

MR CHURCHILL: BERLIN AS GRAVE AS MUNICH
28 June 1948

Mr Churchill, addressing a crowd of 100,000 at Luton Hoo, near Luton, on Saturday, declared that Russia, by her actions in Berlin, had raised issues as grave as those at Munich ten years ago.

He said there was no safety in yielding to dictators, whether Nazi or Communist. The only hope of peace was to be strong. Conservatives would support the Government in the stand they felt bound to make.

The audience was the greatest Mr Churchill had ever addressed. Special trains were run to Luton and a shuttle service of buses ran to the park where he spoke. Mr Churchill was given a tremendous reception before making his speech, which came as the climax to a fete and gymkhana promoted by the Eastern Area of the Conservative and Unionist Association on Major-General Sir Harold Wernher's estate.

As Mr Churchill was escorted to the 12ft-high platform, hats and programmes were waved. Cheering lasted several minutes. Mr Churchill, obviously moved, bowed and smiled his acknowledgments, and then greeted members of the platform party, among whom was the Marquess of Salisbury, Conservative leader in the House of Lords.

Speaking of Berlin, Mr Churchill said: 'We are all naturally anxious about what is happening in Berlin. Last month, on 4 May, our Foreign Secretary, Mr Bevin, said in Parliament, "We are in Berlin as of right. It is our intention to stay there."

'It is certain he would not have said that without having made sure that the United States were equally resolved. On the other hand there can be no doubt that the Communist Government of Russia has made up its mind to drive us and France and all the other Allies out and turn the Russian zone in Germany into one of the satellite States under the rule of totalitarian terrorism.

'This raises issues as grave as those we now know were at stake at Munich ten years ago. It is our hearts' desire that peace may be preserved, but we should all have learned by now that there is no safety in yielding to dictators, whether Nazi or Communist.

'The only hope of peace is to be strong, to act with other great freedom-loving nations, and to make it plain to the aggressor, while time remains, that we should bring the world against him, and defend ourselves and our cause by every means should he strike a felon's blow. I cannot guarantee that even a firm and resolute course will ward off the dangers which now threaten us; but I am sure that such a course is not merely the best but the only chance of preventing a third war, in which the most fearful agencies of destruction yet known to man will be used to the fullest extent. We shall, therefore, support the Government in the stand which, with all their devotion to the cause of peace, they have felt bound to make. I trust that our defences have not been neglected, and that the immense sums of money we have voted for the Armed Forces will have been turned to good account.

'It has often been said that Britain's hour of weakness is Europe's hour of danger. It is our duty to show whatever our party differences may be that in resistance to foreign tyranny we are a united nation. I still believe that by this means peace may be preserved.'

Mr Churchill said that by every test that could be applied the Conservatives had a substantial majority in the country. 'We have good reason to hope that if every man and woman who is a convinced supporter of the Conservative cause works continuously to spread the light of truth, that majority in the country will be reproduced in a new Parliament.

'We are ready at any time to meet the Socialists in the constituencies should this mischievous and incompetent House of Commons be dissolved. But we also have the feeling that time is on our side.'

Though these were inspiring days for the party, our minds were oppressed by the evil plight into which our country had fallen at home and abroad, because in one foolish afternoon the British electorate voted into power a Government and a party in no way worthy of our victories or equal to our strength.

Amid cries of agreement he declared: 'We have had to suffer evils and humiliations almost as bad as those undergone by defeated nations.'

Other points from the speech were:

India: Already there has been something like a collapse in the process of internal administration and we must expect an indefinite epoch of internecine and religious strife.

Burma: 'My solemn warnings have been fulfilled.' Burma has been cast away and is now a foreign country. It is already descending rapidly into a welter of murder and anarchy, the only outcome of which will probably be a Communist republic, affording dangerous strategic advantages to Russia in this important part of the world.

Malaya: The long arm of Communism, unchecked by feeble British administration, has begun a campaign of murdering British planters and their wives as part of the general process of our ejection.

The *Ajax*: Nothing could do more at this moment to humiliate Britain throughout South America than the sale of this ship to Chile. It is like selling the shirt that Nelson wore at the Battle of Trafalgar to General Franco, and getting a little extra for the bloodstains.

Agricultural Charter: In our Charter we have declared that the proper level of agricultural production in this country must be half as much again as pre-war. That is our aim. The Charter shows how it can be won by the well-tried principles of Conservative policy. We repulse the Socialist doctrine of land nationalisation. British farming should be carried on in the future as in the past by private enterprise and management.

US REPLIES TO CHURCHILL PLEA
14 May 1953

The United States State Department today released a statement commenting on Sir Winston Churchill's call on Monday for Big Power talks. The Department made it clear that until Russia demonstrates her sincerity by specific acts, the United States is opposed to any meeting between President Eisenhower, Mr Malenkov and Sir Winston.

The statement suggested that the present Korea truce negotiations at Panmunjom, and negotiations on Austria which are pending, should come first. These gave the Russians an opportunity to demonstrate the sincerity of their statements about a peaceful settlement.

Meanwhile, in the Senate Mr Attlee's speech in the Commons yesterday was criticised with great bitterness. Particular objection was taken to a suggestion that there were elements in the United States which did not want a settlement in Korea.

Leading members of the House of Representatives criticised Mr Attlee's reference to the 'Chiang Kai-shek Lobby' in the United States, and members of both Houses of Congress challenged what they called his attacks on the American constitution.

Criticism of Mr Attlee was coupled in some cases with a warning against starting an angry transatlantic controversy. Senator Wiley, Chairman of the Senate Foreign Relations

Committee, said: 'This is no time for Americans to get bitter. It is a time to keep our heads.'

The statement released by the State Department said:

'Prime Minister Winston Churchill's statement concerning a high-level conference with the Soviets is a further manifestation of his own high purpose and of the fervent desire of all the peoples of the free world to achieve a just and lasting peace.

'Such a peace is a goal towards which we and our free world allies are devoting our constant effort, so that we might help all peoples towards better standards of living.

'Recently, President Eisenhower stressed his willingness to do all within his power to ameliorate existing international tensions and to meet the other side halfway, when, and if, there is concrete evidence that such a meeting would produce positive results.'

'The President indicated in his speech of 16 April those places in Asia and Europe towards which we should look for such evidence. Indeed, at the present time negotiations at Panmunjom and pending negotiations with respect to Austria afford an opportunity for the Soviets to demonstrate the sincerity of their avowals about the peaceful settlement of major international issues.

'Such a demonstration would help to pave the way towards a high-level conference.'

In the Senate a major speech in reply to Mr Attlee and Sir Winston Churchill by Senator Knowland, California, who is Chairman of the Republican Policy Committee, led to a brief debate. Some of the harshest language used about Britain since before the war was heard from both sides of the aisle.

More will be heard tomorrow when Senator McCarthy has promised a speech in which he will deal with what he called the shocking failure of British Government spokesmen to answer Mr Attlee's 'foul and dastardly attack on the President'.

Senator McCarthy did not indicate whether he was referring to Mr Attlee's remark that one sometimes wondered if Senator McCarthy was more powerful than President Eisenhower.

Senator Knowland, referring to the Commons speeches, said: 'In effect, what they have told us is that if we do not accept their advice, and the Chinese Communists persist in war, we must be prepared to go it alone. So be it . . .'

The more responsible papers were trying to find a common denominator between the views of Sir Winston Churchill and Mr Eisenhower on a high-level conference with Russia. They thought they had perhaps found it in Sir Winston's statement that 'settlement of two or three of our difficulties would be an important gain for every peace-loving country'.

If he meant by 'without long delay' after settlements had been reached in Korea and Austria, then his approach would not be very different from Mr Eisenhower's contention that before there is any high-level conference the Russians should prove the sincerity of their peace talk by concrete action.

American officials note that pressure for a high-level conference is undoubtedly strong in most European countries. Before committing themselves publicly on the Churchill proposal they will see if the views of London and Washington can be harmonised. The Administration does not entirely agree that a conference which failed to accomplish anything would do no harm. The Western Powers would leave with more knowledge of the personality and character of Mr Malenkov and the extent to which he has taken Mr Stalin's place.

But a premature conference which raised false hopes and then failed might harm the cause of peace by giving rise to the despairing conclusion that there is no alternative but eventual war.

Chapter 10

Churchill and Europe

On 19 September 1946 Churchill made a speech at the University of Zurich which called for a 'United States of Europe'. The most shocking element of this speech was that the foundation of this union was to be based on a Franco-German alliance. This was very controversial, especially in France, made doubly contentious because of the context in which it was spoken. The Nuremberg trials had not even concluded yet. The Cold War had kicked off, partially because of Churchill's speech in Fulton, Missouri, a couple of months prior. Germany was itself split by the Western and Soviet Powers. These elements made Churchill's proclamations and predictions seem out of touch.

However, his speech in Zurich, and his articles calling for a United Europe, stand as a testament to Churchill's vision for the continent. In 1951 the Treaty of Paris was signed, creating the European Coal and Steel Community, whose principal members included France and West Germany. This was followed by the Treaty of Rome in 1957, which created the European Economic Community and ultimately set the stage for the European Union.

MR CHURCHILL CALLS FOR EUROPEAN UNION
20 September 1946

Mr Churchill, in a 25-minute world broadcast from Zurich University today, called for a United States of Europe.

Remarking, 'I am going to say something that will astonish you,' he declared that the first step in the re-creation of the European family must be a partnership between France and Germany.

On the subject of German war crimes he said that after the guilty had been punished there must be an end of retribution, what Mr Gladstone called 'a blessed act of oblivion'.

A vast concourse of people cheering wildly, waving British and Swiss flags, and throwing flowers, lined the streets through which Mr Churchill passed in an open military car.

Mr Churchill said: 'I wish to speak to you today about the tragedy of Europe, this noble continent, comprising on the whole the fairest and the most cultivated regions of the earth, enjoying a temperate and equable climate, the home of all the great parent races of the Western world, the foundation of Christian faith and Christian ethics.

'It is the origin of most of the culture, arts, philosophy and science both of ancient and modern times. If Europe were once united in the sharing of its common inheritance there would be no limit to the happiness, the prosperity and the glory which its 300,000,000 or 400,000,000 people would enjoy.

'Yet it is from Europe that has sprung that series of frightful nationalistic quarrels, originated by the Teutonic nations in their rise to power, which we have seen in this twentieth century and even in our own lifetime wreck the peace and mar the prospects of all mankind.

'And what is this plight to which Europe has been reduced? Some of the smaller States have indeed made a good recovery, but over wide areas are a vast quivering mass of tormented, hungry, careworn and bewildered human beings, who wait at the ruins of their cities and their homes and scan the dark horizons for the approach of some new form of tyranny or terror.

'Among the victors there is a babel of voices, among the vanquished the sullen silence of despair. That is all that Europeans, grouped in so many ancient States and nations, and that is all that the Germanic races, have got by tearing each other to pieces and spreading havoc far and wide.

'Indeed, but for the fact that the great Republic across the Atlantic Ocean at length realised that the ruin or enslavement of Europe would involve her own fate as well and stretched out hands of succour and guidance – but for that, the Dark Ages would have returned in all their cruelty and squalor.

'Gentlemen, they may still return.

'Yet all the while there is a remedy which, if it were generally and spontaneously adopted by the great majority of people in many lands, would as if by a miracle transform the whole scene and would in a few years make all Europe, or the greater part of it, as free and as happy as Switzerland is today.

'What is this sovereign remedy? It is to re-create the European fabric, or as much of it as we can, and to provide it with a structure under which it can dwell in peace, in safety and in freedom. We must build a kind of United States of Europe. In this way only will hundreds of millions of toilers be able to regain the simple joys and hopes which make life worth living. The process is simple. All that is needed is the resolve of hundreds of millions of men and women to do right instead of wrong and to gain as their reward blessing instead of cursing.

'Much work has been done upon this task by the exertions of the Pan-European Union which owes so much to Count Coudenhove-Kalergi and which commanded the services of the famous French patriot and statesman Aristide Briand. There is also that immense body which was brought into being amidst high hopes after the First World War – the League of Nations.

'The League did not fail because of its principles or conceptions. It failed because these principles were deserted by those States which had brought it into being, because the Governments of those States feared to face the facts and act while time remained. This disaster must not be repeated.

'There is, therefore, much knowledge and material with which to build, and also bitter, dearly bought experience to spur the builder. I was very glad to read in the newspapers a few days ago that my friend President Truman had expressed his interest and sympathy with this great design. There is no reason why a regional organisation of Europe should in any way conflict with the world organisation of the United Nations. On the contrary, I believe that the larger synthesis can only survive if it is founded upon broad natural groupings.

'There is already a natural grouping in the Western Hemisphere. We British have our own Commonwealth of Nations. These do not weaken – on the contrary they strengthen – the world organisation. They are in fact its main support.

'And why should there not be a European group, which could give a sense of enlarged patriotism and common citizenship to the distracted peoples of this mighty continent? And why should it not take its rightful place with other great groupings and help to shape the onward destiny of man?

'In order that this may be accomplished, there must be an act of faith in which the millions of families speaking many languages must consciously take part. We all know that the two world wars through which we have passed arose out of the vain passion of the newly united Germany to play the dominating part in the world.

'In this last struggle, crimes and massacres have been committed for which there is no parallel since the invasion of the Mongols during the thirteenth century, no equal at any time in human history.

'The guilty must be punished. Germany must be deprived of the power to rearm and make another aggressive war. But when all this has been done, as it will be done, as it is being done, then there must be an end to retribution. There must be what Mr Gladstone, many years ago, called "a blessed act of oblivion". We must all turn our backs upon the horrors of the past and we must look to the future.

'We cannot afford to bring forward, across the years that are to come, hatred and revenges which have sprung from the injuries of the past. If Europe is to be saved from infinite misery and indeed from final doom there must be this act of faith in the European family, this act of oblivion against all the crimes and follies of the past. Can the free peoples of Europe rise to the heights of these resolves of the soul and of the instinct and spirit of man? If they could, the wrongs and injuries which have been inflicted would have been washed away on all sides by the miseries which have been endured.

'Is there any need for further floods of agony? Is the only lesson of history to be that mankind is unteachable? Let there be justice, mercy and freedom. The peoples have only to will it and all will achieve their hearts' desire.

'I am now going to say something that will astonish you.

The first step in the re-creation of the European family must be a partnership between France and Germany. In this way only can France recover the moral and cultural leadership of Europe. There can be no revival of Europe without a spiritually great France and a spiritually great Germany.

'The structure of the United States of Europe will be such as to make the material strength of a single State less important. Small nations will count as much as large ones and gain their honour by a contribution to the common cause. The ancient states and principalities of Germany, freely joined for mutual convenience in a federal system, might take their individual places among the United States of Europe.

'I shall not try to make a detailed programme. There are hundreds of millions of people who want to be happy and free, prosperous and safe, who wish to enjoy the Four Freedoms of which the great President Roosevelt spoke, and live in accordance with the principles embodied in the Atlantic Charter. If this is their wish, if it is the wish of Europeans from so many lands, they have only to say so and means can certainly be found and the machinery erected to carry that wish to full fruition.

'But I must give you warning. Time may be short. At present there is a breathing space. The cannons have ceased firing. The fighting has stopped, but the dangers have not stopped. If we are to form a United States of Europe, or whatever name it may take, we must begin now.

'In these present days we dwell strangely and precariously under the shield, and I will even say protection, of the atomic bomb. The atomic bomb is still only in the hands of a State and nation which we know will never use it except in the cause of right and freedom, but it may well be that in a few years this awful agent of destruction will be widespread, and that the catastrophe following from its use by several warring nations will not only bring to an end all that we call civilisation, but may possibly disintegrate the globe itself.

'Our constant aim must be to build and fortify the strength of the United Nations organisation. Under and within that world concept we must re-create the European family in a regional structure called – it may be – the United States of Europe, and the first practical step will be to form a Council of Europe.

'If at first all the States of Europe are not willing or able to join in a union we must nonetheless proceed to assemble and combine those who will and those who can. The salvation of the common people of every race and of every land from war and servitude must be established on solid foundations, and must be guarded by the readiness of all men and women to die rather than to submit to tyranny.

'In all this urgent work France and Germany must take the lead together. Great Britain, the British Commonwealth of Nations, mighty America – and, I trust, Soviet Russia, for then indeed all would be well – must be the friends and sponsors of the new Europa and must champion its right to live.

'Therefore I say to you: "Let Europe arise".'

The speech was heard in attentive silence by the audience of professors and students who had gathered in the great hall of the university. At the end applause broke out, and continued for some time.

The great hall of the university formed a sober setting for the occasion, which had as its outward purpose the presentation of an illuminated address of thanks to Mr Churchill and the British people.

The rector of the university, Dr Anderes, speaking from the flower-decked rostrum and surrounded by the banners of the students' corporations, gave him an academic welcome and the thanks of the university. Extraordinary enthusiasm greeted Mr Churchill as he passed through the streets, giving the famous 'V' sign.

At the seventeenth-century town hall, where he was welcomed as guest of honour of Zurich, he explained that his 'V' sign no longer stood for the victory of one group of nations over another, but for the victory of personal liberty over tyranny everywhere.

The ceremony was attended by councillors, judges, magistrates and officers from all the cantons, and the proceedings were therefore in French. Mr Churchill replied in the same tongue.

'I am convinced,' he said, 'that the natural barriers between nations should not be reinforced by barriers of prejudice, though this has always happened. But why should we not try and work together for the ideas that are dear to us all?' he said.

Thanking Zurich for its welcome, he added: 'I have grasped the fact that my person has been identified to a large extent with the struggle, of value not to one country but to all.

'Here in Switzerland you have solved many of the difficulties which have led other countries into so much suffering and misfortune. You have thus managed to be united in spite of the difference of language and race, and there is no reason why your example should not be followed throughout the whole of this wrecked continent of Europe.

'You have got a stable and solid practical system in which the division of power among so many cantons and districts enables them to take their part, and yet it enables progress to be made steadily in accordance with the movements of the age. And it seems to me that you have a system in which politics is a duty and not a career, in which men serve because they are discharging a civic task and do not grasp the power attached to it.

'All these are matters which should be realised in other lands outside your own. In my own country, dear old England, across the sea, where we kept the flag of freedom flying when we were alone, there are public men who are proud to be servants of the State and would be ashamed to be its masters.'

Mr Churchill was entertained at a farewell banquet given by the university. He will bring his visit to a close tomorrow morning, when he leaves for home from Dubendorf airfield. Mrs Churchill did not accompany him to Zurich, remaining in Berne following her mishap on Lake Geneva last week.

FRENCH CAUTION OVER SPEECH
20 September 1946

Only the Communist organ *Ce Soir* gave any indication tonight of its views on Mr Churchill's speech, the other newspapers contending themselves with printing excerpts from the earlier portions of the speech.

Ce Soir observed: 'There was no reference to reparations, nor did Mr Churchill seem to remember that the war dead, if they could come back, would have much to say on the subject of "friendship" between murderers and their victims.'

In more responsible quarters there are points on which agreement is expressed with Mr Churchill. For instance, it is observed that France is entirely in favour of European unity and would like to see the present gaps in it filled.

France also agrees in principle with a federated system for Germany, but fears that a federal Germany can change too easily into a unified one. In the opinion of those who speak for M. Bidault, only by taking the Ruhr industrial potential away from her can Germany be deprived of the temptation of starting a fresh military threat.

ONE WAY TO STOP A NEW WAR
By the Rt Hon. Winston Churchill, MP
30 December 1946

Eight years have passed since I wrote about 'The United States of Europe', and several things have happened meanwhile. I described the unhappy and dangerous plight of the Continent, torn by ancient quarrels, stirred by modern Nationalism, divided and hampered by a maze of tariff-walls, overshadowed by the Hitler–Mussolini Axis, exhausted and drained by one Great War, and oppressed by fear of another. Now here tonight in my same old room at Chartwell I am writing on the same subject, and I plead the same cause.

Eight years ago I thought the argument was unanswerable. But it proved utterly vain. Within eighteen months Europe was plunged in a war more awful in its devastation than any ever waged by man, and – more than that – once more the European Quarrel dragged America from its isolation, once more it involved the whole world. It almost seems an evil omen.

Certainly the scene we survey in the autumn of 1946 bears many uncomfortable resemblances to that of 1938. Indeed, in some respects, it is even darker. The peoples of Europe have fallen immeasurably deeper into the pit of misery and confusion. Many of their cities are in ruins. Millions of their homes have been destroyed. They have torn each other into pieces with more ferocity on a larger scale and with more deadly weapons than ever before.

But have they found stable and lasting peace? Is the brotherhood of mankind any nearer? Has the Reign of Law returned? Alas, although the resources and vitality of nearly all the European countries are woefully diminished, many of their old hatreds burn on with undying flame. Skeletons with gleaming eyes and poisoned javelins glare at each other across the ashes and rubble-heaps of what was once the august Roman Empire and later a Christian civilisation.

Is there never to be an end? Is there no salvation here below? Are we to sink through gradations of infinite suffering to primordial levels:

> A discord. Dragons of the prime,
> That tare each other in their slime;

or can we avoid our doom?

There is the old story of the Spanish prisoner pining for years in his dungeon and planning to escape. One day he pushes the door. It is open, it has always been open. He walks out free. Something like this opportunity lies before the peoples of Europe today. Will they grasp it? Will they be allowed to grasp it? Will they have time?

The heart of an old man goes out to all these poor ordinary folk. How good, how kindly they are; how helpful and generous to one another in their village life; how capable of ceaseless progress and improvement. And here on their cottage thresholds stand Science, Invention, Organisation, Knowledge – aye, and Power, too. Not only are they offered the simple joys which, or the hopes of which, have cheered the pilgrimage of Man – food, warmth, courtship, love, marriage, a home, little children playing by the fire, the fair fruits of honest toil, rest and serenity when life's work is done. They are offered far more; a wider, more agreeable form of existence, conscious and responsible citizenship, the career open to talent, a richer and more varied dietary, fun, amusements, happy, genial intercourse with one another.

President Roosevelt declared the Four Freedoms. Of these the chief is 'Freedom from fear'. This does not mean only fear of war or fear of the foreign invader. Even more poignant is the fear of the policeman's knock; the intrusion upon the humble dwelling; the breadwinner, the son, the faithful friend, marched away into the night with no redress, no Habeas Corpus, no trial by jury, no rights of man, no justice from the State.

Such are the conditions which prevail today over the greater part of Europe. A horrible retrogression! Back to the Dark Ages, without their chivalry, without their faith.

Yet all this could be ended at a single stroke. Two or three hundred millions of people in Europe have only got to wake up one morning and resolve to be happy and free by becoming one family of nations, banded together from the Atlantic to the Black Sea for mutual aid and protection. One spasm of resolve! One single gesture! The prison doors clang open. Out walk, or totter, the captives into the sunshine of a joyous world.

I do not conceal from the reader that an act of the sublime is required. It is a very simple act, not even a forward bound. Just stand erect, but all together.

I selected France as the land from which the signal should come; first because it involved a finer self-conquest for the

French than for any other great people to take the lead, and secondly because in no other way can France regain her true glory and place in the world. Such are conditions which comprise the elements of the sublime. It is now for France to take the Germans by the hand and lead them back into the brotherhood of man and the family of nations.

I am encouraged by a famous voice from the past. At the National French Assembly in Bordeaux on 1 March 1871, while the French Republic and Germany were still at war, Victor Hugo said:

'And one will hear France cry, "It is my turn, am I your enemy? No! I am your sister. I have retaken all, and I give it all back on one condition: that is that we shall be but one united people, but one single family, but one Republic. I will demolish my fortresses. You will demolish yours. My vengeance, it is fraternity. No more frontiers, the Rhine for all! Let us be the same Republic. Let us have the United States of Europe, let us have Continental federation, let us have European freedom!"'

It was difficult then. The prophetic message was rejected. The poet's inspiration died. Events took a different course. Germany flaunted the laurels of victory and France for more than forty years brooded upon revenge. We had two world wars, in the first of which France was bled white, and in the second laid low and conquered; and in both of which Europe and the whole world were convulsed and shattered. And now they talk of a third world war to finish off what is left of our civilisation and humanity.

The only worthwhile prize of victory is the power to forgive and to guide; and this is the prize which glitters and shines before the French people at this solemn moment in their long history.

The Cause or Question points itself at the United States in a remarkable manner. Isolationism is no more. The Atlantic Ocean is no longer a shield. The Pilgrim Fathers could now cross it in a day; but the troubles from which they fled and the tyrannies against which they revolted can follow just as quick. Not content with tearing their own continent into shreds, the quarrels and hatreds of Europe have now laid their claws upon the New World.

Americans should realise that they must seek the root of these evils. Prevention is better than cure. Why be ravaged every twenty-five years with pestilences bred in Europe? Would it not be reasonable prudence to use the power which has come to the New World to sterilise the infection-centres of the Old? Prolonged and careful study of Europe and courageous, tireless action to prevent the recurrence of war-pestilence would not seem to be a prime interest of every thoughtful American, enjoined upon him by prudence as well as virtue.

The peace and safety of the United States of America requires the institution of a United States of Europe. It is better to face, in an orderly fashion and on high, the remote potential antagonism of two continental groupings than to be dragged for certain into one toil and horror after another by chronic degeneration and the blind convulsions of chance.

The United Nations Organisation is the hope of mankind and the expression in American minds of these ideas and arguments. Regional organisms or federations under the supreme world-organisation are foreseen and encouraged in the San Francisco Charter. It is agreed they are not detrimental to the main structure. It has now to be realised as a fundamental practical truth that without them the central structure cannot stand or function.

Let me use the military modes and terminology with which our sad experience has made us only too familiar. When a great army is formed by a nation or band of allies it has its General Headquarters: who would pretend, with our experience, that any General Headquarters could deal directly with a mob of brigades and divisions, each headed by their own colourful commander, each vaunting the prowess of their own recruiting district or home State, each pleading the particular stresses of their own task and station?

After what we have been through everyone knows that within the Army there must be Groups of Armies and also Army Corps, all with their properly integrated staffs and authority, and that by these alone can the will of the Supreme Command be made effective upon the course of events. Otherwise the great enterprises of war could not be conducted with the slightest hope of success.

In the same way and for the same reasons, unless the intermediate organisms are provided, the World Peace Organisation will either clatter down in ruin or evaporate in empty words. What could be more vain and futile than a crowd of little States, with a few big ones pushing about among them, all chattering about world unity, all working for their separate interests, and all trying to sum up their decisions by votes!

In fact, however, great progress has been made to the creation of these mighty, secondary organisms, and the main pillars of the world-structure are already towering up as realities before our eyes.

There is the United States of America within its larger association of the Western Hemisphere. There is the Soviet Union, with its Slavonic fraternities. There is the British Empire and Commonwealth of Nations spread all over the globe and united by sentimental loyalties which glow to the flame and emerge stronger every time the furnace becomes incandescent.

We must undoubtedly contemplate an Asiatic grouping cherishing the spirit of Asia. The enormous populations of the Far Eastern world, now plunged in defeat or internal confusion, will some day find a coherent expression.

Why then should there not be a place, and perhaps the first place – if she can win it by her merits – for Europe, the Mother Continent and fountain source not only of the woes but of most of the glories of modern civilisation?

Here is an aspect which must be observed. Not only do three at least of the pillars of the world Peace Temple stand forth in all their massive strength. But they are already woven together by many ties of affinity, custom and interest.

The United States of America, as the most powerful country in the modern age, is the guardian of the Western Hemisphere and has connections which are growing everywhere. The vast mass of Soviet Russia in Europe and Asia, with its Slavonic attachments, can only give an improved life to its many peoples through the vivifying but no doubt disturbing tonic of worldwide trade and contacts.

The British nation, lying in the centre of so many healthy and beneficent networks, is not only the heart of the British Empire and Commonwealth of Nations, and an equal partner in the English-speaking world, but it is also a part of Europe and intimately and inseparably mingled with its fortunes. All this interlacement strengthens the foundations and binds together the World Temple.

THE GRAND DESIGN OF A UNITED EUROPE

By the Rt Hon. Winston Churchill, MP

31 December 1946

Let me now set forth tersely what it is we have to do. All the people living in the continent called Europe have to learn to call themselves Europeans, and act as such so far as they have political power, influence or freedom. If we cannot get all countries, we must get all we can; and there may be many. Once the conception of being European becomes dominant among those concerned, a whole series of positive and practical steps will be open.

First there must be a Council of Europe. This Council must look always forward rather than back. Secondly, it must seek the most free and fertile trade between all its members, and must work steadily for the abolition or at least the diminution of tariff and customs barriers between member-States of the Council on the broad principle of the American Inter-State Commerce Act. Thirdly, it must strive for economic harmony as a stepping-stone to economic unity.

Next, the Council of Europe must reach out towards some common form of defence which will preserve order among and give mutual security to its members, and enable Europe to take an effective part in the decisions of the Supreme United Nations Organisation.

Inseparably woven with this is the approach to a uniform currency. As we have to build from chaos this can only be achieved by stages. Luckily coins have two sides, so that one can bear the national and the other the European superscription. Postage stamps, passports, trading facilities, European social reunions for cultural, fraternal and philanthropic objects will all flow out naturally along the main channel soon to be opened.

If at the beginning the Governments of the various countries involved are not able to take official action, strong societies and organisations must be formed of a private and popular character. There is no reason to suppose that existing Governments, although they may not immediately feel able to take the initiative, will be adverse.

Mr Attlee has declared, 'Europe must federate or perish', and he does not readily change his opinions. Prominent names could be cited of men in office and power in many countries in and out of Europe who hold the same view. General Smuts, the South African soldier-statesman-philosopher, has proclaimed himself a champion of the idea. Belgium, Holland and Luxembourg have already begun naturally and unostentatiously to put it into practice.

There is much talk of a 'Western bloc'; but that by itself is too narrow a scheme. Nothing less than Europe and Europeanism will generate the vital force to survive. It may well be that everybody cannot generate the vital force to survive. It may well be that everybody cannot join the club at once. The beginning must be made. The nucleus must be formed in relation to the structure as a whole, so that others can join easily as soon as they feel inclined or feel able. The ideal is so commanding that it can afford a gradual realisation.

But we are told this conception of a free reviving, regenerated Europe is anti-Russian or, to speak more exactly, anti-Soviet in its character, intention and effect.

This is not true. The many peoples of Russia and Asia who are comprised in the Union of Socialist Soviet Republics, and who occupy one-sixth of the land surface of the globe, have nothing to fear and much to gain from the creation of a United

States of Europe, more especially as both these groupings must be comprised within the World Organisation and be faithful to its decisions.

We are also told that International Communism will be hostile; and it may well be that the devotees of this anti-God religion in every country will be enjoined to raise their voices in favour of keeping Europe divided, helpless, impoverished and starving. Such conditions, they may argue cogently, are an essential preliminary to world Communist domination. All this may be so.

But Europe and the great world around it must find their own way through their troubles and perplexity. They must not let themselves be deterred from what is right and beneficial for their own policy and interests by any arbitrary veto.

We must have the four great entities and contributors to world Government all playing their part and bearing their proper weight in the World Organisation. We must hope, indeed, that China will make a fifth. No one party or section of mankind must bar the grand design of a United Europe. It must roll forward, and within its proper limits it will roll forward, righteous and strong.

On my return from Zurich I read in an English newspaper, the *Southern Daily Echo*, the following commentary on what I had said:

'Geographers point out that the Continent of Europe is really the peninsula of the Asiatic land mass. The real demarcation between Europe and Asia is no chain of mountains, no natural frontier, but a system of beliefs and ideas which we call Western Civilisation.

'In the rich pattern of this culture there are many strands: the Hebrew belief in God; the Christian message of compassion and redemption; the Greek love of truth, beauty and goodness;

the Roman genius for law. Europe is a spiritual conception, but if men cease to hold that conception in their minds, cease to feel its worth in their hearts, it will die.'

These sentiments are so beautiful, and their expression so fine an example of English prose, that I venture to quote them with due acknowledgments, and I trust they may resound far and wide and waken their response in every generous heart. Well may it be said, 'Let Europe arise.'

It seems a shocking thing to say that the atomic bomb in the guardianship of the United States is the main safeguard of humanity against a third world war. In the twentieth century of the Christian era, with all the march of science and the spread of knowledge, with all the hideous experiences through which we have passed, can it be that only this dread super-sanction stands between us and further measureless misery and slaughter? Those of us who were born in the broad liberalism of the nineteenth century recoil from such a mockery of all our dreams, of all our defined conceptions.

Nevertheless, I believe the fact is true. Greater divergencies have opened among men than those of the religious wars of the Reformation, or of the political and social conflicts of the French Revolution, or of the power-struggle just concluded with Hitler's Germany. The schism between Communism on the one hand and Christian ethics and Western Civilisation on the other is the most deadly, far-reaching and rending that the human race has known.

Behind Communism lies the military power of Soviet Russia, which, so far as the continent of Europe is concerned, is at the present time overwhelming. This power is in the firm grasp of thirteen or fourteen extremely able men in the Kremlin. We cannot measure the internal pressures to which they are subjected, on the morrow of Russia's sufferings and sacrifices, nor can we tell how far they may be swayed by crude ambitions of world-conquest.

We are confronted at once by a Theme and a Sword. If the issues now afoot in the world were capable of being decided by the strength of ground armies, the outlook for the Western democracies and for modern civilisation would be indeed forlorn.

The atomic bomb is the new balancing factor. Everyone knows it will not be used except in self-defence against mortal injury and provocation. No one can be sure whether it is a final and decisive method of war. Air power, however manifested and armed, may decide a war; but alone it cannot hold a front on land. Still, of all the deterrents against war now acting upon the minds of men, nothing is comparable to this frightful agency of indiscriminate destruction.

While this supreme weapon rests in the hands of the United States alone, it is probable, though we cannot say it is certain, that a breathing-space will be accorded to the world. We cannot tell how long this breathing-space will last. Let us make sure that it is not cast away.

If, in this interval, we can revive the life and unity of Europe and Christendom, and with this new reinforcement build high and commanding a world structure of peace which no one dare challenge, the most awful crisis of history will have passed away and the high road of the future will again become open.

There is no reason why all questions between State socialism and individual enterprise should not be settled gradually and peacefully by the normal workings of democratic and parliamentary machinery. The pyramid of society may become more solid and stable when its top is melted down to broaden its base. If during the next five years we can build a world structure of irresistible force and inviolable authority, there are no limits to the blessings which all men may enjoy and share.

For this purpose few things are more important and potentially decisive than that Europe should cease to be a volcano of hatred and strife and should instead become one of those broad upland regions upon which the joy, the peace and glory of millions may repose.

Chapter 11

Churchill's Postscript

In 1958, the *Telegraph* published this collection of articles by Churchill, which made up a postscript to his illuminating and voluminous war memoirs. Much had changed in the world since 1945 and Churchill felt he ought to comment on the state of international affairs in the post-war world; or as Churchill himself put it, 'to look back and express my views on some of the major events' of the last few years. Though this postscript was included in a one-volume concise edition of Churchill's memoirs, they have received relatively little attention. Despite this, these articles illustrate Churchill's views of the post-war era, the Cold War, the power of nuclear weapons and the role of the UN. They further demonstrate Churchill's hope to use the diplomacy of summit meetings between leaders at the highest levels to bring the Cold War to a close. While these words remain a warning to us today, they also reveal Churchill's optimistic spirit that, despite failures and complications, peace between the great powers would be possible.

FIVE YEARS LATER
21 April 1958

In the extracts from his latest memoirs that will appear on this page this week, Sir Winston Churchill recalls the occasion, almost five years ago, when he launched the idea of a summit meeting with the Russian leaders. It was 11 May 1953, in the House of Commons, a few weeks after the death of Stalin. What he urged was 'an entirely informal conference between the Heads of the leading Powers' which, in his opinion, might avoid the by then customary 'acrimonious exchanges at lower levels'. But, as he now reminds us, 'what I sought was never fully accomplished'. The vaunted Geneva conference took place in the full glare of publicity. Set speeches were exchanged. It was as different from the intimate wartime meetings as is an operatic ensemble from a string quartet.

Coming at a moment when the current spurt to the summit has been slowed down by the diplomatic screeds, this warning, from the still hopeful father of the project, deserves to be most carefully pondered. Certainly another Geneva conference, creating once again the mood of co-existence without its substance, would serve no helpful purpose. But a strictly informal conference, of the kind still envisaged by Sir Winston, is quite another matter. Unfortunately, substantial technical difficulties stand in the way of a four-Power summit meeting of this kind. In this matter, two is company while three or four is decidedly a crowd. Hitherto, however, the West has rejected with horror any suggestion that negotiations with the Soviet Union should be bilateral rather than quadrilateral. Mr Gromyko's latest suggestion, for example, that he should see the Western ambassadors separately rather than together seems to have struck the

Foreign Secretary as just a Russian trick to divide the Allies.

This is surely unduly defeatist. The Allies are not suspect witnesses, unable to tell the same story independently. If the only way to hold a truly intimate exchange is between Russia and one Western Power, then we should not neglect this opportunity out of mutual mistrust. We are trying to avoid a summit propaganda stunt, and that is why we insist on careful advance preparation at diplomatic and Foreign Minister level. But are these same precautions so necessary before we can talk 'at an entirely informal conference'? The great quality of Sir Winston Churchill is that even as a private citizen he can still lift thinking out of a rut. What he had in mind in 1953 was clearly a private meeting between heads of Government lasting perhaps a long weekend. If it had to be bilateral, where is the harm in that? The Churchill touch, it is true, always sets the mind racing. But even if his latest writing does nothing else, it should at least remind us that what he meant by the summit five years ago has not been tried and failed.

SOVIET SHADOW OVER EUROPE
By Sir Winston Churchill
21 April 1958

When I left Potsdam on 25 July 1945, I certainly expected that the election figures would leave me a reasonable majority, and it was startling to be confronted with the facts. Entirely absorbed as I had been in the prosecution of the war and the situation at its victorious close, I did not understand what had taken place in the British Isles.

Otherwise, I thought and still think I could have arranged things differently. Above all, the opinion in the mass of the Army, after so many signs of goodwill, was a great surprise to me.

The election results and figures were an even greater surprise to Europe and America, and indeed to the USSR. They naturally thought that the steadfastness of the British peoples, having survived the grim ordeals of 1940 and having come triumphantly through the five years' struggle, would remain unshaken, and that there would be no change of Government.

During the course of the Conference at Potsdam I had not so far sought to come to grips with Russia. Since Yalta she had behaved in an astonishing fashion. I had earnestly hoped that the Americans would not withdraw from the wide territories in Central Europe they had conquered before we met. This was the one card that the Allies held when the fighting stopped by which to arrange a level settlement. Britain sought nothing for herself, but I was sure she would view the vast advance which Russia was making in all directions as far exceeding what was fair.

The Americans seemed quite unconscious of the situation, and the satellite States, as they came to be called, were occupied by Russian troops. Berlin was already in their hands, though Montgomery could have taken it had he been permitted. Vienna was Russian-held, and representatives of the Allies, even as individuals, were denied access to this key capital.

As for the Balkans, Bulgaria and Rumania had already been conquered. Yugoslavia quivered under Tito, her famous patriotic leader. The Russians had occupied Prague with, as it seemed, the approval of the Americans. Poland, it was agreed, should have her Western boundary moved into the heart of Europe at the expense of Germany.

All these steps had in fact been taken by the Russian armies, which were still advancing. Yet the American view seemed to be that all this was a necessary part of the process of holding down Germany, and that the great national object of the United States was not to get drawn into siding too closely with Britain against Russia.

When the winter came along I went to the United States and remained in the country for several months. I visited the White House and the State Department. I there received an invitation to address the Westminster College in Fulton, Missouri, in March 1946. The President had said he would himself preside.

This was several months ahead, and I kept myself as fully informed as was possible. I made inquiries both at the White House and at the State Department in order to learn whether certain topics would cause embarrassment, and having been assured that I could say what I liked I devoted myself to the careful preparation of a speech.

Meanwhile the dire situation with which the insatiable appetites of Russia and of international Communism were confronting us was at last beginning to make a strong impression in American circles. I showed the notes I had prepared to Mr Byrnes, then Secretary of State, and found that he was very much in agreement with me.

President Truman invited me to travel with him in his train on the long night's journey to Fulton. We had an enjoyable game of poker. That was the only topic which I remember. However, as I was quite sure that his Secretary of State, Mr Byrnes, had imparted my general line to the President, and he seemed quite happy about it, I decided to go ahead. One always has to be very careful about speeches which you make in other people's countries. This is from what I said:

'A shadow has fallen upon the scenes so lately lighted by the Allied victory. Nobody knows what Soviet Russia and its Communist International organisation intends to do in the immediate future, or what are the limits, if any, to their expansive and proselytising tendencies . . .

'From Stettin in the Baltic to Trieste in the Adriatic, an Iron Curtain has descended across the Continent. Behind that line lie all the capitals of the ancient States of Central and Eastern Europe . . . Athens alone – Greece with its immortal glories – is free to decide its future at an election under British, American and French observation. The Russian-dominated Polish Government has been encouraged to make enormous and wrongful inroads upon Germany and mass expulsions of millions of Germans on a scale grievous and undreamed-of are now taking place.

'The Communist parties, which were very small in all these Eastern States of Europe, have been raised to pre-eminence and power far beyond their numbers and are seeking everywhere to obtain totalitarian control.

'If now the Soviet Government tries, by separate action, to build up a pro-Communist Germany in their areas, this will cause new serious difficulties in the British and American zones, and will give the defeated Germans the power of putting themselves up to auction between the Soviets and the Western democracies.

'Whatever conclusions may be drawn from these facts – and facts they are – this is certainly not the Liberated Europe we fought to build up. Nor is it one which contains the essentials of permanent peace.'

The President and Mr Byrnes both expressed their approval. The newspapers, however, were very varied in their comments. When the news reached Russia, it was ill received, and both

Stalin and *Pravda* responded as might be expected. *Pravda* denounced me as 'an anti-Soviet warmonger', and accused me of trying to destroy the United Nations. Stalin, in a newspaper interview, accused me of calling for war against the Soviet Union and compared me with Hitler.

Questions were also asked in the House of Commons, to which Mr Attlee replied that the Government was not called upon to express any opinion on a speech delivered in another country by a private individual.

I had another speech to deliver a few days later in New York, where I was the guest of the Mayor and civic authorities. All round the Waldorf Astoria Hotel at the dinner where it was delivered were marching pickets of Communists, and I was somewhat surprised to learn that Mr Dean Acheson, the Under-Secretary of State, was not coming. When Mr John Winant heard of this change of plan in Washington in the afternoon, he caught a train to New York and arrived in the middle of dinner to support me, and made a most friendly speech. I expressed myself as follows:

'When I spoke at Fulton ten days ago I felt it was necessary for someone in an unofficial position to speak in arresting terms about the present plight of the world. I do not wish to withdraw or modify a single word . . . I am sure that the hope which I expressed for the increasing association of our two countries will come to pass, not because of any speech which may be made, but because of the tides that flow in human affairs and in the course of the unfolding destiny of the world.

'The only question which in my opinion is open is whether the necessary harmony of thought and action between the American and British peoples will be reached in a sufficiently plain and clear manner and in good time to prevent a new world struggle or whether it will come about, as it has done before, only in the course of that struggle.'

The agitation in the newspapers and the general interest, and even excitement, continued to grow. In the autumn of 1946 I paid a visit to Zurich University, and made them a speech about the tragedy of Europe and the plight to which she had been reduced, and I urged the foundation of a kind of United States of Europe, or as much of it as could be done.

'. . . I am now going to say something that will astonish you. The first step in the re-creation of the European family must be a partnership between France and Germany. In this way only can France recover the moral leadership of Europe. There can be no revival of Europe without a spiritually great France and a spiritually great Germany.

'The structure of the United States of Europe, if well and truly built, will be such as to make the material strength of a single State less important. Small nations will count as much as large ones and gain their honour by their contribution to the common cause. The ancient States and principalities of Germany, freely joined together for mutual convenience in a federal system, might each take their individual place among the United States of Europe,

'I shall not try to make a detailed programme . . . But I must give you a warning. Time may be short . . . If we are to form the United States of Europe or whatever name or form it may take, we must begin now.'

Thus ran my thoughts in 1946. To tortured France, lately occupied and humiliated, the spectacle of close association with her finally vanquished executioner seemed at first unthinkable. By degrees, however, the flow of European fraternity was restored in French veins, and natural Gallic pliant good sense overcame the bitterness of the past.

DESIGN FOR THE DEFENCE OF FREEDOM

By Sir Winston Churchill

22 April 1958

I have always held, and hold, the valiant Russian people in high regard. But their shadow loomed disastrously over the post-war scene. There was no visible limit to the harm they might do.

Intent on victory over the Axis Powers, Britain and America had laid no sufficient plans for the fate and future of occupied Europe. We had gone to war in defence not only of the independence of smaller countries, but to proclaim and endorse the individual rights and freedoms on which this greater morality is based.

Russia had other and less disinterested aims. Her grip tightened on the territories her armies had overrun. In all the satellite States behind the Iron Curtain, coalition Governments had been set up, including Communists.

It was hoped that democracy in some form would be preserved. But in one country after another the Communists seized the key posts, harried and suppressed the other political parties, and drove their leaders into exile. There were trials and purges. Rumania, Hungary and Bulgaria were soon engulfed. At Yalta and Potsdam I had fought hard for Poland, but it was in vain. In Czechoslovakia a sudden coup was carried out by the Communist Ministers, which sharply alerted world opinion. Freedom was crushed within and free intercourse with the West was forbidden.

Thanks largely to Britain, Greece remained precariously independent. With British and later American aid, she fought a long civil war against the insurgent Communists. When all had been said and done, and after the long agonies and efforts of the Second World War, it seemed that half Europe had merely exchanged one despot for another.

Today, these points seem commonplace. The prolonged and not altogether unsuccessful struggle to halt the destroying tide of Russian and Russian-inspired incursion has become part of our daily lives. Indeed, as always with a good cause, it has sometimes been necessary to temper enthusiasm and to disregard opportunism. But it was not easy at the time to turn from the contemplation of a great and exhausting victory over one tyranny to the prospect of a tedious and expensive campaign against another.

The United Nations organisation was still very young, but already it was clear that its defects might prove grave enough to vitiate the purposes for which it was created. At any rate it could not provide quickly and effectively the union and the armed forces which Free Europe and the United States needed for self-preservation. At Fulton I had suggested that the United Nations organisation should forthwith be equipped with an international armed force. But both for the immediate future and the long term I had urged the continuation of the special Anglo-American relationship which has been one of the main themes of my political life.

'Neither the sure prevention of war nor the continuous rise of world organisation will be gained without what I have called the fraternal association of the English-speaking peoples. This means a special relationship between the British Commonwealth and Empire and the United States . . . It should carry with it a continuance of the present facilities for mutual security by the joint use of all Naval and Air Force bases in the possession of either country all over the world . . . The United States has already a permanent Defence Agreement with the Dominion of Canada . . . this principle should be extended to all British Commonwealths with full reciprocity.'

The next three years were to see the unfolding of a design that approached but has not yet attained this ideal. I do not wish to claim a monopoly of credit for these conceptions. One of the advantages of being in Opposition is that one can outdistance in imagination those whose fortune it is to put plans into practical effect. The British Government, much inspired by the stout-hearted and wise Mr Ernest Bevin, took the lead in rebuilding something of the Concert of Europe, at least in what was left of Europe.

Initial thoughts were mainly of the dangers of a resurrected Germany. In 1947 Britain and France signed the Treaty of Dunkirk, binding each to come to the other's assistance if there was another German attack. But already the grim realities of the present were overshadowing the fears of the past. After many months of diplomatic activity the Brussels Treaty was signed in 1948. France, Great Britain, the Netherlands, the Belgians and Luxembourg undertook to assist one another against aggression, from whatever quarter it might come. Germany was not mentioned.

Moreover, the beginnings of a military organisation were set up under the chairmanship of Field Marshal Montgomery to assess the resources available for defence and to draw up a plan with what little was available. This became known as the Western Union. I endorsed these measures, but vehemently hoped that the United States, without whose aid they would be woefully incomplete, would soon be brought into the association.

We were fortunate at the time to have as the American Secretary of State the far-sighted and devoted General Marshall, with whom we had worked in closest comradeship and confidence in the war years. Within the limits imposed by American Congressional and public opinion, President Truman and he sought to add weight to what was being done in Europe.

The efforts on both sides of the Atlantic bore fruit, and in April 1949 the North Atlantic Treaty was signed, in which for the first time in history the United States bound herself, subject always to the constitutional prerogative of Congress, to aid her allies if they were attacked.

Certainly in its early stages the Atlantic Treaty achieved more by being than by doing. It gave renewed confidence to Europe, particularly to the territories near Soviet Russia and the satellites. This was marked by a recession in the Communist parties in the threatened countries, and by a resurgence of healthy national vigour in Western Germany. The association of Germany with the Atlantic Treaty remained in the forefront of Western plans. But it was very difficult to overcome French fears of a revived German army, and the topic was a fruitful one for the misguided as well as the mischievous.

In Britain I was conscious of a wide hostility to giving weapons, even under the strictest safeguards, to the new German Republic. But it was unlikely that a Soviet invasion of Western Europe could ever be repulsed without the help of the Germans.

Many schemes were tried and failed. The French had taken the lead in the closer integration of Western Europe in civil matters, and they sponsored a scheme for a European Army with a common uniform, into which German units would be merged without risk to their neighbours. I did not care for this idea. A sludgy amalgam of half a dozen nationalities would find it difficult to share common loyalties, and the trust which is essential among comrades in battle.

It was not for some years that the final simplicity of a direct

German contribution through a national army to the strength of the West was achieved. Even today little has been done to put it into effect. I myself have never seen the disadvantage of making friends with your enemy when the war is over, with all that that implies in co-operation against an outside menace.

Side by side with these developments, many of them lying only in the paper sphere, the United States continued to manifest her determination to assist Europe, and thus herself. Long before the Atlantic Treaty was signed American aircraft were stationed in East Anglia in substantial numbers. Here was a most practical deterrent.

Alas, the splendid structure of the Anglo-American Combined Chiefs of Staff, who had been the architects of so much of our victorious war planning, had been dismantled at American instigation. Nothing has subsequently equalled it, and the best of the NATO arrangements are but a poor shadow of the fraternal and closely knit organisation that formerly existed.

Without the massive dollar aid provided by the American Administration, in spite of some hostility on the part of Congress, Europe might well have foundered into ruin and misery in which the seeds of Communism would have grown at a deadly pace.

General Marshall's decision was on the highest level of statesmanship, and it was a source of great pleasure, but not surprise, to me that my old friend should have presided in America over the two great enterprises of the Marshall Plan and the Atlantic Treaty. Of the launching of the European Movement in 1947, Sir Winston writes:

> In matters of this kind it was not possible to plan movements as in
> a military operation. We were not acting in the field of force, but

in the domain of opinion. The task was to build up moral, cultural, sentimental and social unities and affinities throughout Europe.

The culmination of the many discussions that took place came in the creation of the Council of Europe in 1949, with its seat at Strasbourg. With varying fortunes and shades of publicity much useful work was done there.

There are those who are disappointed that the rapid creation of a federation of European States did not ensue, but there is every justification for a slow and empirical approach. Such weighty matters cannot be imposed on the people from above, however brilliant the planning. They must grow gradually from genuine and widely held convictions. Thus the Council of Europe is serving its purpose and playing an honourable part in a great enterprise.

THE H-BOMB AND OUR FUTURE
By Sir Winston Churchill
23 April 1958

At the stark and glaring background to all our cogitations on defence lay man's final possession of the perfected means of human destruction: the atomic weapon and its monstrous child, the hydrogen bomb.

In the early days of the war Britain and the United States had agreed to pool their knowledge and experiments in nuclear research, and the fruits of years of discovery by the English pioneer physicists were offered as a priceless contribution to the vast and most secret joint enterprise set on foot in the United States and Canada. Those who created the weapons possessed for a few years the monopoly of a power which might in less scrupulous hands have been used to dominate and enslave the entire world.

They proved themselves worthy of their responsibility, but secrets were soon disclosed to the Soviet Union which greatly helped Russian scientists in their researches. Henceforward most of the accepted theories of strategy were seen to be out of date, and a new, undreamed-of balance of power was created, a balance based on the ownership of the means of mutual extermination.

At the end of the war I felt reasonably content that the best possible arrangement had been made in the agreement which I concluded with President Roosevelt in Quebec in 1943. Therein Britain and America affirmed that they would never use the weapon against each other, that they would not use it against third parties without each other's approval, that they would not communicate information on the subject to third parties except by mutual consent, and that they would exchange information on technical developments. I do not think that one could have asked for more.

However, in 1946 a measure was passed by the American Congress which most severely curtailed any chance of the United States providing us with information. Senator McMahon, who sponsored the Bill, was at the time unaware of the Quebec Agreement, and he informed me in 1952 that if he had seen it there would have been no McMahon Act.

The British Socialist Government certainly made some sort of a protest, but they felt unable to press it home and they did not insist on the revelation of the Quebec Agreement at least to the McMahon Committee, which would have vindicated our position and perhaps saved us many years of wearisome and expensive research and development.

Thus, deprived of our share of the knowledge to which

we had a most certain right, Britain had to fall back on her own resources. The Socialist Government thereupon devoted vast sums to research, but it was not until 1952 that we were able to explode our first atomic bomb. The relative stages of research and development remain unknown, but experimental explosions are not the sole criterion, and we may perhaps in some ways claim to have outdistanced even the United States. But research is one thing, production and possession another.

It was in this then, the American possession or preponderance of nuclear weapons, that the surest foundation of our hopes for peace lay. The armies of the Western Powers were of comparative insignificance when faced with the innumerable Russian divisions that could be deployed from the Baltic to the Yugoslav frontier. But the certain knowledge that an advance on land would unleash the devouring destruction of strategic air attack was and is the most certain of deterrents.

For a time, when the United States was the sole effective possessor of nuclear weapons, there had been a chance of a general and permanent settlement with the Soviet Union. But it is not the nature of democracies to use their advantages in threatening or dictatorial ways. Certainly the state of opinion that prevailed in those years would not have tolerated anything in the way of rough words to our late ally, though this might well have forestalled many unpleasant developments.

Instead the United States, with our support, chose a most reasonable and liberal attitude to the problems of controlling the use of nuclear weapons. Soviet opposition to efficient methods of supervision brought this to nothing.

In former days no country could hope to build up in secret military forces vast enough to overwhelm a neighbour. Now the means of destruction of many millions can be concealed in the space of a few cubic yards.

Every aspect of military and political planning was altered by these developments. The whole structure of defence had to be altered to meet the new situation. Conventional forces were still needed to keep order in our possessions, and to fight what people call the small wars, but we could not afford enough of them because nuclear weapons and the means of delivering them were so expensive.

The nuclear age transformed the relations between the Great Powers. For a time I doubted whether the Kremlin accurately realised what would happen to their country in the event of war. It even occurred to me that an announced, but peaceful, aerial demonstration over the main Soviet cities, coupled with the outlining to the Soviet leaders of some of our newest inventions, would produce in them a more friendly and sober attitude. Of course such a gesture could not have been accompanied by any formal demands, or it would have taken on the appearance of a threat and ultimatum.

But Russian production of these weapons and the remarkable strides of their air force have long since removed the point of this idea. Their military and political leaders must now be well aware of what each of us could do to the other.

Hopes of more friendly contacts with Russia remained much in my mind, and the death of Stalin in March 1953 seemed to bring a chance. I was again Prime Minister. I regarded Stalin's death as a milestone in Russian history. His tyranny had brought fearful suffering to his own country and to much else of the world.

The Soviet leaders must not be judged too harshly. Three times in the space of just over a century Russia has been invaded by Europe. Stalin tried not only to shield the Soviet Republics behind an Iron Curtain, military, political and cultural. He also attempted to construct an outpost line of satellite States, deep in Central Europe, harshly controlled from Moscow, subservient to the economic needs of the Soviet Union and forbidden all contact or communion with the free world, or even with each other.

No one can believe that this will last forever. Hungary has paid a terrible forfeit. But to all thinking men certain hopeful features of the present situation must surely be clear.

The doctrine of Communism is slowly being separated from the Russian military machine. Nations will continue to rebel against the Soviet Colonial Empire, not because it is Communist, but because it is alien and oppressive.

An arms race, even conducted with nuclear weapons and guided missiles, will bring no security or even peace of mind to the Great Powers which dominate the land masses of Asia and North America, or to the countries which lie between them. I make no plea for disarmament. Disarmament is a consequence and a manifestation of free intercourse between free peoples. It is the mind which controls the weapon, and it is to the minds of the peoples of Russia and her associates that the free nations should address themselves.

But after Stalin's death it seemed that a milder climate might prevail. At all events it merited investigating, and I so expressed myself in the House of Commons on 11 May 1953. An entirely informal conference between the heads of the leading Powers might succeed where repeated acrimonious exchanges at lower levels had failed.

I made it plain that this could not be accompanied by any relaxation of the comradeship and preparations of the free nations, for any slackening of our defence efforts would paralyse every beneficial tendency towards peace. This is true today.

What I sought was never fully accomplished. Nevertheless, for a time a gentler breeze seemed to blow upon our affairs. Further opportunities will doubtless present themselves, and they must not be neglected.

It is not my purpose to attempt to assign blame in any quarter for the many disagreeable things that have occurred since 1945. Certainly those who were responsible in Great Britain for the direction of our affairs in the years that followed the war were beset by the most complex and malignant problems both at home and abroad. The paths by which they chose to solve them were often forced upon them by circumstances or by predetermined doctrinaire policies, and their results were not always felicitous either for Britain or the free world.

The granting of independence to the Indian sub-continent had long been in the forefront of British political thought. I had contributed a good deal to the subject in the years between the wars. Supported by seventy Conservative members, I had fought it in its early stages with all my strength. When I was at the head of a Coalition Government I was induced to modify my former views.

Undoubtedly we came out of the desperate world struggle committed to Dominion status for India, including the right to secede from the Commonwealth. I thought, however, that the method of setting up the new Government should have given the great majority of the Indian people the power and the right to choose freely for themselves. I believed that a constitutional conference in which all the real elements of strength in India could participate would have shown us the way to produce a really representative self-governing India which would adhere to the British Empire.

The 'untouchables', the Rajahs, and many other different, vital, living interests, the loyalists, of whom hundreds of millions existed, all would have had their share in the new scheme. It must be remembered that in the last year of the war we had had a revolt of the extremists in the Indian Congress party which was put down without difficulty, and with very little loss of life.

The British Socialist party took a violently factional view. They believed that the advantage lay in the granting of self-government within the shortest space of time. And they gave it without hesitation – almost identifiably – to the forces which we had vanquished so easily. Within two years of the end of the war they achieved their purpose. On the 15 August 1947, Indian Independence was declared.

All efforts to preserve the unity of India had broken down, and Pakistan became a separate State. Four hundred million inhabitants of the sub-continent, mainly divided between Moslem and Hindu, flung themselves at one another. Two centuries of British rule in India were followed by greater bloodshed and loss of life than had ever occurred during our ameliorating tenure.

Fortunately at the head of the larger of the two new States erected on this bloody foundation was a man of singular qualities. Nehru had languished for years in jail or other forms of confinement. He now emerged as the leader of a tiny minority of the foes of British rule, largely free alike from two of the worst faults of human nature, Hate and Fear. Gandhi, who had so long led the cause of Indian independence, was murdered by a fanatic shortly after Nehru's installation as head of the Government. Jinnah presided over the Moslem State, Pakistan. We are on easy terms with the two Republics which have come into being. Their leaders attend the meetings of the Commonwealth, and their power for good or evil in Asia and the world is undeniable. I will not attempt to prejudge the future.

'WE HAVE NOT TRIED IN VAIN'
By Sir Winston Churchill
24 April 1958

Within the briefest interval of the news of the invasion of South Korea, President Truman had reached the conclusion that only immediate intervention by the armed forces of the United States could meet the situation. They were the nearest to the scene as well as by far the most numerous, but this was not the point.

As he has said in his memoirs, 'I felt certain that if South Korea was allowed to fall, Communist leaders would be emboldened to override nations closer to our own shores. If this were allowed to go unchallenged it would mean a third world war.' His celerity, wisdom and courage in this crisis make him worthy, in my estimation, to be numbered among the greatest of American Presidents. In Britain the Government endorsed and sustained the Americans.

British and Commonwealth forces made a small but robust contribution, but America carried almost the whole burden and paid for it with almost a hundred thousand casualties.

I will not dwell on the pendulum of military success and failure in Korea. The outcome can scarcely be thought of as satisfactory. However, South Korea remained independent and free, the aggressor suffered a costly repulse and, most important of all, the United States showed that she was not afraid to use armed force in defence of freedom, even in so remote an outpost.

After writing of Indo-China and the Dutch East Indies Sir Winston adds:

The changes in Asia are immeasurable. Perhaps they were inevitable. If a note of regret is to be found in this brief account, let it not be supposed that it is in hostility to the right of Asian peoples to self-determination, or a reflection on their present standing and integrity. But the means by which the present situation was reached give pause.

Was so much bloodshed necessary? Without the haste engendered by foreign pressure and the loss of influence inherent in our early defeats in the Far Eastern war, might progress to the same end have been happier, and the end itself more stable?

A great part of the Second World War had run its course to defend the land-bridge where Africa and Asia meet, to maintain our oil supplies and guard the Suez Canal. In the process the Middle Eastern countries, and notably Egypt, had enjoyed the advantage of protection from German and Italian invasion at no cost to themselves.

Throughout this region the world has witnessed a surge of nationalist feeling, the consequences of which have yet to run their course. From Indonesia to Morocco the Moslem peoples are in ferment. Their assertiveness has confronted the Western Powers, and especially those with overseas responsibilities, with problems of peculiar difficulty.

Amid jubilant cries for self-government and independence, it is easy to forget the many substantial benefits that have been conferred by Western rule. It is also hard to replace the orderliness which the Colonial Powers exercised over these large areas by a stable new system of sovereign States.

The most intractable of all the difficulties that faced Britain in these regions was that of Palestine. Ever since the Balfour Declaration of 1917 I have been a faithful supporter of the Zionist cause. I never felt that the Arab countries had had anything from us but fair play. To Britain and Britain alone they owed their very existence as nations. We created them; British money and British advisers set the pace of their advance; British arms protected them.

As mandatory Power [in Palestine] Great Britain was confronted with the tortuous problem of combining Jewish immigration to their national home with safeguarding the rights of the Arab inhabitants.

Few of us could blame the Jewish people for their violent views on the subject. A race that has suffered the virtual extermination of its national existence cannot be expected to be entirely reasonable. But the activities of terrorists, who tried to gain their ends by the assassination of British officials and soldiers, were an odious act of ingratitude that left a profound impression.

There is no country in the world less fit for a conflict with terrorism than Great Britain. This is not because of weakness or cowardice; it is because of restraint and virtue, and the way of life which we have lived in our successfully defended island. Stung by the murders in Palestine, abused by the Middle Eastern countries, and even by our allies, it was not unnatural that the Socialist Government should finally wash its hands of the problem and in 1948 leave the Jews to find their own salvation. The brief war that ensued dramatically dispelled the confidence of the Arab countries who closed in for an easy kill.

The infective violence of the birth of the State of Israel has sharpened the difficulties of the Middle East ever since. I look with admiration on the work done there in building up a nation, reclaiming the desert and receiving so many unfortunates from Jewish communities all over the world. But the outlook is sombre.

The frontiers of Israel flicker with murder and armed raids, and the Arab countries profess irreconcilable hostility to the new State. It is a black and threatening scene of unlimited violence and folly.

One thing is clear. Both honour and wisdom demand that the State of Israel should be preserved, and that this brave, dynamic and complex race should be allowed to live in peace with its neighbours. They can bring to the area an invaluable contribution of scientific knowledge, industriousness and productivity. They must be given an opportunity of doing so in the interest of the whole Middle East.

Before I complete this brief survey of the things that have struck me since the war, let us have a look at the United Nations. The machinery of government may easily fail in its purpose. My idea as the end of the war approached was that the greatest minds and the greatest thoughts possessed by men should govern the world. This entailed, if all countries great and small were to be represented, that they must be graded.

The spectacle presented by the United Nations is no more than a vain assertion of equality of influence and power which has no relation to the actual facts. The result is that a process of ingenious lobbying has attempted to take possession of the government of the world. I say attempted, because the vote of a country of a million or two inhabitants cannot decide or even sway the actions of powerful States. The United Nations in its present form has to cringe to dictatorships and bully the weak.

Small States have no right to speak for the whole of mankind. They must accept, and they would accept, a more intimate but lower rank. The world should be ruled by the leading men of groups of countries formed geographically. The mere process of letting the groups shape themselves and not judging by their power or their numbers would tell its own tale.

I do not intend to suggest that all the efforts and sacrifices of Britain and her Allies recorded in the six volumes of my War Memoirs have come to nothing and led only to a state of affairs more dangerous and gloomy than at the beginning. On the contrary I hold strongly to the belief that we have not tried in vain.

Russia is becoming a great commercial country. Her people experience every day in growing vigour those complications and palliatives of human life that will render the schemes of Karl Marx more out of date, and smaller in relation to world problems than they have ever been before.

The natural forces are working with greater freedom and greater opportunity to fertilise and vary the thoughts and the power of individual men and women. They are far bigger and more pliant in the vast structure of a mighty empire than could ever have been conceived by Marx in his hovel.

And when war is itself fenced about with mutual extermination it seems likely that it will be increasingly postponed. Quarrels between nations, or continents, or combinations of nations there will no doubt continually be. But in the main human society will grow in many forms not comprehended by a party machine. As long therefore as the free world holds together, and especially Britain and the United States, and maintains its strength, Russia will find that Peace and Plenty have more to offer than exterminatory war.

The broadening of thought is a process which acquires momentum by seeking opportunity for all who claim it. And it may well be if wisdom and patience are practised that Opportunity-for-All will conquer the minds and restrain the passions of Mankind.

Chapter 12

Churchill's Pets

Winston Churchill was a certified animal lover. Some of the earliest evidence for this dates back to 1891 when he sold his bicycle to buy a bulldog named Dodo. And his love for animals went far beyond conventional pets. In 1926 when Churchill sold off some of his livestock, he could not bear to part with all his pigs. He famously quipped, 'I am very fond of pigs. Dogs look up to us. Cats look down on us. Pigs treat us as equals.' Chartwell, Churchill's country estate overlooking the weald of Kent, practically became a menagerie with all manner of beasts and fowl.

Churchill's love of animals has also created some interesting myths and stories. There was a parrot called Charlie which Churchill was supposed to have taught to swear profanities against Hitler and the Nazis. Unfortunately, no one has been able to prove that Churchill owned the colourful parrot. He did build a butterfly house and in 1946 L. Hugh Newman, a butterfly breeding expert, was called in to help set it up. Churchill also looked into the practicalities of keeping kangaroos in his orchard at Chartwell. He was even given a lion named Rota in 1943 by George Thompson for his 'lion-hearted efforts' during the Second World War.

He did not have the ability to keep Rota at Chartwell, so Rota lived in London Zoo and Churchill would come by and feed her fairly regularly.

His pets became a way for Churchill to forget the pressures of being an eminent statesman and as he grew older the animals of Chartwell became an asylum for him. In 1955, he even donated some tropical fish to the London aquarium, though Churchill kept goldfish and golden orfe for himself. They remained in the pools in Chartwell's garden and, in his later years, he would sit for long hours and feed the fish, lost in silent reflection.

Of course, as Churchill aged, so did his pets. In 1955, at the age of seventeen, Rota the lion passed away. Much to Churchill's delight a lion cub named Rusty was given to him shortly after and he also lived in London Zoo. However, when poodle Rufus II, Churchill's trusted companion for years, passed away while Churchill was convalescing from a broken hip at the hospital in 1962, there was no replacing him. It is perhaps remarkable that Churchill's love of his pets was so prominent that when one of his pets died or was lost it was considered newsworthy.

PREMIER LOSES BLACK SWAN
2 June 1954

A black swan belonging to Sir Winston Churchill flew away from Chartwell, Kent, yesterday. It was one of four presented to him by Australia four years ago, and has a red bill with a white tip. Ponds, pools and lakes near Chartwell were searched.

Anyone with information can communicate with Chartwell or 10 Downing Street. A black swan that flew away from

Chartwell last October was never found. Another has been lent by Sir Winston to the Severn Wildfowl Trust for breeding, and a clutch of four eggs was recently hatched.

SWAN FOUND IN HOLLAND LIKE PREMIER'S
8 June 1954

A black swan found by a farmer at the small south Holland town of Uden is believed to be one missing from Chartwell, Kent, the home of Sir Winston Churchill, since Tuesday. Interpol, the International police organisation, and the British Embassy at The Hague are trying to identify it.

The red beak with white markings is said to be similar to that of the missing swan. The Prime Minister's swan carried no identification.

The Dutch farmer gave the swan shelter when it landed on Sunday. He informed the police.

If it proves to be the missing bird it will have flown about 240 miles from Chartwell. If the flight was direct the swan would have set a course crossing the English coast at Margate and passing south of Flushing.

None of the bird parks in Holland is missing a black swan. The bird did not seem especially tired when it landed.

Our nature Correspondent writes: 'A movement of 240 miles in a direct line would represent little more than five hours' flying time for a swan, their measured speeds in the air being around fifty miles per hour.'

SIR WINSTON'S LION MAKES FRIENDS
10 August 1955

Although Sir Winston Churchill's new lion is still in quarantine at the Zoo, he is on view and has already made many friends through the double wire-netting required by quarantine regulations. The ferocity he showed on arrival, after being kept in a crate for his flight here, has disappeared as he has settled down.

He is affectionate to his keeper and on good terms with a young lioness, Okene, who shares his home. Sir Winston has not yet named his lion, but the keeper calls him Rusty, as his coat has a reddish tinge.

SIR WINSTON'S PET BIRD LOST
15 February 1961

Sir Winston Churchill, who has been staying since last Saturday at the Hotel de Paris, Monte Carlo, tonight offered £22 reward for anybody bringing back Toby, his pet green and white budgerigar.

Toby, who has travelled with Sir Winston on all his flights and cruises of the past few years, disappeared this afternoon. After lunching with Prince Pierre, father of Prince Rainier of Monaco, Sir Winston went up to his suite on the eighth floor, to find the door of Toby's cage ajar and the windows of the room wide open. Sir Winston's private detective saw Toby perched in a palm tree on the Casino terraces. It flew away.

SIR WINSTON'S POODLE DIES
17 August 1962

Sir Winston Churchill's brown French poodle Rufus II died in his sleep at Chartwell on Wednesday night and was buried in the garden yesterday near Rufus I, a former pet of Sir Winston. Rufus II was fifteen years old and his sight was failing fast.

Lord Moran, Sir Winston's physician, who paid him a routine visit at Middlesex Hospital yesterday, said he was 'very well'. Asked when Sir Winston would be leaving hospital, Lord Moran replied, 'Nothing is fixed yet.'

Lady Churchill, who spent an hour with her husband yesterday, said: 'He is not coming out this week. I hope it will be sometime next week. The reconstruction work at home is not quite ready yet.' Another of Sir Winston's visitors yesterday was Lady Violet Bonham Carter.

Chapter 13

Churchill in Twilight

Once Churchill left his last premiership in 1955, he was able to retire to a relatively private life. He continued to be MP for Woodford until 1964 and he enjoyed regularly going to Parliament. He was still considered an elder statesman and was written to by his successor Anthony Eden on several occasions. However, without a sense of purpose, Churchill increasingly grappled with his melancholy. In 1956, he rebuffed his Private Secretary Anthony Montague Browne's insistence of his achievements by saying, 'Yes, I worked very hard all my life, and I have achieved a great deal – in the end to achieve nothing.' He further confessed to Browne that he felt like 'an aeroplane at the end of its flight, in the dusk, with the petrol running out, in search of a safe landing'. Despite this, Churchill still enjoyed travelling, to the South of France, to the US on Aristotle Onassis's yacht and elsewhere. He also took solace in his country home Chartwell and in his family.

HOW SIR WINSTON WENT
By Donald McLachlan
21 April 1955

For Sir Winston's leave-taking there was no public demonstration of farewell, no processional occasion. Without their newspapers to remind them of days and times, to confirm forecasts and rumours, people could not make a date to see their Prime Minister.

Instead there was a sequence of intimate and miniature ceremonies: first at No. 10 Downing Street, then at the Palace, then again at No. 10.

After the parting audience with the Queen on Tuesday afternoon, 5 April, there were hundreds only to cheer and run with Sir Winston's car. But at teatime on Wednesday, when it was known for certain that he had laid down his office, there were thousands in Whitehall to watch him leaving No. 10 for good.

It was only a few dozen, assembled outside the gates of Chartwell, who heard the last recorded remark of three memorable days: 'Come into the grounds, all of you, and see my goldfish.'

On Monday 4 April we were still guessing. Would the constitutional processes go forward as forecast by the newspapers, now silent? Would there be only what Lord Samuel has called a 'muted farewell'?

So it was to be, but no one outside No. 10 on the Monday night could be quite certain. We were waiting to see the Queen and the Duke of Edinburgh leaving the party of distinguished guests which we knew to be assembled for dinner behind the blinds of the first floor.

Would it or would it not be a poignant scene: the aged statesman, still Prime Minister, conducting to her car the young Queen whose great-great-grandmother he had served as a cavalry subaltern? When the front door opened and the floodlights came on in the Foreign Office opposite, the doubt remained. The picture was too brilliant to be sad.

There seemed to be no special significance in Sir Winston's deep bow and Lady Churchill's graceful curtsey. Only when the Queen's car had gone and the host stood alone on his doorstep was the cheer of affectionate sympathy heard: and even then it was rather timid.

Not till the next afternoon, Tuesday, were doubts resolved. Just after 4.30 Sir Winston, with black frock-coat, top-hat, gold-headed cane and cigar, arrived at Buckingham Palace by car. Three-quarters of an hour later it was all over.

The Queen, in the words of the official announcement, had been 'graciously pleased to accept his resignation as Prime Minister and First Lord of the Treasury'. Not till the next day would the name of the new Prime Minister be known, so it was still Sir Winston's hour.

As he left the Palace, calm and cheerful for all to see, the crowd cheered, waved and ran. Back in Downing Street another small throng was waiting for him, and was rewarded for its patience by the 'V' sign. Indoors, all those Ministers who had not been in the Cabinet were waiting to shake hands. To the Cabinet itself Sir Winston had said goodbye before lunch.

On this same Tuesday afternoon a packed House of Commons hoped against hope that it might take fond and formal leave of the Prime Minister. To see him standing for the last time in the place from which he had hurled the great defiances of May 1940, would have been a dramatic and moving experience – perhaps too moving for the great man himself.

When Mr Crookshank made it clear he would answer for Sir Winston the galleries thinned and the mood of the House suddenly turned skittish. Questions were asked to which no one expected any answer. Mr Emrys Hughes, for instance, wanted to know if Caesar would be buried in the House of Lords or would be allowed to come back to the Commons to worry Anthony.

The next day, Wednesday, was shared between Sir Winston and Sir Anthony.

At midday we heard that Sir Anthony Eden had been received in audience by the Queen, had accepted her Majesty's offer of the succession and had kissed hands upon appointment. By the afternoon the new Prime Minister was replying in the House of Commons to the tributes paid to his predecessor.

He spoke above all of his courage, 'the courage which expresses itself not only in the first enthusiastic burst of fervour but that endures also; perhaps the rarer gift of the two.' Mr. Attlee's voice sounded not only respect but also affection. Mr Walter Elliot caught exactly the mood of the House when he said it had 'lost one of the greatest front-benchers, but the back-benchers had gained the greatest back-bencher of all time'.

In the House of Lords the mood was the same; unity in admiration and regret. Lord Salisbury said that Sir Winston's passionate love of freedom made him 'one of the greatest Liberals, in the fullest sense of the word'. Lord Jowitt, for the Labour Party, bore witness 'to that underlying unity which adds to confusion of our critics and the consternation of our enemies', and paid warm tribute to the devotion and public spirit of Lady Churchill.

To the chorus of praise and regret Britain's national

newspapers could add nothing. But abroad Sir Winston's resignation and Sir Anthony's succession were treated as one of the great stories of the century.

In the United States, especially, it thrust aside all other news – twenty-nine columns in the *New York Herald Tribune*. President Eisenhower made of his tribute a special ceremony, before newsreel and television cameras. Standing in the rose gardens of the White House he spoke movingly of his 'very old and very dear friend', and insisted that his advice would still be sought by old comrades in arms.

The sentiment was echoed by Mr Nehru, who spoke of Sir Winston's departure as a tremendous event. From Mr St Laurent in Canada and Mr Menzies in Australia came tributes to the inspiration of his leadership; from the New Zealand Parliament a resolution expressing appreciation for his services to the Commonwealth. French statesmen, including M. Faure, M. Mendes-France and M. Reynaud, spoke warmly of Sir Winston's affection for their country. Dr Adenauer in Bonn and Mr Hatoyama in Tokyo expressed their deep regret.

Meanwhile Sir Winston was moving deliberately, and doubtless sadly, through his last day at No. 10, his home for five years of war and three and a half years of peace.

He had written to the Conservatives of Woodford to assure them that he would stand for Parliament in the next general election. He referred to Sir Anthony Eden, his successor, as a leader 'who will, I am sure, sustain the highest interests and traditions of Britain, and uphold the cause of Tory democracy which Lord Beaconsfield proclaimed, which Lord Randolph revived, and which I have tried to serve.'

There was a farewell tea with the staff at No. 10 and those waiting outside could hear it ending to the strains of 'For He's a Jolly Good Fellow'. Then came the departure, with everything the crowd wanted to see: the cigar, Rufus the poodle, the budgerigar, the 'V' sign.

Just a week later Sir Winston and Lady Churchill, bound for the painters' paradise of Syracuse, stepped into the Sicilian sunshine from their Viscount airliner, which had made record time from London to Catania. The aircraft flew the standard of the Lord Warden of the Cinque Ports.

PREMIER WRITES TO SIR WINSTON
14 May 1955

Sir Anthony Eden has sent the following letter to Sir Winston Churchill:

My Dear Winston,

I have written, as you used to do, to all our candidates giving them, I trust, encouragement in the great battle which lies immediately in front of us.

You, of course, need no such message. You have been the architect of our successes, just as you were the architect of victory in the great war, and to you I send our gratitude and lasting affection for all you did for us while you were the Leader of our Party and Prime Minister.

It would be inappropriate for me, as the new Leader of our Party, to commend you, who were so long our Leader, to the electors of Woodford. They are too deeply conscious of their privileged position in having had you as their Member and in fighting for you now as their candidate to need any encouragement from outside.

May I then wish you, as the Leader under whom I have been

so proud to serve, a happy campaign and a magnificent majority on 26 May.

This was Sir Winston's reply:

My Dear Anthony,

Thank you so much for your most kind letter, which gives me, and I am sure my supporters in Woodford and Wanstead, great pleasure. I rejoice your campaign is going so well.

SIR WINSTON'S GOLDEN WEDDING TODAY
12 September 1958

Sir Winston and Lady Churchill celebrate their golden wedding at Cap d'Ail, on the French Riviera, tomorrow. 'It will be very much a family affair,' said Mr Anthony Montagu Browne, Sir Winston's secretary.

So the grounds of Lord Beaverbrook's Provençal-style Villa Capponcina will remain closed to well-wishers, photographers and others. Mr Randolph Churchill arrived in Nice by air this afternoon with his eight-year-old daughter Arabella.

Later Sir Winston took his grand-daughter for a swim at Monte Carlo. British tourists cheered and waved as Sir Winston and Lady Churchill drove to the beach with her and her father.

Sir Winston, wearing a grey suit and his famous Mexican sombrero, took Arabella's hand as she went to swim in the pool. He sat on some steps as she splashed about.

Then Arabella helped him up some steps to a terrace. There

the party had tea and cakes, with no limit on cakes for Arabella.

Gifts and congratulations were coming in from all over the world today. The Cap d'Ail post office has had to make special arrangements to deal with the bulk of mail for the village's famous guest, who is also its honorary mayor.

A chocolate cigar weighing 25lb is on its way by air from Geneva. It is the gift of the Swedish Countess Coudenhove-Kalergi. Presents already received include a gallon bottle of 119-year-old cognac from the Chateau de Madrid restaurant at Villefranche, where Sir Winston often dines. A champagne firm has sent twelve bottles of its best vintage. There are flowers from the Cap d'Ail municipality, and pictures by many amateur painters.

Messages from the Queen, Mr Macmillan and many Commonwealth and foreign Governments are on their way. No list of guests for the celebrations has been made public, but M. Pierre-Jean Moatti, Prefect of the Alpes Maritimes Department, is expected to be among them. Last night he gave a dinner for Sir Winston and Lady Churchill.

Mr Onassis, the Greek ship owner, and Greta Garbo were reported to be among those who would drop in during the day. But they are said to be far away in Mr Onassis's yacht in Greek waters. Mr Somerset Maugham is a likely guest.

Tomorrow, too, Sir Winston and M. Jean Cocteau should have met for the first time. M. Cocteau wishes to present Sir Winston with a medal. But the meeting of the former *enfants terribles* of politics and poetry has been postponed indefinitely.

The case of M. Cocteau and the medal is still a bit vague, like the mist shrouded above Monte Carlo this morning. He was to have presented it on behalf of the Committee of l'Ordre de la Courtoisie Française, an organisation which is understood to have an ill-defined connection with French tourism.

Sir Winston would then have become the holder of the Grand Croix of the order, although he would actually have received a silver medal decorated with a symbolic lion on one side and a woman holding a sheaf of flowers on the other.

Unfortunately the committee of the order was unable to obtain the Churchill family motto, which it wished to engrave on the medal. The British Embassy in Paris declared itself unable to help.

Last night, when the committee's plans for the presentation were, it seemed, running smoothly, M. Raymond Rodel, president of the committee, read me M. Cocteau's speech for the occasion.

Apart from his office with the order, M. Rodel is also president of the Committee of Prestige and National Propaganda, president of the Committee for the Promotion of Tourism, International Delegate of the 'Lions Club' and president of honour of the French Lawn Tennis Association.

The speech was brief, sonorous and extremely graceful. 'It needs a poet to decorate a poet,' M. Cocteau was to have said.

And then, with possibly more foresight than he realised: 'You are the Prince of a mysterious kingdom where the titles are not bequeathed, but are gained by the universal suffrage of the living and the dead, from the present which observes us and the past which judges us.'

But perhaps M. Cocteau, thinking it over in his villa at Cap Ferrat, will not be too annoyed with Sir Winston, who will spend the day reading telegrams and opening presents. A box of cigars from a Mme Barande, of Nice, bears the legend:

'To Winston Churchill, who saved the world.'

Chapter 14

Remembering Churchill

Churchill passed away on 24 January 1965, on the same day as his father seventy years prior. The entire nation mourned his loss. He was given a magnificent state funeral, though initially he'd hoped to be cremated and his ashes scattered at his beloved home Chartwell. The funeral itself was a global event with over 350 million people watching on their televisions across the world. More than 7,000 soldiers and nine military bands participated in the funeral precession and over a million people gathered in the streets of London to watch. The *Telegraph* remembered Churchill in a series of eulogies and reports on the funeral and lying in state of the Great Man, Sir Winston Churchill.

W.S.C.
25 January 1965

Men and women in many lands will mourn the passing of Winston Leonard Spencer-Churchill, for they know well that if he had never lived they might not be alive today. Never was more justified the saying of Pericles that 'the whole earth is the sepulchre of the renowned and their memorial is written not on tablets of stone but on the hearts of men'. Few of our great men have been more British, but also few have been more international. In every land where a trace of freedom remains, and perhaps in many where freedom seems to have been snuffed out, the name of Churchill evokes the admiration of the noble and silences the gibes of the petty. To those abroad who found consolation in despair from his indomitableness and caught fire at the flame of his courage, it will always be a puzzle that the British people temporarily discarded one whom they would have been proud to acclaim. It is our way not to treat our great men well, though it does not follow that we are unworthy of them. At least today our reactions will not bewilder our friends, for all will join in deep homage to one whose memory will never die.

It was said of the late Lord Balfour that 'he saw a great deal of life from afar'. Churchill saw a great deal of it from close. No man, until the last few lingering years, ever lived every moment of his life more fully, with more zest and with less aloofness. The dazzle of his war leadership is so great that we are apt to be blind to the forty years of sailing in the rough seas of democracy that preceded the fearful storm through which he guided us. Yet there was material enough in those forty years to form a not inconsiderable pedestal. Moreover, among this material were disappointments. The bitterest in his life was probably the failure of the Dardanelles expedition. Unjust censure for that tragedy has already been converted by history into triumphant vindication. The second most bitter may have been the rebuffing for seven long years by the blind or calculating of his warnings of the renewed German menace. History has atoned to him for that. Let us hope that she may not have to atone to him for other occasions on which a majority of the nation rejected his counsel.

Again, his achievements in war were so great that many have misjudged his character and forgotten his achievements in peace. Deep study of the art of war or of military history, immense courage and capacity in war, do not make a man a warmonger. He hated war as much as any pacifist, because he knew its horrors better. All the time that he was warning us about Germany he was beseeching us to put strength into the League of Nations, and in the post-war years he sought to give substance to the hope of world peace by promoting cohesion between the still free States of Europe. Nor should it be forgotten that he who gave us victory gave us also, as much as any single man, the structure of our social services.

It is, of course, natural and right that his chief title to fame should rest upon 1939–45. He became Prime Minister at the darkest hour in our history. The heavier the odds, the greater the achievement. His was not marred by any pretensions to be indispensable. He did not exclaim, like Chatham, 'I know that I can save this country and nobody else can.' He offered only, like Garibaldi, 'blood, toil, tears and sweat', and, like Clemenceau, to fight. For he was, as he said himself, 'the child of the House of Commons', as resigned to bow as he was resolute to rule, if called upon to do either. He well knew that there is no substitute for sweat, and he worked hard – in office and out of it. The reason why he could withstand so great a strain so long was only that he was always at peace with himself.

In the achievement of this inner quietude he was continuously fortified by a serene and cloudless marriage. To say, as he said himself: 'I married and lived happily ever afterwards', is the simple epitome of a companionship unaffected by any buffets of fortune, and immune to even the most viperish tongues. He had his moments of despair, of bitterness, of impulse, and of revolt. In all such, his wife was steadfast and wise, neither assertive nor overawed, neither too outspoken nor too restrained. His affection for her was founded on the deepest respect, and if he was sometimes deaf to others he was ever attentive to her.

It is tempting to make a comparison between Churchill and other great war leaders who have helped this country to ride similar storms. The closest analogy in spirit, skill and eloquence is Elizabeth I. Many of her phrases have the true Churchillian ring. Chatham's genius had a touch of the feverish. He too was equal to his hour; he had his element of flamboyance and his moments of unquestioned grandeur. But his mind havered on the borderline between brilliance and insanity. Pitt had stubborn resolution and far sight. But he was broken by his disappointment.

There remains Lloyd George. He was spurred to rise to a stature which nobody thought he possessed. He spoke with the tongues of men and of angels. He defied the lightning. But he had brains rather than character. He could 'charm the birds off the trees', but one felt all the time that he was better at conjuring tricks than genuine magic. On the whole, therefore, with the possible exception of the splendid but slightly misty figure of the first Elizabeth, Churchill outshines all his competitors to the title of chief architect of national salvation.

Such a man has the power to lift up the hearts of men. That was his supreme gift to us in life, and it may be his legacy to us in death. If he could send any message from the shades to the people whom he loved so well, we may be very sure that it would be a call to quit ourselves like men. Did he not prove that his country in the storm of calamity has 'a secret vigour and a pulse like a cannon'? 'He does not die,' says the poet, 'who can bequeath some influence to the land he knows.' If so, and it surely is so, Winston Churchill, acknowledged and acclaimed as a paladin in and architect of the past, has still a contribution to make to the history of the future.

'My friends' – the familiar exordium of Churchill's broadcasts – was no mere formal phrase. It reflected a direct relationship between him and his listeners. They mourn him, one and all, a friend as well as a deliverer.

But while their sorrow bites deep, its edge is tempered, if not turned, by pride; pride, yes, and thanksgiving that this country could breed a man capable of moving among the towering and terrible events of those five years with a stature which matched their own: who could on Atlantean shoulders raise us from the pit, and for a time plant us on the top of the world.

His genius was not static. The Churchill of under thirty, a politically immature knight errant, avid beyond measure for peril and personal adventure, is not the Churchill who by 1906 had won his political spurs and between then and 1930 filled almost every public position except the highest; nor yet the seasoned veteran whose prescience from that time on persistently envisioned the death-grapple with the Nazis; and whose sage, tempered valour resolved it, when it came, in our favour.

Each of these phases revealed in some degree a different man. But all change implies a persistent, underlying identity. In the first place, he was endowed at birth with two or three times the normal human allowance of vitality. He brought to any undertaking he approached, were it some fateful decision of policy, or the design of a swimming pool, or the punctuation of an Admiralty minute, an *attaque*, a concentration, a gusto the possession of which was in itself a kind of genius.

Men supercharged with energy often find an outlet for it in physical adventure. He did. All his life he had a passion for courage as a master-virtue and for peril as the condition of its exercise. He loved the razor's edge.

But with all this 'fire in his belly', with all his rare and radiant intellect, he combined from the first to last a moral outlook markedly normal. There was much in him of John Bull; tenacity, intolerance of dictation, refusal to own defeat, simplicity and affection in all family relations, a love of plain dealing, fidelity to friends, a good sound hatred of enemies who were silly enough to remain such; and with this an unflagging passion for the glory and greatness of Britain (which he often referred to as 'Britannia') and of the British Commonwealth (which he was not afraid to call 'the Empire'). These qualities are the traditional norm and staple of our race. In this anything but normal man they were strong, salient, ineradicable.

Winston Churchill's 'knight errant' phase lasted from 1895 to 1901. By the age of twenty-seven he could look back on four campaigns – in Cuba, on the Northwest frontier of India, on the Nile, on the Veldt. At the Battle of Omdurman he managed to take part with the 21st Lancers in almost the only cavalry charge of modern times; and in the Boer War, when he was taken prisoner, his captor had to be no lesser man than the future General Botha.

Between the general election of 1905–6 and the rise of Hitler, Churchill held a prodigious range of offices. His tenure of some of them, for instance that of First Lord of the Admiralty at the time of the Dardanelles expedition, led to controversies over which the dust has not yet settled. But to almost all he brought some notable contribution. As Under-Secretary for the Colonies it fell to him to submit to the House of Commons the measure for conferring self-government on the Transvaal. As President of the Board of Trade he introduced, with the help of Lord Beveridge, the Labour Exchange, or Employment Exchange as we now call it. The melodrama of Sidney Street has obscured a fuller recognition of many wise reforms he projected during his short stay at the Home Office.

It is not necessary to recall his exclusion from the Coalition of 1915 (insisted on by the Conservatives as a condition of coalescing), his period of service on the Western Front, the gamut of offices which he ran through under Mr Lloyd George's Coalition, or his Chancellorship of the Exchequer in Mr Baldwin's Government of 1925. The interesting question is how the highest office managed to elude him. Why was this?

Two factors here seem to have concurred. One was a certain personal unpopularity, strange as it seems that this should have attached to one who was to become the idol of a nation. The other was a widespread belief that one sovereign gift, often denied to genius and accorded to mediocrity, the gift of judgment – the faculty of being right – had been withheld from him; and this must now seem almost equally strange, for from 1930 onwards he was not only right but displayed a gift almost of divination.

Unpopularity, up to a point, was easily accounted for. Almost at the start of his political life he had crossed the floor of the House, abjured the party in which he had been cradled, and of which his father had been a brilliant, if heterodox, member and from this act of apostasy (for such it must have seemed to Tories) he had, owing to the Liberal tidal wave of 1905–6, reaped a glittering reward.

Resentment ascribed his conduct to calculating ambition. In fact, no one foresaw the landslide of 1906, and no one who did not could be certain that the path of apostasy would be particularly profitable. It was at best a gamble. And few of his Conservative critics were charitable enough to consider that conviction may have played a part in determining his action.

He himself was impenitent. Friends warned him that one who changes his party should walk delicately, feel his way, disarm hostility when and how he could. Churchill's sanguine temperament did not take kindly to such counsels. He was combative. Though not rancorous, he had a quick temper. He did not suffer fools with rapture, and could not always repress the 'flash and outbreak of a fiery mind'.

The other retarding factor was his alleged want of 'judgment'. Critics of the dash to Antwerp; critics of the Dardanelles expedition; critics, later, of his abortive Russian campaigns in support of Kolchak and Denikin relied on these incidents as proof that he lacked this vital quality.

Yet if these criticisms had any substance at the time it is beyond question that in the crowning and crucial phase of his career he brilliantly lived them down. Argument still seems possible about the Munich Agreement. Even so, the preceding policy (or want of it) finds today few defenders; and it was these precedent transactions which furnished the occasions for Churchill's most searching criticisms and for his most penetrating prophecies. From the first significant emergence of Hitler until the end of the war, and indeed beyond (for we must not forget the Fulton speech and its sequels), the mantle of Calchas (and, alas! that of Cassandra, too) descended on his shoulders.

One earlier forecast is so striking that it can fittingly find a place here. It is mainly remarkable because of its date. 'May there not be methods of using explosive energy incomparably

more intense than anything heretofore discovered? Might not
a bomb no bigger than an orange be found to possess a secret
power to destroy a whole block of buildings? . . . Could not
explosives of an existing type be guided automatically in flying
machines by wireless or other rays, without human pilot, in
ceaseless procession upon a hostile city, arsenal, camp or
dockyard?'

This was written by him in 1925; eighteen years before V1
or V2, and longer still before Hiroshima and Nagasaki. Yet it
may be doubted whether Churchill was ever more importantly
right than he was about Hitler's reoccupation of the Rhineland
in March 1936. The resumption of this area by the Germans
was, as is now common knowledge, a bluff, from which Hitler
would have receded if the bluff had been called. In the debate
which followed this demarche, Churchill predicted the consequences of permitting it to go unchallenged.

After pointing out that the 'demilitarised' – now reoccupied
– area would as a matter of course be fortified (as it was by
means of the 'West Wall'), he said:

'It will be a barrier across Germany's front door which will
leave her free to sally eastwards and southwards by the other
doors . . . The creation of a line of forts opposite to the French
frontier will enable the German troops to be economised on
that line, and will enable the main forces to swing round
through Belgium and Holland . . .

'Then look East . . . The Baltic States, Poland and
Czechoslovakia, Rumania, Austria and some other countries,
are all affected very decisively the moment that this great work
of construction has been completed . . .'

This was all said, not in the atmosphere of after-knowledge,
but on the morrow of the reoccupation. When we consider
the fate of Austria, Czechoslovakia and Poland in 1938 and

1939, and that of Belgium, Holland and many other countries a little later, we may well ask what prophecy has been more pitilessly vindicated.

But apart altogether from the evidence of specific comments on particular events or phrases of policy, Churchill's foresight is attested by an accumulation of warnings, disregarded by those in control of policy, but verified, tragically, in their despite. He never doubted that Hitler (after his reoccupation of the Rhineland at least) was 'running for blood': was unappeasable by art or skill. This being so, he was never satisfied with the tempo or scale of rearmament.

It was principally these pronouncements which clinched his succession to the office of Prime Minister as soon as it was vacant. Nor did his judgment desert him then. He divined the temper of the nation. He struck the exact note which Britain expected and longed to hear, and to which she was most likely to respond. 'Blood, toil, tears and sweat' – after being fed on so much optimistic nonsense, Englishmen craved for this stern tonic. On no other fare could they face what confronted them; a lonely, dragging rearguard action against a seemingly invincible foe. Who that heard it can ever forget that glorious voice roaring defiance in 1940 against the triumphant, the unbeatable enemy of mankind?

The raw material of British heroism was always there, but it always needs concentration and a focus. How he knitted together the dispersed courage and resource of the people, doggedly rearmed our gunless, tankless Army, infected all with his own grim buoyancy, weathered the endless storm and led the nation to one of the most overwhelming victories in history, is an epic still fresh in our minds.

Churchill the man is hardly separable from the statesman. It has been said that at least three accomplishments go to the making of an ideal statesman: command of the spoken word, at the hustings and in debate; grasp of administration; and weight in council. These three elements are not often found in combination; more seldom still in perfect balance.

Churchill's powers of speech were beyond admiration. The sentence (worthy of Simonides) about the 'few' and the 'many' is graven on our hearts, but by way of contrast, it may be permissible to recall a famous bit of satire in a speech criticising the Baldwin Government in 1936:

'The Government cannot make up their minds, or they cannot get Mr Baldwin to make up his mind. So they go on in strange paradox, decided only to be undecided, resolved to be irresolute, adamant for drift . . .'

So exuberant was his rhetorical fancy that in leisure moments he would burlesque his own periods.

As a departmental administrator he was classed in the first rank by those best qualified to judge. He was exacting. He expected everyone who served him to be at his beck and call at most hours of the day and night, and to put aside all other work, however urgent, on demand. But should a war leader of such inspired quality, in a war so deadly as the last, need any excuse for being coercive, pre-emptive, exacting? Had he any right to be considerate?

Of his sagacity in council during the war, again there can be little question, since the major decisions must be assumed to have been arrived at, if not on his initiative, at least with his concurrence, and they led to victory. Some again say that Churchill was not the ideal chairman of a deliberate body. He could, it is acknowledged, state his own view with vivid and fierce force, but he was by some alleged not to encourage the 'cross-fertilisation of minds' by which an individual opinion is submitted to check and review.

It would be unreasonable to suggest that Churchill never made mistakes, or had no limitations; nor would the suggestion find favour in an age when hero-worship is at a discount and the deflation of renown has become almost a profession. But would it not be more unreasonable still to doubt that his shortcomings were dwarfed by his achievements? When we consider, as dispassionately as we can, the situation which Churchill took over in 1940, and that which he left in 1945, who can fail to marvel at the 'dead-heave' given to our national fortunes, and to the cause of civilisation, mainly by one man; the measureless danger in which from 1940 to 1942 the Allied cause stood; its appalling military weakness; the unimaginably horrible sequels of defeat; and then ask if ever our country has thrown up a more wonderful leader at a more critical time.

LONDON DAY BY DAY
25 January 1965

Sir Winston Churchill will lie in state in Westminster Hall.

Not since 1898 has that honour been accorded to an English statesman. From then, with one exception – the victims of the R101 disaster in 1930 – it has been a tribute reserved for members of the Royal family.

Mr Gladstone's body was brought from Hawarden and lay in state in Westminster Hall for two days. During this time 250,000 filed past the bier.

Had it been decided to bury Sir Winston in the Abbey, precedent would have required Parliament to move an address to the Queen, as was done for Mr Gladstone, praying that her

Majesty be graciously pleased to direct that the remains be interred at the public charge.

During his years in the Commons since 1955, Sir Winston occupied a distinctive place.

He sat always in a corner seat on the first bench below the gangway. While there he was, at least to the public gallery, still the central figure.

Though he did not speak, Sir Winston came quite often, for the last time on Monday 27 July last year, the day before all-party valedictory tributes delivered in his absence.

To the end he remained obstinately independent, and although usually escorted to the entrances of the Chamber he very much disliked doors being held for him.

His dress for these occasions was invariable – a black jacket and long white cuffs.

Sir Winston's style of oratory was unique. So were the accoutrements which were indispensable to all his major performances in public – a box at the right level for notes and special lenses that picked up the typescript without the need for his stooping.

For many years he had delivered no big speech extempore. His notes were typed on octavo sheets. A former principal private secretary, Mrs Thompson, has commented:

'The result had the appearance of rather eccentric blank verse; a "verse" represented a sentence and this was subdivided into phrases – sometimes even words – on separate lines, so that, as he read it, he could tell at a glance where emphasis was required.'

Though on some occasions he could be abrupt, cross and disgruntled, Sir Winston never departed from the strict code of courtesy which the best of his generation observed.

In attire, manners and address he had his own standards.

When younger men entered or left his room at Downing Street or the House he would usually rise from his chair. Some pictures taken with parting guests from Downing Street illustrate his rule of politeness.

But he could be most disconcerting – as he was with the very young politician who lunched with him and was given an exceptional glass of claret. He sipped it carefully and murmured appreciatively. Sir Winston was not impressed. 'Sip burgundy, swill claret,' he grunted. There was a long silence.

With all members of the Royal family he combined close friendship with strict decorum. Of these relations future biographers will reveal more. It is permissible to recall one dinner at which Sir Winston and the Queen, then Princess Elizabeth, were present.

With the coffee, Sir Winston began to express his feelings strongly and loudly about something. The company fell silent and looked at him with mixed respect and apprehension.

All save Princess Elizabeth. Her own features revealed a mixture of affection, tolerant amusement and wise regard. Into that moment a lot of English history could be written.

During his lifetime little was said or written, no doubt from feelings of delicacy, about Sir Winston's remarkable physical attribute – his digestion.

In an age when nearly all his younger colleagues suffered some duodenal trouble, an occupational disease of modern statesmen, Sir Winston enjoyed the serenest of stomachs. Nearly all his constitutional trouble occurred early in life.

He would eat and drink with an appetite which astonished and often defeated his young companions, especially in the late hours. He smoked cigars less heavily than many supposed, but hard enough, and through a long life his constitution received enough punishment to cripple a weaker man.

Some attributed his immunity to the inflexible habit of working from bed first thing in the morning and taking a sleep after lunch. It lay rather, I believe, in Nature's gift of an altogether exceptional interior economy. He liked to work with a whisky and soda within reach, but it often lasted him three or four hours.

Of hobbies he had less need than most men. He found relaxation and peace of mind in changing his manifold activities. His goldfish at Chartwell were a hobby. He took an immense interest in their welfare and displayed them with much pride.

Once he took a visitor to the pond, where nothing was visible. To attract the fishes' attention he shouted loudly. Nothing appeared. He shouted again. No goldfish.

Then he dipped his hand into a tin and scattered titbits on the water. The fish responded eagerly. 'Very much as your electors behave,' observed the visitor. Sir Winston looked thoughtful and, for once, had no adequate rejoinder.

His Harrow days were not, Sir Winston afterwards confessed, the happiest of his life. In the last years of them, however, he found some happy moments there. He left Harrow in 1892 and returned in 1900 to give a lecture. Then there was a gap of forty years.

Not until the autumn of 1940 did he pay the first of what became a series of annual visits to Harrow's Speech Room to take part in the singing of school songs. Harrow's songs fill a volume. With his memory for poetry and prose Sir Winston could sing many of them by heart.

After songs Sir Winston would go to the headmaster's study. There a few guests and senior boys assembled. The guests amused themselves. The boys gathered about Sir Winston in a separate corner apart.

What they said to each other was, traditionally, quite

private. This custom began during the war. As Prime Minister he never refused an answer. Nor was he ever let down – an incomparable bit of training in public life for the young.

Sir Winston's philosophy on exercise might be summed up in a minute written in February 1941, when he heard of a Division in which every officer and man was required to do a seven-mile run:

'Who is the General of this Division, and does he run the seven miles himself? If so, he may be more useful for football than for war . . . In my experience, based on many years' observation, officers with high athletic qualifications are not usually successful in the higher ranks.'

Later he had cause to revise this judgment of Lord Montgomery.

His repartee – especially at question time in the House – was helped by his slight deafness.

Sir Winston's hearing aid was in fact a two-edged weapon. He was as adept at failing to hear what interrupters desired him to hear as at picking up *sotto voce* remarks not intended for his ears.

After one inconclusive private interview, a young Member of Parliament was heard to exclaim ruefully: 'He used his hearing aid to speak to me, and laid it down when I began to talk.'

Even in his twilight years, Sir Winston was capable of devastating flashes.

One day, after he had moved with difficulty into his usual seat in the Commons, two Members behind commented with pity on the deterioration of his faculties.

To their horror a great head swung round to look at them and a rasping voice remarked:

'And, they tell me, he's very deaf too.'

CHURCHILL AS THE ARCHITECT OF VICTORY
25 January 1965

If Sir Winston Churchill, who has died at the age of ninety, had never, as the architect of victory in the 1939–45 war, written such an imperishable page in the story of Britain and of civilisation, his genius, which flowered in several forms, would still have ensured him a place in history.

He was an acknowledged master of the written and spoken word, and would have been remembered in the world of literature if only for his life of Marlborough.

He held more ministerial posts than any other politician including two memorable terms as First Lord of the Admiralty when Britain was embarking on both world wars. He was twice Prime Minister, holding office at two critical stages of our history.

He was the only member of the War Cabinet to remain in office from 3 September 1939 until victory had been achieved in Europe. Finally, his brilliant and versatile temperament found such fluent expression at the artist's easel that he was, at the age of seventy-three, elected an honorary Academician Extraordinary of the Royal Academy.

The threads of his life story were woven, unobtrusively enough at first, in the tapestry of British history. Winston Leonard Spencer-Churchill was born at Blenheim Palace, historic home of the Marlboroughs, on 30 November 1874, the son of Lord Randolph Churchill, third son of the seventh Duke of Marlborough.

His mother was formerly Miss Jennie Jerome, of New York, a fact he was not slow to recall, with impish humour, when his audience was American.

His schooling at Harrow and at Sandhurst was undistinguished. He declared modestly later in life that book-learning was not his forte, and that he had had to pick up things as he went along. His commission in the 4th Queen's Own Hussars in 1895 was not achieved without difficulty in passing the necessary examinations.

But he displayed signs quite early of that restless independence, and spirit of adventure, which was later to figure so prominently not only in his military, but also in his political career. He secured permission to serve with the Spanish forces in Cuba in the Spanish-American war, and in 1897 he was attached to the Punjab Infantry with the Malakand Field Force. He subsequently served with the Tirah and Nile Expeditionary Forces and was present at the Battle of Khartoum.

In 1899 he found time to contest, unsuccessfully, Oldham in the Conservative cause before service in South Africa with the Light Horse. Here, while acting as war correspondent of the *Morning Post*, he was the central figure in an escapade of the type in which he revelled.

Captured when a troop train was ambushed by the Boers, he escaped within a month, jumped a goods train and travelled to neutral territory hidden in bales of wool. Among the officers who had interrogated him was one Jan Christiaan Smuts, later to fill his own particular niche as a great soldier-statesman and to become a firm friend of his former captive.

Sir Winston Churchill's political career began in earnest in 1900 with his success, at the second attempt, at Oldham. He retained the seat until 1906, but his differences with the party leaders on several matters of policy, including that of Tariff Reform, led him to join the Liberal Party. From 1906 to 1908 he was Liberal MP for North-West Manchester, and he had his first experience of office as Under-Secretary for the Colonies.

For the next fourteen years, in the course of which he held eight offices and saw some more active service, he represented Dundee. He was President of the Board of Trade 1908–10, and Home Secretary 1910–11. The Sidney Street affair, in which armed anarchists barricaded themselves in a Whitechapel house, occurred while he was at the Home Office.

Sir Winston, determined to meet force with force, ordered a detachment of Guards to the scene, which he visited personally. The anarchists finally set fire to the house, in which their charred bodies were found.

In 1911 came the start of his initial term as First Lord of the Admiralty, an appointment for which the nation subsequently had cause to be profoundly grateful.

As well aware of the German menace at that period as he was a quarter of a century later, he saw that the Royal Navy was brought to such a pitch of preparedness that at the outbreak of war it slipped quietly, but with deadly precision, into action. It was conceded on all sides that most of the credit for this was due to the foresight, vigilance and energy of the First Lord.

When in 1915 the failure at Gallipoli caused his undeserved and temporary political extinction, his desire for a more active part in the war led to his command in 1916 in France, as a lieutenant-colonel, of the 6th Royal Scots Fusiliers.

But he was recalled in 1917 to become successively Minister of Munitions, Secretary for War, and Secretary for Air. Colonial Secretary 1921–22, he was elected for Epping in 1924, and having returned to the Conservative fold he was appointed Chancellor of the Exchequer from then until 1929.

As Hitler loomed large on the European horizon, Sir Winston's forebodings, which he characteristically expressed on every possible occasion, began to irritate those who adhered to the policy of appeasement which culminated in Munich.

His ceaseless warnings of the wrath to come were regarded contemptuously as the meanderings of a man with an obsession, and resulted in a 'sojourn in the wilderness' which caused him grim amusement, and brought a sense of despair and frustration to his sympathisers.

The relief which accompanied his appointment in 1939 for the second time as First Lord, and the affection in which he was held in naval circles, were demonstrated by the single message which was flashed round the Fleet – 'Winston is back'.

A sense of strength and confidence permeated this maritime nation at the realisation that at least one of the most important posts had been more than adequately filled.

The refusal of the Socialists in 1940 to serve in a Coalition under Mr Chamberlain, and their enthusiastic acceptance of Sir Winston as Prime Minister, led to the magnificent culmination of his career at the head of a country more closely united than ever before.

He started immediately to fulfil his onerous dual role of Prime Minister and Minister of Defence with an energy and determination that did not relax until the surrender of Germany.

That his wartime travels to conferences, often accomplished in the face of difficulties and dangers that many would have considered risks outside the line of duty, amounted to more than 40,000 miles was a striking example of the eager, almost ferocious way he set about the tasks before him.

He ranged from America, where he talked with Mr Roosevelt and drew tumultuous applause from both Houses of Congress in the United States and the Canadian Parliament, to Cairo and Moscow, where he first met Marshal Stalin, in 1941–42.

There followed visits to Casablanca, Turkey, Tripoli, Teheran and to America again in 1943. Two attacks of pneumonia, one suffered in England and the other in Carthage, created public alarm, but failed to shake the determination of this indefatigable and indomitable man.

He was back in England by January 1944, and six days after D-Day he was beaming with pleasure at the rousing welcome accorded him by the troops on the beaches of Normandy.

Two more visits to Northern France were followed by conferences in Italy with Tito, Umberto and Badoglio, and a call on the troops preparing for the invasion of Southern France. Within a fortnight he flew to Quebec for another conference with Mr Roosevelt, and then on to Moscow, accompanied by Mr Eden (now the Earl of Avon).

On Christmas Day, a month after his 70th birthday, he flew with Mr Eden to Athens to study the problems raised by the internecine warfare which had broken out in Greece.

At Yalta, in the Crimea, in February 1945, he met Mr Roosevelt, in company with Marshal Stalin, for the last time. The shock, and the sense of personal loss, with which the Allies received the news of Mr Roosevelt's death in April aroused its deepest echo in the heart of Sir Winston, whose unbounded admiration for 'that great and good man' was fortified by the bonds of genuine, and reciprocated, affection.

The defeat of the Conservative Party in the general election of 1945, at which Sir Winston was first returned for Woodford, was due in no way to any diminution in the esteem in which he was personally held.

This was proved not only by the tremendous reception he received on his 1,000-mile electioneering tour of Britain, but by the many tributes which have since been paid to his war leadership by even his bitterest political opponents.

Six years were to pass before he was in office again. But no temporary setback at home could deprive him of the extraordinary influence and prestige which he enjoyed abroad.

In addition to delivering many vigorous and powerful assaults on the Government in his role as Leader of the Opposition, he had worked arduously, and with a moving sincerity, for European co-operation. His speeches to the International Council of the European Movement, and at the Congress of Europe and the Council of Europe, bore eloquent testimony to his passionate desire for unity among the Western nations.

He was no less anxious for full Anglo-American accord. In speeches at Fulton, Missouri, and in Massachusetts he pleaded for a perfect understanding between the two countries that would perpetuate their war-time comradeship.

Much of the credit for the North Atlantic Treaty, as well as for the movement towards a united Europe, must in justice be awarded to him. His profound warnings on the attitude and activities of Russia drew caustic comments from sympathisers with that country, and allegations of warmongering. He remained unmoved by both, and waited calmly for time to prove him right, as it had done so frequently, and so painfully, in the past.

The election of 1950 left the House of Commons almost equally divided. A further eighteen months, notable for a further slide towards insolvency and for the loss of more of our hard-won prestige, had to pass before the nation once more entrusted its destinies to Sir Winston's care.

The gravity of the times, exemplified by the outbreak of war in Korea, must have made many feel that he was the man for the hour; but there is good reason to suppose that a widespread fear of war, which was unscrupulously exploited by his opponents, did much to reduce the Conservative majority in the House of Commons.

With the energy and realism that had characterised the whole of his political career, he quickly tackled the problems which lay before him on assuming office for the second time.

In Parliament he refrained from any attempt to make capital out of the parlous situation inherited by his Government, and in a sombre but confident broadcast, in the course of which he warned his hearers of the rough road Britain had to travel, he appealed for an end to bitter party strife.

Overshadowing in world interest his many other important activities, however, was his arrangement to visit Mr Truman at Washington. There can be no doubt that he fulfilled his purpose of giving new tone to Anglo-American relations. His speech to Congress was acclaimed as fully up to his own high standard. Some observers detected signs that the physical though not the intellectual machine was running down.

He was not the type, however, to permit a decline in health to halt the vigour of his control of the nation's affairs. On his return to England he made several personal interventions into vexed problems which displayed all his old mastery. None felt with a greater sense of loss the death of King George VI. As Monarch and Prime Minister in the years of Britain's greatest trial, they had formed bonds of the deepest affection and respect.

In 1953, when Mr Churchill became Sir Winston as a Knight of the Garter, he played his full part in the Queen's Coronation and presided over all five plenary sessions of the Commonwealth Prime Ministers' Conference in London.

When Mr Eden, as he then was, fell ill that year he also took over the Foreign Office, and he made plans for another Atlantic crossing to meet President Eisenhower in Bermuda.

Fears that all these burdens would overtax his strength were realised when his doctors ordered a month's complete rest just before he was due to sail. The Bermuda talks were postponed but not abandoned.

The following year he was off again, flying to Washington for further talks with the President and Mr Dulles. These were followed by a visit to Canada. On his eightieth birthday in 1954 he was still at the head of affairs, after months of rumours about his impending retirement. His birthday was greeted by gifts and tributes from all over the world, among them a controversial portrait by Graham Sutherland presented to him in Westminster Hall by both Houses of Parliament.

President Eisenhower wrote: 'We Americans salute you as a world statesman, as an unconquerable warrior in the cause of freedom, as our proven friend of many valiant years.' Earl Attlee described him as 'the last of the great orators'.

With money gifts Sir Winston formed the Winston Churchill Memorial Trust, with the object, among others, of endowing his country home, Chartwell, as a museum containing 'relics and mementoes of my long life'. From the £259,175 received he founded scholarships at his old school, Harrow, to encourage the study of English language and literature. He also gave £25,000 to assist the foundation of Churchill College, Cambridge, created for scientific studies.

Sir Winston eventually handed over the Premiership to his partner for so many years in war and peace, Sir Anthony Eden, who had married his niece, Miss Clarissa Spencer Churchill, in 1952. But his retirement, announced on 6 April 1955, in the midst of a national newspaper stoppage, was not his farewell to politics. A few weeks later he was fighting his fifteenth general election.

He did not speak, though he was in the House, during the

Suez crisis in 1956. But the following May, after Sir Anthony Eden's resignation, he publicly praised his 'resolute action' and condemned the United Nations. He was one of the two elder statesmen, the Marquess of Salisbury was the other, consulted by the Queen when Sir Anthony resigned in January 1957, and his advice was frequently sought by Sir Anthony's successor, Mr Macmillan.

In 1958 an attack of pneumonia while he was on holiday in the south of France caused worldwide anxiety. It forced him to postpone an informal visit he had planned to the United States.

But he made the journey the following year and, at the White House dinner in his honour, called for new efforts to build Anglo-American unity. He spent three days as President Eisenhower's guest and visited his friend, Mr Bernard Baruch, in New York.

In the general election of 1959 he stood again at eighty-four as candidate for Woodford. On his return to Parliament he became Father of the House of Commons, an honour he would have achieved long before but for his two years out of Parliament after his defeat at Dundee in 1922.

The same year his old friend, Field Marshal Viscount Montgomery, unveiled a bronze statue of him at Woodford, and in November 1959 he went to Paris to receive from General de Gaulle the Cross of Liberation, one of France's highest awards.

Among the thousands of congratulatory messages he received on his eighty-fifth birthday was one from Mr Khrushchev.

The breaking of a small bone in his back as a result of a fall at his London house in Hyde Park Gate caused further anxiety about his health in 1960, but he made a good recovery.

The following spring he went for a three-week cruise to the West Indies in the yacht of his friend Mr Aristotle Onassis, the ship owner.

In 1960–61 he drew for the first time his full annual pension of £2,000 as a former Prime Minister. Because of uncertain health he was unable to lay the foundation stone of Churchill College in the autumn of 1961, and the annual Songs of Harrow School were postponed until November so that he could attend, for the twenty-first time.

On his eighty-seventh birthday, which brought more worldwide tributes, among them one from President and Mrs Kennedy, he was applauded in the Commons, a breach of the rules of the House to which the Speaker turned a blind eye.

Sir Winston broke his thigh in a fall in Monte Carlo in 1962. Then came nearly two months of anxiety, with an emergency operation, a flight back to London and fifty-two days in the Middlesex Hospital. After this he had his first outing in the following November when he dined with friends of The Other Club, which he formed with F.E. Smith, later the first Earl of Birkenhead, in 1911.

On 1 May 1963, Sir Winston announced that he was giving up his seat at Woodford at the general election. In the previous October he had completed sixty years as an MP.

Last year he still attended the Commons and in February went to another dinner of The Other Club.

On 5 June, Prince Philip, in the presence of Lady Churchill, Mrs Christopher Soames, her daughter, Mr Randolph Churchill and Mr Winston S. Churchill, Sir Winston's grandson, paid tribute to Sir Winston in performing the official opening of Churchill College, Cambridge.

Party politics were forgotten on 28 July, when the Commons paid tribute to the Father of the House on his retirement. They gave unanimous assent to a motion which put on record their 'unbounded admiration and gratitude for his services to Parliament, to the nation and to the world'.

Sir Alec Douglas-Home, the then Prime Minister, left with a delegation of MPs to present the resolution, printed on vellum, to Sir Winston at his home at Hyde Park Gate, Kensington.

On Sir Winston's ninetieth birthday on 30 November messages of good wishes broke all records. As a crowd outside his London home sang 'For He's a Jolly Good Fellow' Sir Winston came to the window.

There were telegrams from the Pope, President Johnson, General de Gaulle and other world leaders. Mr Johnson proclaimed the day 'Sir Winston Churchill Day'.

The years following Sir Winston's resignation of the Premiership saw the publication, between 1956 and 1958, of his *History of the English-Speaking Peoples* in four large volumes. This was the last of more than thirty books from his pen. The first was *The Story of the Malakand Field Force* in 1898. His other works included *Lord Randolph Churchill* (1906), a study of his famous father, *The World Crisis* (1923–29), a masterly review of the 1914–18 war and its origins, and *Great Contemporaries* (1937). He reached the peak of his literary prowess with the publication of his history of the 1939–45 war, extracts from which were serialised in the *Daily Telegraph*.

In 1953 he received the Nobel Prize for Literature, one of a host of honours showered upon him by countries all over the world, among them honorary citizenships, some fifteen foreign decorations, gold medals of cities, the freedom of more than forty boroughs and cities.

The knighthood conferred on him by the Queen at Windsor in 1953 when she invested him with the Insignia of a Knight

Companion of the Garter was offered to him at the end of the war. He declined it on that occasion and in 1946 accepted the Order of Merit instead.

He took particular pride in his appointment in 1941 as Lord Warden of the Cinque Ports and also in the fact that he was an Elder Brother of Trinity House (1913). In 1963 he became an honorary citizen of the United States. A Privy Councillor since 1907, he was also a Companion of Honour (1922), a Fellow of the Royal Society (1941), an honorary Bencher of Gray's Inn (1942), honorary Academician Extraordinary of the Royal Academy (1948) and an honorary Fellow of Merton College, Oxford (1942).

In 1908 he married Miss Clementine Hozier, daughter of Colonel Sir Henry and Lady Blanche Hozier. She survives him with one son, two daughters, ten grandchildren and three great-grandsons.

Mr Randolph Churchill, MP for Preston 1940–45, married in 1939 the Hon. Pamela Digby. There was a divorce in 1946. In 1948 he married Miss June Osborne. The marriage was dissolved in 1961. There is one child of each marriage.

Miss Diana Churchill married first in 1932 Mr John Bailey, afterwards second baronet, and there was a divorce in 1935. The same year she married Mr Duncan Sandys, MP, former Commonwealth and Colonial Secretary. There are three children of the second marriage, which was dissolved in 1960. She was found dead in her Belgravia flat in 1963.

Miss Sarah Churchill, the actress and a wartime section officer in the Women's Auxiliary Air Force, married Vic Oliver, the comedian, in 1936. There was a divorce in 1945. Her second marriage in 1949 was to Mr Anthony Beauchamp, the photographer, who died in 1957. She subsequently married Lord Audley at Gibraltar. He died in July 1963.

Sir Winston's youngest daughter, Miss Mary Churchill, married Mr Christopher Soames MP, former Minister of Agriculture, in 1947. There are five children of the marriage.

Another daughter, Marigold Frances, born in 1918, died in 1921 at the age of two.

THE HOMAGE OF THE MANY
By Dermot Morrah
25 January 1965

All down Whitehall, that first evening of the lying-in-state, the pavements were crowded with people, all hurrying southward to where the illuminated face in the Clock Tower showed a quarter to six. At the corner of New Palace Yard the police with megaphones directed us to turn left across Westminster Bridge.

As the pattering feet sped on along the paved walk below the windows of St Thomas's Hospital on the Surrey side, an ageing memory cast back to the last time of being thus diverted, when a junior Civil Servant seeking his second-rank office on Millbank (it has since blossomed out into the Ministry of Power) stumbled upon the funeral cortège of Queen Alexandra making its stately progress in a silence made ghostly by the muffling of thick snow. That was forty years ago; and one reflected that even then Winston Churchill was a long-established statesman and a veteran of four or five campaigns.

The bright sunshine on the snow that far-off day contrasted with the damp gloom this evening. A sharp north wind blew in the faces of the crowds as, having regained the Westminster bank by Lambeth Bridge, they were shepherded into Victoria

Tower Gardens; but no one seemed to be complaining of the cold. Hereabouts the cloud of molecules began to coalesce into a solid queue.

Mostly, at this hour, it seemed to consist of workers in shops and offices, just as they had come off duty: but not all. Just ahead was a youngish man whom one put down tentatively, from the cast of his features and the shape of his head-dress, as a Persian; he gazed straight ahead of him and spoke to no one. Here and there were the darker skins of Africa and the West Indies. On the flank of the queue, now nine or ten abreast, walked a pair of young lovers, who remained clinging in one another's arms all through the long trudge.

Whether what they whispered had to do with the great man dead, or with more personal intimacies, none could guess; but to swathe them both from head to foot the young man had put on a black cloak which almost exactly reproduced those worn by the civilian mourners as they are drawn in the emblazoned volume at the College of Arms which records the State funeral of Lord Nelson.

As the queue became more closely knit, conversation, always quiet, became more continuous. There seemed to be a feeling for Churchill as the Great Commoner. 'He wouldn't have a title.' 'He could've been a Duke, couldn't he?' 'Yes, the King wanted him to have it, but he wouldn't.' 'They ought to have made him Duke of Marlborough.' 'But I think there is one already.' 'Anyhow, he turned it down.' 'Shows what a great man he was really.'

Much disjointed reminiscence seemed to be claiming slight but affectionate association with the dead. One aged man was saying to another, 'Yes, I saw him wearing it there – it wasn't his fault that we couldn't hang on', and one caught the word 'Antwerp'. Two or three obvious survivors of a later conflict were recalling that once they were brigaded with the 8th Hussars – it wasn't the 4th, but since that day the two regiments have been amalgamated to form the Queen's Royal Irish Hussars. So there was a link; and any link, however indirect, was something to hug to one's bosom.

There was talk of the coming procession, with all Churchill's medals, decorations and heraldic insignia carried before the coffin. Somebody remarked that there ought to be a procession of his hats, and someone else was a little shocked at the ribaldry on such an occasion. But no, thought queue opinion, Winston loved a joke even in tragic circumstances; there was nothing of the stuffed-shirt about him.

A lady joining in the conversation revealed that she was a schoolmistress come up from Windsor to make her obeisance; she was proud that she had actually given her children a lesson in the Castle, where Sir Winston walked in procession with his knightly brethren of the Garter; she drew from her handbag a coloured snapshot taken on the day. It didn't actually show Churchill, but he had been there.

Next morning the queue was a quarter-mile longer and rather different in texture: perhaps more varied. There were several crocodiles of uniformed schoolgirls, one of them led by a nun; and a crew – if that is the correct noun of assembly – of Wrens. There were very few visible signs of mourning, even of black ties – which means nothing except that fashion has changed, for there was no mistaking the sorrow that had brought them all together.

A young mother in brilliant scarlet oilskins led by the hand a three-year-old in equally vivid yellow with red gumboots; far on in the twenty-first century he will no doubt be telling his unbelieving grandchildren that he actually remembers the coffin of that old man in the history books who was born in

1874. His little sister in the pram will not be able to do that, but Mother thought it important she should be there. Many another housewife had evidently left the breakfast washing-up for the evening.

One caught murmurs of splendid and familiar phrases – 'grim and gay' – 'the Few' – 'fight on the beaches' – 'you can always take one with you' (this from a man carrying his wartime gasmask in its haversack). Anecdotes of the hero were being exchanged – some seemed to have developed since first told – and one had glimpses into the growth of a legend. Also, one realised that the wealth of stories about him was part of his hold on the people's heart – for England cannot dwell continuously in the epic mood.

We had reached St Stephen's entrance and the platform that looks down the broad steps into Westminster Hall. The murmuring ceased, gave way to a sort of sigh as we surveyed the simplicity and grandeur of the scene.

It was more austere than the lying-in-state of kings. There were fewer guards – an officer at each corner of the catafalque and one on the bridge of steps leading to the Grand Committee Room, all motionless, heads bowed over their drawn swords. The tall yellow candles of mourning stood round about the coffin. Instead of the royal draperies of velvet and cloth-of-gold, the Union Flag draped only the top of the catafalque, leaving the lower half stark and black. No flowers lay upon it, only a cushion on which lay the insignia of the Garter.

For a moment, with the severe dignity, one felt most of all the awful loneliness of death. Then the eye, led by the lines of the cross towering at the head of the coffin, travelled up to the golden angels supporting the ancient roof; and there came a feeling that the great spirit was mysteriously not alone after all. Those angels had looked down upon so many a leader of the people, who 'lay like a warrior taking his rest'.

Moving slowly with the stream of mourners past the coffin, imagination called up the vision of some of those other makers of history, who had lain in state in this august hall or other ancient buildings, before being borne in majesty to their obsequies under the Earl Marshal's sceptre. There were few without some title to call cousin with Churchill in Valhalla.

Lord Roberts – with the same nostalgia for the sound of the guns. Mr Gladstone, another great orator, another passionate hater of cruelty, in Bulgaria as at Belsen. Wellington, the only rival to Churchill's versatility as soldier-statesman, the Iron Duke who wept over the casualty lists of Waterloo as his successor wept over bomb-blasted tenements in London. William Pitt, the pilot who weathered the storm, a storm unparalleled for fury till the blitzkrieg broke. Marlborough – but what to say of him except what is said by a character in one of James Bridie's plays: 'It's not that we're *like* our parents – we *are* our parents.' George Monk, Duke of Albemarle, the rock of support for the English monarchy, the father-figure of constitutional government in his day. And Philip Sidney, the epitome of the high Elizabethan magnanimity, the pattern of chivalry, the fine spirit who more than any other in that age bridged the gulf that separates the worlds of literature, politics and war.

We had passed the guarded catafalque, some with a shy bow, many with tears in their eyes. On the further threshold we turned for a last backward look at the severe, the noble scene, the symbolic representation of the terrible and glorious Churchillian age through which we had lived. 'What shadows,' some of us may have thought with Edmund Burke. 'What shadows we are and what shadows we pursue.' Little people, who had had a moment's communion with greatness, we passed out into Palace Yard, leaving the Titan in the ghostly company of his peers.

FAREWELL
30 January 1965

There are few, high or low, eloquent or not, who have not tried this week in some way to express the gratitude, the love, the admiration that they feel for Winston Churchill. It has not been easy for anyone to say things that are new or original in expressing the feelings that are shared by all. The old exploits have been recalled; the famous sayings repeated; the precious little anecdotes retold. We are all conscious of the inadequacy of what we say. But at such a time words, like flowers, lose nothing of their freshness or sincerity by repetition. We may be sure that the broken, murmured phrases of gratitude and grief from the hundreds of thousands coming out from Westminster Hall would have been no less welcome to Winston Churchill himself than the eloquent tributes of Prime Ministers and Presidents. He identified himself with the ordinary people of Britain as they have identified themselves – this week more unmistakably than ever – with him. Their tributes have come more easily because they have been expressions of affection, loyalty and sympathy rather than of distant praise.

Today we bid him farewell. There is not one of us who does not feel that we are bidding farewell also to a part of our own past; not one of us who does not know that we owe to him our past, our present and our future, that Britain, in the worst dangers that ever confronted her, was inseparable from his leadership. There can scarcely be one who dares to think what Britain might be if he had not lived. But not Britain alone. At St Paul's today will be Kings and Princes, Presidents and Chancellors, Ministers and Marshals. Many of them would dare as little to think what their world would have been, or the world that their peoples have to live in, had it not been for the brave and steadfast heart that inspired courage and unity in his own country and for the ringing voice that lifted up men's spirits in so many others. Freedom, which knows no national frontiers, is paying its homage today to one of her greatest servants.

This day is a day of grief and mourning, of memories of the 'finest hour' which his deeds made possible and his words immortalised. It is right that our minds should dwell on past glories that were incarnate in him. Yet he would have wished, too, that our minds should dwell on the freedom, the future opportunity for achievement and for human progress, that his leadership secured for this and other nations. 'This day': the phrase that came so often from his pen is itself a reminder of the way in which he used to make out of words deeds already half-done. For him, one achievement was but the prelude to another. It is a day for sad and proud remembrance, yes. It is also a day for us all to re-dedicate ourselves to the service of the free world which he cherished and championed and of the Britain which he so deeply loved and so mightily protected. Let that be at least one of our thoughts as, whether we stand along the route or watch on the television screen, the stately procession winds its way from Westminster Hall to the service at St Paul's and thence Winston Churchill goes to his last resting place in a country churchyard.

SPIRIT OF THE FINEST HOUR
By Douglas Brown
31 January 1965

It was surely the greatest funeral ever for its public memories and meaning. As twilight fell over the churchyard at Bladon, and Lady Churchill with her children and grandchildren moved sorrowfully from the graveside, trumpet notes were still ringing in the nation's ears.

For this had been a day when the history of this century had been solemnly re-enacted in slow motion so that the imperishable Churchill story might be told at his passing.

'Lead out the pageant, sad and slow.' And pageant it was. From the moment the gun-carriage rolled out of New Palace Yard it was clear that the silent crowds were doing more than express their sorrow at the death of a great friend and leader, or even their gratitude for a life to which they owed their own.

They had suddenly become a sentient nation, marvelling at their remembered deliverance and beginning to wonder again about their destiny. For all the sad splendour and the deep-felt grief, this was nothing less than VE-Day recollected in tranquillity.

They were all there in the great procession, his comrades in arms – the sailors, the soldiers, the airmen, the civilian fighters of the blitz. But these were more than portrayers, twenty-five years later, of that Finest Hour.

Churchill's wide-ranging spirit had caught them up into a grander perspective so that the youthful spectators, of whom there were so many, though they might remember nothing of 1940, began to realise why they felt so strangely proud and sad.

Inextricable strands of history and memory ran through all the funeral pomp. Sir Winston came from Westminster Hall as a Garter knight, preceded by banners, as though out of the mist of the past.

But he came also from our workaday quarrelsome Mother of Parliaments whence he had drawn his strength and where he had fought more than his share of losing battles.

He was taken along Whitehall, past the end of Downing Street, where he had wrestled with the complexities of power.

In the great cathedral, passing from the people's view, he was awaited for the last time by his Sovereign supported by all her most illustrious people – heralds, officers of state, judges, counsellors, captains, scholars.

The nation in its formal and executive aspect was ranged there to greet him. Among old friends and enemies there were many new faces, expressing new aims and ambitions, but the great pyramid of State was intact – and it was he who had kept it so.

Under that mighty dome he received the homage of the world. Kings and Presidents and statesmen had come from all corners of the earth. These presented a more complex picture, as the man they had come to honour would have been the first to remark. Churchill will never stand again at a watershed of world history, and neither, perhaps, will England.

Allies, former enemies, the Commonwealth itself have changed, often out of all recognition. Some of the countries represented might never have existed at all if Churchill had had his way.

But his mark is on them all, and those who still live in freedom do so because of him.

'Who would true valour see, let him come hither.' The confident hymns filled the vast church and the mood of the day's ceremony leaped dramatically from this world to the next.

In the midst of this congregation of earthly kings and captains the Christian message of hope rang out unequivocally.

It was on this note that the Queen and her past and present Ministers, the eminent pallbearers out of Churchill's varied past and the representatives of all the great troubled world, bade him farewell.

Down at the Tower, where the Beefeaters were on duty, the salt Thames awaited the Former Naval Person. To the wail of pipes he was carried aboard his simple funeral launch and as it cast off, all the slow marches forgotten, a naval band struck up 'Rule Britannia'.

So, still irrepressible, Winston Churchill returned up river towards political Westminster, among the screeching gulls. The great had said goodbye to him, but the humble could still watch him from the bridges.

Only at the Festival Pier did London, and Britain, at last entrust him to that family who had followed him, on foot, and in coaches, through all this sad triumph.

It was too soon to say whether this surge of emotion, contained and controlled by the splendid exactitude of British high ceremonial, had produced besides a forgivable nostalgia any lasting sense of re-dedication. But that the day had set young people thinking, there could be no doubt.

London returned to its Saturday pursuits and from the railway station of Waterloo, well-named, Winston Churchill was carried out into the English countryside in the bosom of his family. What had been a State funeral had become something more universal, more fundamental, and therefore, in truth, more majestic. 'God accept him, Christ receive him.' Winston Churchill was laid to rest in a village churchyard among the graves of his ancestors and of local farmers, far from the stirring scenes of his active life.

His grave had been dug beside that of his father, on which stands, as memorial, a cross of the local Bladon stone. This, which marks the ultimate victory, is the enduring 'V' sign.

WE START AGAIN WITHOUT CHURCHILL
31 January 1965

When historians in the future write long works about England there will always be a volume called simply 'The Age of Churchill', and all of us alive today, children for whom he is only a name no less than their elders, will appear to posterity as part of that age. The period between the great man's retirement ten years ago and his death – which seem so important to us – will probably be compressed into a few pages with the names of Eden, Macmillan, Home making brief appearances before the curtain is rung down with the bells tolling for the death of Churchill.

This will not be strictly accurate, for in a sense the Age of Churchill ended many years ago, before the younger generation were born. It was, too, a very short age, in terms of years in power. Yet such was the stature of the man, and the uniqueness of his contribution, that although in fact the last ten, possibly the last twenty, years have been shaped by different hands, with Churchill dominating the scene less and less, they will nevertheless appear in the history books as the last days of the Age of Churchill.

Perhaps it is because we have all known this in our bones,

known that our role in history while Churchill was still with us would inevitably be merely an epilogue to a volume whose climax was already past, that during these last ten years so many have been content to behave as befits people who expect to be little more than footnotes. What was the point in the fifties and sixties of striving to succeed when the standard of comparison, so long as Churchill was alive, would be Britain's 'finest hour'? How could we, with the great man still among us – physically so in the House of Commons until last year – hope to do deeds and say words that could ever equal, let alone surpass, those done and uttered by him many years ago? Who in British public life would hope or want to outshine the title figure of the age or, so long as he lived, to seize its mantle from his shoulders?

Imagine how different history might have been in the United States if Franklin Roosevelt had lived on in retirement instead of ending the Age of Roosevelt while still in the White House. He would certainly, as the great architect of victory and the father of his people, have pre-empted the role which Eisenhower, *faute de mieux*, came to play; Ike could never have enjoyed that particular star billing if the great showman himself had still been around, even if only in the wings.

And as for John F. Kennedy, one wonders whether his lustre would have shone in quite the way it did if that other sun had still been in the sky, even if only as a fading hue slowly setting over the horizon. One rather doubts it. If Roosevelt had lived on in retirement the scope for succeeding Presidents to assume the mantle of popular leadership and blaze new trails would have been subtly and significantly reduced. So long as 'FDR' had been alive a young man like Kennedy, brought up to revere the master, would have felt it almost blasphemous to aspire to comparable greatness.

But Churchill did live on. Unlike the Age of Roosevelt, which ended in 1944, the Age of Churchill lasted until 1965. No one can deny that this has brought Britain many advantages. So long as he lived these islands enjoyed an extra respect both in our own eyes and in those of others. It is something, after all, to have the greatest man alive in one's midst. With so very special a passenger on board, the British ship of state could expect to receive special treatment, even when she went off course or lay helpless and becalmed. Memory of what that very special passenger had once done when he was at the helm continued to ensure Britain a respected place long after he had disappeared from the quarter-deck to rest in his hammock down below.

But his marvellous longevity has also encouraged the prolongation in the mood of an age that should have died long ago. Unwittingly Churchill became for England a kind of Ancient Mariner holding us all transfixed with his tales of Britain's island story. But so great was the magnetism of the man, and the scale of his own deeds, that it became impossible so long as he was with us to conceive of the story having a further chapter. England without Churchill became to seem like *Hamlet* without the Prince. We shrank back, fearful of anti-climax. While there were even a few embers of the Churchill fire still to warm our hands at, who could bear to tear himself away and face the cold dawn of a new and as yet unvaliant age?

But now the embers are at last quite cold. No longer can we sit around warming our hands at the remains of that once glorious blaze which, nearly a quarter of a century ago, fired the spirit of one nation, and sparks from which kindled the flames of freedom throughout the world.

It is time to seek to light a new fire. It will never be the same, never as fierce and golden, as joyous and crackling, as warm and kindly. It will be a different kind of fire, electric as against the blaze of oak, in a smaller and less imposing grate, in a modern house rather than a mansion. Not a fire, no doubt, fit for the Age of Churchill.

But that age is now over. A new age must begin. It will not be an age of giants. There are certainly none at hand, at least judging by the measurements of the Churchill Age. But these are no longer the right measurements. Against the Churchill scale everything is bound to look small. But the whole world, with the exception perhaps of France, is living in its equivalent to a post-Churchill age – America without Roosevelt, without even Kennedy. Russia without Stalin. Now Britain without Churchill.

There has been a period of mourning and burial; of solemn panegyric and stirring pageantry. But let us not, as we cherish remembrance of the funeral day, relapse into nostalgia, into somnolent sweetness recalling the past. To do so may be one way of burying Churchill, but certainly not the way to praise him. True praise would be to make sure by our present exertions that the island story which he told so superbly and enacted so gloriously is as immortal as he believed it to be. And the only way a nation remains immortal is to stay vigorously alive.